PROJECT TIGER

GAVIN NEWSHAM

PROJECT TIGER

THE BIRTH OF GENIUS AND THE PRICE OF GREATNESS

DIVERSION BOOKS

For more information, email info@diversionbooks.com

Diversion Books
A division of Diversion Publishing Corp.
www.diversionbooks.com

First Diversion Books Edition: March 2026
Hardcover ISBN: 9798895150948
e-ISBN: 9798895150955
Design by Neuwirth & Associates, Inc.
Cover design by Jonathan Sainsbury // 6x9 design

Printed in the United States of America
1 3 5 7 9 10 8 6 4 2

For Betty Farragher (1933–2024)

&

Geraldine Newsham (1944–2013)

PROJECT TIGER

TABLE OF CONTENTS

INTRODUCTION

When Tiger Woods was seventeen, a friend of mine, Tim Southwell—award-winning journalist and my fellow cofounder of *Golf Punk* magazine—visited Woods in Cypress to interview him for the first issue of a new magazine he was about to launch in the United Kingdom called *loaded*. Back then, there was no media circus around Woods. There were no publicists, security staff, or entourage. All Southwell had to do was ring up the Woods house on Teakwood Street and ask to speak to Tiger, at which point Earl, who had taken the call, hollered for his son to hurry out of the shower and come to the phone. Amazed that Southwell was prepared to fly five thousand miles just to play golf with him, Tiger and Southwell arranged a date, and soon, Southwell found himself hitting balls with Tiger on the range at the Navy Golf Club in Los Alamitos, California.

We didn't know a lot about Tiger Woods back then. This was an age where there was no internet, no social media, and where people didn't have cell phones filming anything and everything that moved—and most things that didn't too. People in the world of golf knew, of course, but he hadn't become the household name he would be in just a couple of short years. What struck Southwell was not just how relaxed and at ease Tiger seemed in his company, despite his burgeoning reputation, but how normal he was.

That day, the two played a round together and chewed the fat over Mexican food at a nearby restaurant. After their time together, Tiger told him he had had a great day, adding, "Next time you're in town and you want a game of golf, look me up."

Ten years later, Southwell was in Isleworth, Florida, working on a story for *Golf Punk* when he decided to take Tiger up on his offer. By now, Woods had already won eight major titles, including the unprecedented "Tiger Slam" in 2000–2001, and was fast on his way to becoming golf's first billionaire player. As one the richest and most recognizable sports stars in the world, Woods now was living in a private, gated community, enjoying the perks of not having to pay state taxes as he would if he had stayed in California. When Southwell spoke to the guard sitting in the security hut at the entrance, he was told that Tiger wasn't at home and that he wasn't likely to be in the foreseeable future. In other words: Please leave immediately.

Southwell left his number and did as requested.

Today, getting to Tiger is like trying to complete a Rubik's Cube blindfolded; it is possible, but you will probably be wasting a lot of your time. Never a fan of the media or their demands on his time, even when he was being paid handsomely for it, Woods can be reclusive and unreachable. But more than that, he just looks, well, sad. And the contrast between the kid who would happily entertain TV crews and journalists in his young life, armed only with his clubs and that mile-wide killer smile of his, couldn't be more pronounced. But it is why this book exists—to chart those formative years and the remarkable journey from child prodigy to turning professional, aged twenty, with $60 million in the bank.

When I decided to write a book about one of the most famous sports stars that has ever existed, there are many moments when I wondered just what have I gotten myself into. On one hand, it is extremely useful having such a wealth of readily available resources to call upon, especially when a life like that of Tiger Woods has been so heavily documented; but, on the other, it can prove difficult when trying to find something new, something different, to the received wisdom.

One of the first books on Tiger Woods, released in the wake of Tiger's breakthrough major win at the 1997 Masters Tournament at Augusta National, was John Strege's biography, entitled simply *Tiger: A Biography of Tiger Woods*. On the inside cover, it speaks glowingly of the impact that Tiger Woods was having on the game of golf and how this "popular and admitted" golfer was now "a role model for young and old alike."

Nearly thirty years on from its publication, though, you wonder where it all went wrong. For everything that Woods has achieved on the golf course, most of which will never be matched, his slow and sorry decline in recent years has been difficult to watch at times. Waylaid by injury after injury and sidelined by scandals, it is difficult to imagine him ever returning to regular tournament golf—whether that is in majors, the occasional PGA Tour event, or maybe even the pipe-and-slippers world of the Champions Tour—now that he is eligible.

Yet despite everything, Tiger Woods remains the biggest draw in golf, and that in itself speaks volumes, not only about Tiger's greatness but also the current state of professional golf, which has been ripped apart by the emergence of the Saudi-backed LIV Golf series as it lures the world's best players over to their competition with the kind of money they simply couldn't make on the PGA Tour. There was a moment in 2019 when, after eleven years without winning a major championship, Woods returned to the winners' circle in Augusta at the Masters, at age forty-three. His lifelong pursuit of Jack Nicklaus's record tally of eighteen majors seemed to be back on track. But a serious car crash in 2021, where Tiger nearly lost his leg, put an end to that.

But we know about that. We know about the serial infidelity and the DUI busts. What we don't really know is how he got there, especially those years when, as a junior and an amateur, he rewrote the record books in spectacular and seismic fashion. What Woods pulled off before he turned twenty-one will likely never be replicated. In many ways, it's even more remarkable than his success as a professional because you could see that coming. The young Tiger won three consecutive United States Golf Association (USGA) National Junior titles, often playing against boys who were as much as five years older than him. He also secured three US Amateur championships in succession, something nobody has ever done before or since (not even Bobby Jones, the most lauded amateur golfer in history). Then there was the six Junior World Golf Championship titles and more than two hundred other junior titles in the United States and beyond.

But you need to look beyond the trophies and the accolades to examine the factors that caused this prodigious talent to blossom and how Tiger Woods's strange, dysfunctional, and stage-managed childhood (if, indeed, he had a childhood) then burgeoning celebrity impacted his development.

His father, Earl Woods, is central to all of this. From Tiger's birth, Earl had all but mapped out his son's life, believing that his son, with his multiracial heritage, would achieve a level of global celebrity and influence that transcended sports. Earl often described how Tiger was marinated in this messianic vision throughout his formative years, and although he never embraced his father's belief that he was destined to be the savior of mankind, the grandiose scale of Tiger's success, fame, and wealth *did* enable him to achieve a kind of immortality even before his fortieth birthday.

It is hard to imagine the immense pressure placed on Tiger from an early age to meet the exacting expectations of his father and just how he dealt with the unstoppable transformation from Tiger the person to Tiger the persona, a billionaire-dollar global brand.

Yes, Tiger's complex and painful trade-offs in the pursuit of greatness helped him rise to unparalleled achievements on the golf course, but away from the sport he loved, his success somehow dehumanized and, ultimately, immiserated him. Of course, the genius of Tiger Woods is beyond dispute, but this story is to understand the price he paid for it.

Tim Southwell, incidentally, is still waiting for Tiger's call.

PROLOGUE

It was a routine birdie putt. Maybe eighteen feet at most, with just a hint of borrow from the left. But when it dropped, as they nearly always did for Lee Elder, the magnitude of what he had achieved suddenly hit home.

Not because it gave him victory over England's Peter Oosterhuis and his first ever victory on the PGA Tour. Nor because winning the Monsanto Open title at Pensacola Country Club came with a winner's check for thirty thousand dollars.

No, its true significance lay in the fact that Lee Elder—a thirty-nine-year-old journeyman pro from Dallas via Los Angeles, who cut his teeth on the United Golf Association (UGA) Tour for Black players excluded from the Professional Golfers' Association (PGA) of America—had just become the first African American in history to qualify for the Masters, the one major championship that had never featured a Black player.

But there was no time for celebration.

As soon as he holed out, the PGA Tour director Jack Tuthill appeared at the greenside and whisked Elder off in a police car, rather than risk a public trophy presentation on the final green.

"There have been death threats, Lee," warned the former FBI man.
Elder sighed. "Not again . . ."

April 1974 was a historic month for America's Black athletes. In baseball, Hank Aaron of the Atlanta Braves broke Babe Ruth's all-time home run record when the man they called "the Hammer" crushed a pitch from the LA Dodgers' Al Downing high over the left-centerfield wall at Atlanta–Fulton County Stadium and reached 715 career homers.

It had been nearly twenty-seven long years since Jackie Robinson had broken Major League Baseball's color barrier by turning out for the Brooklyn Dodgers, but it still hadn't been easy for next-generation Black players like Aaron. As he closed in the record, he had been deluged with hate mail and death threats.

The letters, which the Braves kept or handed over to the FBI, were unremittingly racist. One, addressed to "Dear Mr. N*****," wrote, "I hope you don't break the Babe's record. How do I tell my kids that a n***** did it?" Another, written on August 21, 1972, and signed "A has-been fan," asked, "Who told you a *bunch of n****** can play ball? . . . Home Run King his Black *ass*." "Retire or die," demanded another. While Aaron handled the situation with grace, he still needed an armed bodyguard to accompany him in his day-to-day life. Even his children had police escorts when they went to school. There was never any question that Hank Aaron would surrender to the white supremacists. "Dammit all, I had to break the record," he wrote in his 1991 autobiography, *I Had a Hammer: The Hank Aaron Story*. "I had to do it for Jackie [Robinson], and my people and myself and for everybody who ever called me a n*****."

Thirteen days after Hammerin' Hank finally broke Babe Ruth's record, Lee Elder triumphed in the Monsanto Open, a victory that gave him nearly a year to prepare for what would be a landmark appearance at the 1975 Masters, scheduled to be played at its home at Augusta National Golf Club from April 10–13.

But as the Masters drew ever nearer, Elder's game fell apart. He was missing more cuts than he made, hadn't finished higher than thirty-third in a tournament, and had made less than five thousand dollars. "I go to bed thinking about the Masters," Elder told Bob Greene of the *Associated Press* in March 1975. "I dream about the Masters. I wake up thinking about the Masters."

As news of Elder's achievement spread, the hate grew. At one tournament, he had to change into his golf shoes in the car park because, as a Black man, he still wasn't welcomed in the clubhouse. On another occasion, in Memphis, he found the ball he had hit into the middle of the fairway had been tossed into a thick hedge. Even on the night before his final round in Pensacola, Elder had taken a call in his hotel room in the early hours of the morning. "N*****," the voice said, "you better not win this golf tournament."

When Elder finally arrived at Augusta, what was already a hard week suddenly got a whole lot more difficult, thanks largely to Clifford Roberts, the Masters' autocratic chairman. A former Wall Street stockbroker, Roberts had cofounded the Masters in 1934 alongside fabled amateur player Bobby Jones on a redeveloped plantation in Augusta, Georgia.

Ever since, Roberts's word had been God when it came to the running of Augusta National. Although *The New York Times* once called him a "benevolent dictator," his benevolence was lost on most members. Roberts's insistence on the strictest adherence to the rules—*his* rules—meant that only people he invited could play his golf course . . . and that definitely meant no Black players. "As long as I'm alive, golfers will be white and caddies will be Black," he told Augusta's members.

In the teeth of the Civil Rights Act and the ending of formal segregation, Roberts had successfully ignored the claims of pioneering Black professionals like Charlie Sifford, the first Black player on the PGA Tour, and Pete Brown, the first Black winner of a PGA Tour event when he won the Waco Turner Open in Burneyville, Oklahoma, in 1964—both of whom Roberts continued to exclude from the Masters. He had even rebuked a group of congressmen who had written to him demanding change, telling them, "We are a little surprised as well as being flattered that eighteen congressmen should be able to take time out to help us operate a golf tournament."

However, thanks to a PGA Tour rule change in 1972 that saw winners on the circuit receive an immediate invitation to the Masters, Roberts was powerless to prevent Lee Elder teeing up at Augusta in early April 1975.

Publicly, at least, Roberts welcomed Elder to Augusta; but, privately, he loathed the idea that his sacred slice of Georgia would soon be hosting African American players.

Lee Elder's week at the Masters would be a nightmare. Inundated with interview requests on one hand and death threats on the other, he and his wife, Rose, were forced to rent two homes in the area—one on Washington Road and another on Wheeler Road, switching between the two for their own safety.

On the first evening in Augusta, Elder, his wife, and ten other guests called in to a local restaurant at 5:00 p.m. and, seeing it was empty inside, asked to be seated. "They turned us away, said they were booked up," Elder explained. "I'd seen this type of thing before." When the press reported this, the president of nearby Paine College, Dr. Julius Scott, invited Elder and his guests to eat at the college every night he was in town, rather than run the gauntlet of the local restaurants again. "I took him up on that, and it was a highlight of the week. Nice and quiet, so welcoming. Good food too," said Elder later.

By the time Elder was finally announced on the first tee at 11:15 a.m. on April 10, 1975, he was exhausted. Playing with the 1961 US Open champion Gene Littler and the Ryder Cup player Miller Barber, Elder started wonderfully, making a par at the opening hole and a birdie at the second. But he faded badly, finishing with a round of 74.

It got worse the following day. A second round of 78 left Elder four strokes adrift of the halfway cut mark, and Elder's Masters experience was over almost as soon as it had begun.

Over two thousand miles away in Cypress, California, Earl Woods had watched Elder on TV with fascination and pride. As an amateur Black golfer, he knew only too well how America's clubs treated players like him and Elder. But in Cypress, twenty-five miles southeast of Los Angeles, Earl had lucked out. A five-minute drive from their new house at 6704 Teakwood Street was the military-owned Navy Club, and Lieutenant Colonel Earl Woods, with his proud record as a Green Beret and two tours of Vietnam under his belt, was only too welcome to play there whenever he liked.

His second wife, Kultida, meanwhile, had more pressing issues to worry about. If only Earl would quit talking about Lee Elder and the Masters for a moment, she might be able to tell him her good news—*their* good news.

A year or so later, Tida was cooking Thai food again, as she did so often. Though they had been married for six years, Earl Woods never had the heart to tell his wife how much he really hated it. As the aromas from the lemongrass and tamarind drifted out of their kitchen and around their home, Earl did what he always did: He went to the garage to hit some golf balls.

At least now he had some company as he gathered up his little boy to come and admire his swing as he crushed ball after ball into the net he had rigged up.

When he wasn't at the golf course, the garage was Earl's haven; a place where he and the son he called Tiger could disappear for an hour or two, with Earl honing his game and his baby boy watching from his high chair.

Then, in October 1976, something happened. As Earl moved through his clubs, Tiger motioned to his father to be lifted out of his chair. When his father obliged, the toddler picked up a tiny putter that Earl had made for him and hit a ball. Then he hit another. And another.

Earl Woods couldn't believe his eyes. Tiger wasn't swinging and missing. Instead, he was catching each ball flush on the clubface, displaying the kind of hand-eye coordination he might expect from a ten-year-old kid, not a ten-month-old toddler.

Earl yelled for Tida, and she, too, was amazed. It was a pivotal moment, not just in Tiger's development but also in Earl and Tida's marriage. "We made a personal commitment to each other that we would devote all of our energies and finances to assure that he had the best we could give him," he said later.

Project Tiger had begun.

CHAPTER 1
CAPTURED BY GOLF

"There are only two colors in the United States: white and non-white."
—Earl Woods, 1968

House-hunting in Southern California was hard enough, but for a Black man and his Thai wife in the 1970s, it was close to impossible. From Pasadena to Palm Springs, San Bernardino to Santa Ana, Earl and Tida Woods had been stymied at every turn in their search for a new home.

One vendor had raised the price by five thousand dollars (around thirty thousand dollars today) the moment Earl walked through the door. Another pulled their property off the market rather than sell it to the Woods family. *It was like the Civil Rights Movement had never happened*, thought Earl.

Running out of options, they decided to take up their broker's offer to rent one of his condos in Los Alamitos, a blink-and-you'll-miss-it town wedged between Long Beach and Anaheim. The condo wasn't ideal, but compared to the postage-stamp-sized apartment they had in New York City, it felt palatial. Besides, they would only be there a year at most, just till they found somewhere to buy.

After three years in the Big Apple, Earl and Tida couldn't wait to leave New York. The city had changed beyond all recognition.

In the mid-1970s, crime had exploded, drug use was out of control, and unemployment rates were in the double figures. With the city on the verge of bankruptcy and the middle classes fleeing for the suburbs, Earl and Tida knew it was time to move on. At the end of his first marriage to Barbara (or Ann, as she preferred to be known), Earl had told his three children—Earl Jr., Kevin, and Royce—that he would one day move closer to their home in San Jose, California. Now, with the Big Apple bruised and busted, he decided to make good on his promise.

Earl had landed a good job as a senior buyer at the aerospace company Arrowhead Products in Los Alamitos, but living there wasn't ideal either. When Tida Woods left Thailand and arrived in America in 1968, it was the first time she had left her home country. Earl had warned her about what to expect from her new life in the United States, telling her that, in America, there are only two colors—white and non-white. "Whites will let you know without a doubt that you are non-white," he said. "You'll see it in their actions and reactions to you."

As soon as the Woods family moved into their rented condo in Los Alamitos, they knew they were not welcome. "When I would come out to the pool and hug my wife, everyone would scatter," recalled Earl Woods. "Suddenly, stony silence would descend as they would get out of the water and leave. We knew we weren't welcome."

When Earl's oldest son, Earl Jr., came to stay, he was dragged out of his father's 1965 Mustang by local cops, who slammed him against a wall and accused him of stealing the vehicle. "We're not accustomed to seeing people like you in this neighborhood," said one police officer.

Earl and Tida wouldn't have to wait long to leave Los Alamitos. A house had come on the market in nearby Cypress that ticked all their boxes: 1,474 square feet, single story on a corner plot, two bedrooms, a backyard, and a garage wide enough for two cars or, as Earl had already planned, a homemade golf-practice facility.

Thirty miles south of Los Angeles, Cypress was once known as "Waterville" on account of the abundance of artesian wells helping fuel a thriving agricultural community. By the early twentieth century, the growing settlement had gained a stop on the Pacific Electric Railway line, taking on the new name Cypress in 1957 after the distinctive evergreen trees found in the area. A school, newspaper, post office, and bank followed, marking its steady, if modest, growth. Originally a rural dairy town where cows once outnumbered humans by fifty to one, Cypress was eventually swept into Los Angeles's urban sprawl. As demand for land in the city pushed dairies out, Cypress was only too happy to accommodate the overspill, transforming its pastures into hundreds of cookie-cutter houses on mirror-image roads, including that of 6704 Teakwood Street.

While they loved the house that they had found, the real estate agent handling the sale advised them against buying it, saying it wasn't their kind of area. In other words, it was a white neighborhood. As a former Green Beret, Earl Woods wasn't dissuaded. Besides, he had been through much worse than just a few bricks hurled from some ignorant local bigots.

But as soon as they moved in, the Woodses realized just what the realtor had meant. Barely a day went past without an orange or a lime splattering against their windows. Soon, the panes would rattle with pellets fired from BB guns too. Still, though, the Woodses refused to move, and, slowly, peace won.

Within days of moving into their new home, though, Earl had set to work making his own personal golf facility. In the couple's garage, he rigged up a net, and with a slab of artificial grass stuck to the floor, he began working on his swing. Spending hours a day in his garage after work, Earl's golf game improved dramatically. Within a year, his handicap of 12 had dropped to 7 and, soon after, to a 4.

Earl Woods had been bitten by the golf bug when he and Tida lived in New York City. As he saw out the last few months of his time in the US Army at Fort Hamilton in Brooklyn, Woods had started playing at Dyker Beach, a municipal course in the shadow of the Verrazzano Bridge linking Brooklyn to Staten Island. He was immediately hooked.

In California, he could play all year round—in shorts too. And with the Navy Club so close, he could easily put all of those endless hours in his garage into practice too. So what if there were no other Black or brown faces in the neighborhood? Nobody said you had to be neighborly.

Born in Manhattan, Kansas, in 1932, Earl Woods was one of his father's eleven children from his two marriages. A street cleaner and a caretaker, Miles Woods was a devout Baptist, albeit one with a penchant for profanity. His first marriage, to Viola, yielded five children, of which Earl was the youngest, while his second, to Maude, resulted in another six. But both of Earl's parents were dead before he reached the age of thirteen.

While Miles Woods wanted Earl to play baseball for the Kansas City Monarchs in the Negro Leagues, his mother, Viola, was adamant he got a good education instead. Earl ended up going to Kansas State College (now Kansas State University) on a baseball scholarship, graduating with a Bachelor of Science degree in sociology in 1953. Soon after, Earl Woods enlisted with the US Army and served two tours in Vietnam, the first as an infantry officer in the early 1960s, and the next as a member of Army Special Forces. When he returned to the United States, he rose to the rank of lieutenant colonel before his final posting took him to Fort Hamilton. Then, at the age of forty-two and with just months before the end of his military career, he got captured. By golf.

"I wasn't just captured by golf. I was shanghaied," he said.

Playing with colleagues, he snuck on to the Dyker Beach course on the second hole, out of the view of the starter and the clubhouse, and with some borrowed clubs, shot a score of 91 for seventeen holes. Woods hadn't felt such a buzz since he had played baseball at Kansas State College. "I considered golf a little old girl's game. I never held a club in my life, not even a putter. I had no desire to play, and I got hooked in that one afternoon," Earl recalled.

Soon after, in the spring of 1975, just as Lee Elder became the first Black player to appear at the Masters at Augusta National and the war in Vietnam finally came to its inglorious end, Tida Woods was pregnant. Earl, with three kids from his first marriage to support already, wasn't exactly thrilled. "I wasn't looking forward to it," he said. "But Tida was because, in Thai culture, the marriage is not fully consummated until you have a child."

Tida Woods gave birth to a baby boy at Long Beach Memorial Hospital at 10:50 p.m. on December 30, 1975. After missing the births of his first three children when he was serving in Vietnam, Earl Woods was present this time as his new son entered the world.

"God, he is ugly," he said.

The couple deliberated long and hard on choosing the name for their new addition but settled on Eldrick, because it not only meant "wise ruler" in Old English, which appealed to Earl's grandiose ambitions for his child, but it started with an *E*, for Earl, and ended in a *K*, for Kultida. They added a middle name too: Tont, a traditional Thai name meaning "beginning."

When the couple came home from the hospital, their new child in Tida's arms, the first thing Earl did was place his son gently in his crib and spin some jazz records, in a preemptive attempt to dictate his son's future taste in music. Despite the image that Earl Woods would create for himself as the pushy parent intent on driving his son on to ever greater heights, he had always maintained that he had no expectations for Eldrick. "I certainly wasn't pondering how to turn this wonderful creature into an international superstar," he said.

But Eldrick was never called by his given name. Instead, Earl nicknamed him "Tiger," in honor of his close friend, a South Vietnamese lieutenant colonel whom he served with in Vietnam by the name of Vuong Dang Phong. "He was a tiger in combat, so I began calling him Tiger," Earl explained. Throughout his time in the conflict, Phong had been by his side, saving his life on several occasions, and though the pair had lost contact after the war had ended, Earl had always pledged to pay tribute to him by giving his son the same nickname, hoping, against hope perhaps, that one day Phong might see Tiger on television or read about him and realize just who he was named after.

But he never did.

When Earl Woods became a father for the fourth time, he pledged he would do things differently this time. No more would he be away from home for months on end. No more would he struggle to get involved with his kids' upbringing. From now on, he pledged, Tiger and he would always be there for each other, without fail. His time in Vietnam was never out of his system and had taught him many things about himself and life. Often, he would talk about the mental fortitude it took to survive combat—the unwavering focus, the sheer stubborn will required to stay alive. For Earl, these were the qualities that made a man and the lessons he needed to teach his new son. In that sense, Vietnam wasn't just a footnote in Earl's life; it was almost a blueprint for Tiger's.

It was also why a few racist thugs in his new neighborhood were nothing to get worked up about, not least because Earl Woods had become wearily accustomed to racism throughout his life. When he played baseball for Kansas State College in the 1950s, becoming the first Black player to play in the Big Eight Conference (which was then the Big Seven Conference), for example, he often had to stay in a separate accommodation than his white teammates when the team was on the road. Even in the army, where he attained the rank of lieutenant colonel, Earl Woods would have white subordinates saluting him during the day, but then, on the way home each evening, he would have to sit at the back of the bus while the same juniors took the seats in the whites-only section at the front. Ironically, Earl had only joined up because he thought it was the one vocation where he might receive equal treatment.

When Earl Woods was sent to Germany in the mid-1950s with the army, bringing his first wife, Ann, with him, he was taken to see a potential apartment for the couple to live in, but as soon as they got out of their car, they were met with scores of people, all staring and pointing at them. "People got out of their cars, pointing at us as though we were aliens," he recalled in 2006. "I asked the landlord what they were talking about. 'They're looking for your tails,' he said."

One evening, as Tiger slept at Teakwood Street, Earl stood over him and imagined what life would have in store for his baby boy. Whatever it was, and based on how little had really changed for people of color in the United States, all he knew was that Tiger Woods was going to face many more challenges than most. "But I knew Tiger was special the day he was born," he said.

CHAPTER 2
KINDERGARTEN WUNDERKIND

"In the picture business, I've seen too many precocious kids like this sweet little boy and too many starry-eyed parents."
—Actor James Stewart, October 1978

Word was spreading fast about Earl Woods's brilliant boy, largely because Earl Woods never stopped talking about him. Down at the Navy Club, Earl's friends couldn't wait for him to bring Tiger along, just so they could marvel at this cute little kid with the big talent. Now, following a phone call from Earl where he told producers that his two-year-old son was not just going to revolutionize golf but race relations in the United States as well, a TV crew from Los Angeles cable channel KCBS, along with sportscaster and former NFL defensive back Jim Hill, were on their way to film a short segment with Tiger at the club.

During the piece, Jim Hill turned to the camera and declared that "this young man [Tiger] is going to be to golf what Jimmy Connors and Chris Evert are to tennis." Later, in what passed for an interview with young Tiger, Hill pressed him repeatedly about what he liked so much about golf, but the toddler, clearly uncomfortable, was reluctant to offer any answer. That said, he did have more pressing concerns. "I gotta go poo-poo," he announced. Earl, Tida, Jim Hill, and the crew all collapsed in laughter.

Earl Woods knew what he was doing. As soon as the report was broadcast, the phone at Teakwood Street started ringing, with the producers of *The Mike Douglas Show* first in line. A keen golfer, Mike Douglas had seen Jim Hill's report, and Tiger Woods, not surprisingly, had really caught his eye. Within a few days, his production team had tracked down the boy and his parents and booked him and his father for the show. "[Tiger] stood out like a sore thumb, because they were all swinging like babies, and he swung like he does now," Douglas said in an interview with *The Cincinnati Enquirer* in 2000.

On October 6, 1978, ten weeks shy of his third birthday, Tiger Woods made his first television studio appearance hitting some balls on *The Mike Douglas Show.* It was a memorable TV debut, not least as his two fellow guests that evening were genuine Hollywood legends in the shape of Bob Hope and James Stewart. Dressed in shorts, a T-shirt, and a red cap, and carrying a big red bag of golf clubs on his back, Tiger wandered on to the studio floor and hit a few putts on a makeshift green to the amazement of guests and audience alike. But the little boy, just as he was with Jim Hill and KCBS, was clearly very uncomfortable with all of the attention.

Earl Woods, on the other hand, dressed in his turtleneck and wearing a gold medallion, seemed to revel in the occasion, basking in his son's limelight. But as young Tiger Woods would soon discover, this was just the start of a childhood—an entire lifetime, in fact—living in the public eye and something he would somehow have to find a way of getting accustomed to.

Certainly, Stewart was taken with Tiger, but speaking to host Mike Douglas in the green room after the show, the *It's a Wonderful Life* star, then seventy, expressed his concern about just what a stage-managed childhood like his could do to a youngster like Tiger. "In the picture business, I've seen too many precocious kids like this sweet little boy," he ventured, adding, "and too many starry-eyed parents."

On the way home, meanwhile, Tiger had something to get off his chest. The makeshift putting green they had erected in the studio for him to play on, he said, was sloping too much, and that's why he missed his putt on the show. Earl and Tida chuckled. That was their little Tiger all over.

Even at the ages of two and three, Tiger Woods could tell a good golf swing from a bad one, nudging his dad when some player or other at the Navy Club carved a ball into the rough or shanked one into the trees, or recognizing when someone's swing was unorthodox, unwieldy, or just plain wrong. Before he reached kindergarten, and even before he could count, Tiger knew the golf scoring system and how it worked, and he would watch video tapes of old Masters tournaments, mimicking the swings of Player and Nicklaus, of Watson and Ballesteros, with his dog Toba sitting by as a ready-made gallery.

Instinctively, he seemed to know his way around a golf course, too, hazards and all. When he played with his father, carrying just three clubs in his bag (a driver, a 7-iron, and a putter), Earl would ask him why he was hitting a ball in a certain direction. "Because there's a sand twap," he would reply, or "because there's wawa."

The only condition ever imposed on Tiger, from his mother at least, was that when he finally went to school, he would only ever be permitted to play golf once his schoolwork was not just done but done to the highest possible standard. There would be no exceptions.

Armed with his dog-eared copies of Ben Hogan's *Five Lessons: The Modern Fundamentals of Golf* and *Golf My Way* by Jack

Nicklaus, and his experience as an instructor of Military Science and Tactics, Earl Woods set about building his son into a sporting legend. As soon as Earl got home from work at McDonnell Douglas, the pair would head to the garage to hit some balls, or sit together as Earl explained what all the instructional photographs were about in his coaching manuals. And, as the months passed, Earl's hunch that he might just have a golf prodigy on his hands seemed to be borne out.

For Earl, the secret in keeping his young son enthused and engaged lay not so much in teaching the technical aspects of the golf swing ("How are you gonna explain a grip to a ten-month-old?" he once said) but in the manner in which he communicated with his young son. "We transcended the parent-child relationship and became best friends," he said. "I never treated Tiger like a kid. I treated Tiger as an equal."

When Earl took Tiger to the practice range at the Navy Club, the toddler hit ball after ball, each with unerring accuracy. Earl even let him play a hole on the club's challenging Destroyer Course—a 410-yard par-4, which the tot completed in eleven shots (eight to the green and three putts).

Not everybody was delighted to see young Tiger doing his thing at the Navy Club. For one, Earl Woods wasn't universally popular among the members. The idea of a Black man being a member of a golf club, even one owned and operated by the military, presented problems. When he played at the Navy Club, other members jokingly called him "Sgt. Brown," as though it was inconceivable for a Black man like him to ever rise to the higher rank of lieutenant colonel that he achieved, let alone be an ex–Green Beret and two-time veteran of Vietnam. Worse still was the fact that he also had a child who was in danger of becoming better than anyone else at the club, even though he hadn't even started kindergarten. Suddenly, after several complaints, the club informed Earl that Tiger was not allowed to play until he was ten years old. Those were the rules, they said. Only it wasn't true; all too often, Earl would see other kids, much younger than ten, playing at the course or practicing on the range without an accompanying adult in sight. But these other kids were different. They were white.

In the spring of 1980, Earl and Tida (although, to be accurate, it was more Earl than Tida) decided that Tiger's talents needed some professional guidance, but the prohibitive cost of lessons and, for that matter, the wholesale lack of junior programs in the Southern California area, and especially ones for children as young as Tiger Woods, meant their options were extremely limited.

There was one possibility, however.

Set in the northeast corner of Long Beach, about seven miles from Teakwood Street, Heartwell Golf Park was an eighteen-hole, par-3 course measuring a little over 2,100 yards. Short and relatively straightforward, it was the kind of nonthreatening golf course that was perfect for those taking up the game and who wanted to get a feel before they took the leap and stepped up to golf courses that were longer and more challenging. It was perfect for kids like Tiger Woods, at least in the short term.

A few weeks after the dashing young Spaniard Seve Ballesteros had cruised to his first Masters victory at Augusta, Tida Woods took her son along to Heartwell, his three little, cut-down clubs his dad had made for him slung over his back. When they reached the pro shop, Tida found the assistant professional Rudy Duran standing behind the counter. Before he started working at Heartwell, Duran had tried his hands in the purgatory of the minitours, bouncing around the Canadian Tour and satellite tours in the

United States, all the while dreaming of one day making it into the bright lights and big paychecks of the PGA Tour. The son of a car upholsterer and a housewife, Duran grew up without access to any golf. He had first picked up the clubs in 1968 during his time serving in the US Air Force, before spending many years as an educator and counsellor in New Mexico, teaching biology, guiding teenagers, and coaching everything from baseball to basketball. But he found his calling in golf.

When he was discharged from the air force in 1971, Duran had decided to turn pro but also took jobs as a club professional, just so he always had some money coming in. Which is why there was now a very shy, cherubic four-year-old boy peering up and over the shop counter at him.

Tida informed Duran that her son was showing a real talent for golf and that she was keen to get her son some lessons. Duran told her to bring him in, at which point Tida pointed to Tiger, smiling up at him. Despite his appearances on *The Mike Douglas Show* and Jim Hill's KCBS show, Duran had no idea who this little kid was. "Most nights I was working at the club, so didn't really watch any TV," he said. "So that was the first time I ever saw him, when he turned up at Heartwell."

Duran stepped out from behind the counter and asked Tida and Tiger to follow him to the practice ground, just so he could take a look at what he might be working with.

"How old are you, Tiger?" asked Duran.

"I'm four . . . and a half," replied Tiger.

At the range, Duran teed up three balls and watched intently as Tiger used his sawn-off driver to hit three arrow-straight shots into the distance. "They were just perfect little shots," recalled Duran. "I just remember being shocked at how someone so small could get the golf club back over his shoulder and whack it out there. It went nowhere really—maybe sixty or seventy yards—but he hit it perfect each and every time."

His audition over, Duran informed Tida that Tiger was more than welcome to come and play at Heartwell, and, better still, he could do so free of charge, so impressed had Duran been with the prodigious talent he had just witnessed. Whether he knew it or not, suddenly, Rudy Duran—the thirty-one-year-old club pro with the *Magnum, P.I.* mustache—was now a fully integrated member of Project Tiger. "The kid's not exceptional," Duran told the media soon after. "He's way beyond that."

Soon, Rudy Duran, just like his contemporaries at the Navy Club, would be inundated with calls from the media, eager to see the little kid with the big talent. Invariably, Earl Woods signed off most requests with almost indecent haste, even though Duran wasn't entirely sure just how happy young Tiger was with all the attention he was receiving. "I mean, he did it," said Duran, "but when we're done, it was, 'Let's go play golf.'"

While Tiger clearly understood the mechanics of the golf swing, he still found the par-54 course at Heartwell a little on the long side. He was, after all, not even five years old yet. Which was why Rudy Duran developed a new kind of game for his new star player: Tiger Par. Put simply, Tiger Par was a way of keeping Woods motivated and engaged whenever he thought his game wasn't up to the demands of Heartwell. "When he started, Tiger couldn't reach nearly all of the holes with his tee shots, so we ignored the scorecard and gave each hole a Tiger Par for him to play to," said Duran. It was under the Tiger Par scoring system that Tiger, age just five, shot eight under for a round at Heartwell.

What Duran's Tiger Par game also meant was that, from a very young age, Woods had the opportunity to develop his short game, pitching, chipping his way to the putting surface when the other, older kids on the junior program were capable of reaching the green in a single shot. "I think it has a lot to do with why he was always so good on or around the greens in later life," added Duran.

Recognizing the huge potential of Tiger and knowing that Earl and Tida Woods were not in the position financially to help their son not just with lessons but with equipment as well, Duran also got him some new clubs. "Junior clubs weren't really available in the late seventies, but I managed to get him some clubs and then cut them down in the little workshop I had at the back of the pro shop," said Duran.

The difference it made to Tiger's development was key. Now, rather than trying to swing a club that was too long for him, or gripping down it just to try and make it work, Tiger had clubs that fitted him and his game correctly. "No one was really getting the right-sized clubs ordered for juniors, but I tried to make his clubs fit so that he could maintain his swing," added Duran.

It's a valid point. After all, look at John Daly, winner of two majors and a player known for one of the most unorthodox over-swings in the professional ranks. His unique "killer swing" was the result of using full-size adult clubs when he was a child, and to this day, his swing is still unlike anything in the game. "There I was, age six, trying to swing a man-sized driver. Not only was the club far too long for me, but it was far too heavy for me too. It would be the same as an adult trying to swing a driver that is sixty inches long instead of forty-three inches, and that weighs something like thirty ounces instead of thirteen," he once said. "The result was that these clubs were so long and heavy that they swung me."

With clubs that fitted him, Tiger was good to go.

On his sixth birthday, he, or rather Earl, accepted an invitation Rudy Duran had received to put on an exhibition at Redlands

Country Club near San Bernardino—one of the oldest clubs in the United States. After impressing the members with his range of shots, Tiger and Earl took on Rudy Duran and a local twelve-year-old, Michele Lyford, whose father, Ted, had played golf at Arizona State University and nearly made it through qualifying school for the PGA Tour in the fall of 1969. "I was nervous," Lyford told the *Redland Community News* in 2019. "I couldn't let this six-year-old beat me. I was twice as old as he was, and he was half my size."

She didn't. Team Tiger was taken down by Lyford and Duran, with the twelve-year-old shooting 41 over the nine-hole contest, and Tiger trailing with 51.

The opportunities that being at Heartwell and working with Rudy Duran had afforded Tiger, like the exhibition at Redlands, had impressed Earl Woods, and, for once, Tiger's presence there had happened largely by chance and not because it was part of Earl's grand master plan for his son. "Why was he at Heartwell Golf Park, on a par-3 golf course? It wasn't my decision," he said later. "Things have always happened for a reason in the lives of Tiger and me. It was just meant to be."

To his credit, Duran had realized, almost immediately, that the primary task with a talent as huge as young Tiger's was to nurture his love for the game, to keep things fun and engaging, and to not bog him down with the technical aspects of the game. There would be plenty of time for that in the years to come. Instead, he taught Woods the fundamentals of the grip, the stance, and the swing, but he did so in a way that tapped into Tiger's natural athletic ability. He wasn't trying to build a machine; he was simply helping a future force of nature find his rhythm. In other words, he quickly recognized that he wasn't dealing with an ordinary child. If anything, he was simply facilitating a genius.

When he wasn't at Heartwell, Tiger spent his spare time playing golf wherever and whenever he could. He would stand on his front lawn at Teakwood Street, imagining there was a lake between his house and the neighbor's lawn—the putting green—across the road, before clubbing lightweight plastic balls over the "water hazard" and onto the putting surface. He would even hit balls over the roof of the family home, never once breaking anything.

Even when he attended golf events, he was more interested in playing than watching. When Rudy Duran took Tiger to the Los Angeles Open at Rancho Park in 1983, he sat him down at the greenside to watch the household names his father was forever talking about, like Tom Watson, Johnny Miller, and Lee Trevino. But Tiger couldn't care less. "He maybe lasted fifteen minutes before he jumped up and asked me when we were going to play golf," he said.

Duran headed to the phone box at the clubhouse, made a few calls, and, an hour later, the pair were playing nine holes on the way back home. "He really wasn't interested in watching the touring pros," he added. "Earl used to watch golf on TV and read about it, but I don't think Tiger really did."

It was a little different when Tiger had the chance to play with them though. Later, in 1982, Tiger was given the opportunity to play two holes with Sam Snead at Soboba Springs in San Jacinto, thanks to Rudy Duran and the reputation of his junior program. Slammin' Sam, now sixty-nine, was not only the seven-time major winner who also held the record of eighty-two PGA Tour wins but also one of the most famous golfers who had ever trod the fairways. Excitedly, Duran told Tiger of his date with one of the game's true greats.

"Is he any good?" asked Tiger.

"He's only one of the best players ever," replied Duran.

Snead had already played several groups when he met Tiger and Earl Woods, as well as Duran and his father, at the designated tee and posed for a photograph. After hitting his tee shot on the green, Snead and the group moved forward to the next tee where Tiger teed it up and, without even considering the layout of the hole ahead of him and the fact he still couldn't reach the putting surface, proceeded to smite his ball down the right side of the fairway, at which point it bounced right and rolled down a hill and into a water hazard. When Tiger reached his ball, he found it partially submerged in the sludge at the side of the pond. Most players would have taken an unplayable lie and their medicine. Not Tiger Woods. "He just went down there, took out his club, and whacked it out of the water and onto the green." Duran smiled.

Snead did a double take and laughed while Rudy Duran just shook his head in disbelief. Two putts later, meanwhile, Tiger had a bogey, or a Tiger Par as Duran deemed it. "He just wasn't fazed by anything—the crowd, Sam Snead, nothing. It was all so natural to him," added Duran.

After their game, Sam Snead posed for another photo with Tiger, signing an autograph for him as the youngster sipped on a soda. Still, though, young Tiger had no idea of whom he had just played with.

CHAPTER 3
EARLY LEARNING

"When I met Tiger, aged four, I quickly realized I was signing up to be a student."
—Rudy Duran, Tiger's first golf coach

On September 14, 1981, still age five, Tiger Woods started kindergarten at Cerritos Elementary School, a drive and a long iron away from the family home on Teakwood Street. Opened in September 1969, Cerritos was an unremarkable building in an unremarkable part of town, with just two kindergarten rooms to accommodate each year's thirty-strong intake. Until now, Tiger's short life had been little more than an extended play date with his dad, albeit one in which all they ever played was golf. On the first day, Tiger was nervous, but his father reassured him that every other kid would be too. Tida Woods was less compassionate, keen to get over her message. "If you don't study hard," she said, "your golf clubs are going in the closet."

The first day at any new school can be tough for children, but according to Tiger Woods, his was almost enough to make him never return. "A group of sixth graders tied me to a tree, spray-painted the word 'n*****' on me, and threw rocks at me," he recalled. "And the teacher really didn't do much of anything." Instead, Woods was told he could go home but still had to sprint the short distance back to Teakwood Street just to avoid further attacks.

It was, he later said, the first time he "became aware of my racial identity."

The story, told to NBA star Charles Barkley for his 2005 book, *Who's Afraid of a Large Black Man*, was shocking when it emerged, especially for those who were at Los Cerritos Elementary School at the time, as it was the first they had ever heard of it. Then principal Donald Hill said no report of any incident like this was ever made, nor did either of Tiger's parents ever lodge a formal complaint. Besides, the playground at Los Cerritos was always heavily supervised at all times and surrounded with the kind of fencing that would make a swift escape home almost impossible, especially for a traumatized five-year-old on his first day at school.

Meanwhile, Tiger's teacher that day, Maureen Decker, was still incensed about the claims nearly thirty years later. Hiring the attorney Gloria Allred in her bid to get a full apology from Woods, Decker said the claims had ruined her life. "I am asking Tiger for a private and public apology to put my mind at ease and set the record straight," she told a press conference in April 2010. "I was shocked, saddened, and disappointed by his false allegations of physical and racial abuse on his first day of school in my kindergarten class," adding that the only explanation she could give was that Earl Woods had invented the story for "publicity." Maureen Decker never did get her apology.

For young Tiger, school life suddenly represented an entirely new challenge. From a life where all he ever had to worry about was where his next birdie was coming from, there were now other, more serious concerns for him to deal with—and he didn't like it.

Tiger was shy at the best of times, but his anxiety increased to the point where he developed a stammer. He took to sitting at the back of the class in the hopes teachers wouldn't call on him to speak, in case he embarrassed himself. The only time he ever spoke normally, where he ever felt truly comfortable, was when he was talking about or, better still, playing golf. He was in complete charge then.

Earl and Tida couldn't understand why it was happening, and even several sessions with a speech therapist failed to determine the root of the problem. Tiger even tried talking to his new dog Boom Boom (named after PGA Tour winner Fred "Boom Boom" Couples) to help him through it. "Then it dawned on us," said Earl. "Tida talked to him in Thai, and I talked to him in English. When Tiger spoke, he talked in English. The thing was, he didn't want to listen or speak in Thai. His mind was rebelling. We stopped talking in Thai, and his stuttering ceased."

The stammering always stopped, however, when Tiger had a point to make. With a birthday on December 30, Tiger always received his presents for Christmas and then another set five days later, but when he was five, he suggested to his parents that, through no fault of his own, he was being shortchanged when it came to gifts simply by dint of his birth date. A family meeting was convened, and Tiger stated his case, omitting Santa Claus from his argument and instead blaming his parents for the discrepancy. The following year, Tiger got all the presents he felt he deserved, and the issue was never raised again. "He just thought we bought one batch of presents and split them," said Earl. "I never could convince him otherwise."

Tida Woods's strict rules regarding school and golf, meanwhile, was the only encouragement—or threat—the young Tiger needed to put in as much work in his lessons as he did on the golf course. And he was doing things on a golf course that suspended disbelief. He had already completed nine holes at the Navy Club in just forty-eight shots at the age of three (although Earl let him tee the ball up for each shot). Aged four, he had beaten a sixteen-year-old in a minor competition at the Mile Square Golf Club in nearby Fountain Valley. At five, he had been profiled in *Golf Digest* magazine by writer Lyla Dusing, which had described him as "about as tall as a ball washer" and an "incredible" talent. "He has been the subject of a profile on CBS and was scheduled this fall to appear on the TV show *That's Incredible!*" it read. Tiger, however, told them it was no big deal. "After all, golfers get on television lots of times," he said.

When Tiger duly appeared on *That's Incredible!*, he did so alongside Tammy Stafford, a nine-year-old female weightlifter who lifted hosts Cathy Lee Crosby, Fran Tarkenton, and John Davidson off the ground. After the show, an audience member had even asked for Tiger's autograph; never having practiced his signature, he printed his name in block capitals.

There was also an appearance on the *Today* program where presenter Bryant Gumbel called him "the most amazing five-year-old golfer you have ever seen." During the segment, his coach Rudy Duran highlighted young Tiger's impressive golf game and predicted great things for him, while his mother, Tida, said that he only ever wanted to play with his putter and never any of the other toys that she and Earl had given to him. When Gumbel asked him what he wanted Santa to bring him for Christmas, Tiger looked genuinely uncomfortable, his eyes staring at the ground, just as they did in all the other TV interviews. Eventually, after some encouragement, he had an idea. "How 'bout a 1-iron and a 2-iron?" he replied.

In all of his television appearances in his very young life, Tiger Woods never once looked at ease with a TV camera in his face or a microphone shoved under his nose, but why would he? He had no choice. Each time, there seemed to be a palpable sense that he was now having to navigate a world he hadn't chosen, but rather one thrust upon him by his talent or by his father, or a combination of the two. The only times he ever looked happy in these early media events was in those segments when he was actually playing golf, not being asked questions he didn't understand or care to answer.

Despite the constant media clamor for his attention and Earl's seemingly inexhaustible desire to expose him to it, Tiger's appetite for the game never dimmed. Indeed, with each passing week, he just got better. When he was six, Earl decided it was high time Tiger tested himself in an altogether more serious competition and entered his son in the Junior World Golf Championships, which, for Tiger's age group, was held over the par-3 course at Presidio Hills. Established in 1968 by the San Diego Junior Golf Association, it brought together over one thousand players from scores of countries and virtually every state in America, and Earl liked the idea of Tiger participating because there was precious little traveling involved. Tiger, meanwhile, liked it because it was a title with the word *world* in it, which could only ever mean that it really was very important.

Yet it didn't quite pan out the way they planned. Having made a par on one hole, the scorekeeper for Tiger's group marked him down for a birdie, and at the end of the round, Tiger signed the card accordingly, earning him an instant disqualification. While Tiger protested his innocence, Earl remonstrated with the scorekeeper, even though both he and the scorekeeper knew his son had messed up.

"Did you sign this?"

"Yes."

"Did you check it?"

"No, Daddy."

It was a lesson learned, and one Tiger would never forget. "I told him to never trust anyone else with your scorecard. Never," Earl said in 2006. "Tiger's little eyes were as big as teacups. That was the end of it. He hasn't signed a wrong scorecard since."

For Earl Woods, lying about your score or cheating at golf constituted the worst kind of crime on the golf course. He believed that anyone who did it was merely cheating themselves and that, ultimately, it devalued any achievement. He told his son as much too. "To this day he's incapable of lying. He may not give you a full answer, but he never lies," he added. "The one time Tiger lied as a boy, he got physically ill."

As Tiger grew taller, many of Heartwell Golf Park's greens soon became in reach and on May 12, 1982, Tiger Woods at age six-and-a-half recorded his first hole in one when he aced the twelfth hole. Having hit his tee shot, Woods could see his ball carry the bunker guarding the front of the green, but he still wasn't tall enough to see exactly where it landed. Then he heard the cheers as one of Rudy Duran's friends lifted him up, high above his head, so he could see that his ball wasn't on the green but actually in the cup itself. Elated, Tiger ran to the green to collect his ball until his celebration was cut short. "You idiot!" shouted one of his playing partners. "You left your golf bag back on the tee!" And Tiger trudged back, still smiling.

At home, Tiger watched videos of old Masters tournaments, when Jack Nicklaus, Craig Stadler, and Seve Ballesteros won—all the time fine-tuning his swing and picturing the day when he, too, would stride up the eighteenth fairway with a three-shot lead and doff his cap to the Augusta National patrons rising as one to salute their new champion. Earl also bought some audio cassettes, filled with a variety of motivational messages, and Tiger would listen before writing them down and pinning the maxims to his bedroom wall. "I will own my own destiny," he told himself. "I smile at obstacles. My will moves mountains. I do it with all my heart."

It wasn't the only trick Earl Woods employed to make sure Tiger maintained focus ahead of his matches. Before one Saturday tournament, Tida and Tiger sat in the car waiting to go when Earl noticed that Tiger's clubs were still in the living room. Smuggling them to the car, Earl hid them under a blanket on the back seat, and the three set off. When they arrived at the course, Tiger opened the car's trunk, only to find that his clubs weren't there. His lip trembled. "Dad! I left them in the living room!" he said.

Earl shrugged. "Well, Tiger, I guess you won't be playing golf today."

With Tiger on the verge of tears, Earl produced the golf bag from the backseat before giving Tiger another lecture about personal responsibility. "He never left anything behind ever again," said Earl.

All of Earl's instruction, be it technical or motivational, was designed to achieve the same objective: to create a golfer equipped with unshakable focus and perseverance under what could be crushing pressure. In other words, the kind of traits that Earl needed during his time in Vietnam. But it wasn't just Earl Woods pushing Tiger ever onward. At times, Tida Woods could be just as forthright, perhaps even more so. "In sport, you have to go for the throat," she told Tiger. "Because if [you are] all friendly, they come back and beat your ass. So, you kill them. Take their heart."

Yes, behind the cherubic face and the purest of smiles, Tiger was growing up quickly, maybe quicker than he needed to, but gradually becoming the cold-blooded golf assassin that Earl Woods had always envisaged. Just before he turned seven, and on one of the rare occasions he was allowed back on the Navy Club course, for example, Tiger won the Drive, Pitch, and Putt competition—in the

Under 10 category. On another occasion, Rudy Duran arranged for Tiger to play a round with a local club professional by the name of Stewart Reed. By the time they reached the turn, Tiger was ahead before Reed gathered himself and emerged victorious, leaving Woods in tears at the end of the contest. Woods also came in eighth out of 150 kids, all of them at least three years older than him, at the Optimist Junior World Under 10 division at Presidio Hills in San Diego.

Disappointed again, Tiger vowed to return the following year and make amends.

CHAPTER 4

A TOUR PRO IN A KID'S BODY

"He never rebelled once. I never smacked him or chastised him or punished him. He was the closest thing to a perfect child you will ever run into."

—Earl Woods, 2002

Six years after Los Angeles had been awarded the rights to host the Summer Olympic Games, and fifty-two years after it had first staged them, the city stepped up and delivered an opening ceremony unlike any other in the event's long history. On Saturday July 28, eight-year-old Tiger Woods sat with his parents in front of the television at Teakwood Street and watched, along with 180 million other Americans, as Bill Suitor, the self-styled Rocketman, flew across the Los Angeles Coliseum field on his space-age jet pack, signaling the start of the Games. His son's interest piqued, Earl Woods decided that maybe the two of them should go and see some of the sports on offer and bagged a couple of tickets to see the archery competition. That said, young Tiger still couldn't understand why golf wasn't a part of the Olympic Games too. After all, he reckoned, it was every bit as valid as archery, if not more so.

As the Olympic Games captured the world's attention and America's Carl Lewis matched the achievements of Jesse Owens at the 1936 Berlin Games, winning four gold medals in the same events, Tiger dreamed of one day slipping a gold medal over his neck, if only golf ever got the green light after its eighty-year absence from the Games.

With Rudy Duran's input, though, Tiger's game had moved on apace, and at the age of eight, he triumphed in the ages 9–10 category at the Junior World Golf Championships in San Diego, the first win of what would be six victories in the event. He also broke 80 for an eighteen-hole round for the first time.

Young Tiger was quite the competitor, even when he wasn't playing a round. With Earl working, Tida would jump in her Plymouth Duster with Tiger beside her and drop him off at the golf course where she would routinely leave with him twenty-five cents for a hot dog, twenty-five cents for the payphone to call her when he needed picking up, and another twenty-five cents for emergencies, which, in Young Tiger's mind, meant his stake money for emergency putting contests against other kids for cash. Inevitably, Tiger walked away with a pocketful of quarters, storing them away in his bedroom when he got home, all the while keeping his little side hustle quiet from his father. Or so he thought. When Earl finally got wind of it, he lectured Tiger about the perils of gambling and that from now on, if he insisted on continuing with the putting competitions against the other children, then he could only do so if he told his father first and then made him his designated playing partner.

While he was yet to develop his trademark length with his tee shots, Tiger's short game already set him apart from his contemporaries. and his rare ability to salvage potential round-ruining situations was already becoming apparent. He always ended up having a wedge in his hand, having to improvise or fashion his shots after short tee-offs unlike other players. "He could really pitch and chip, but his putting was exceptional," said Rudy Duran. "Sometimes I would just throw some balls down on the green and watch as he made a whole bunch of them. What was interesting was when he did miss one, he really didn't like it."

Four years after Rudy Duran started coaching him, Tiger Woods duly became the Heartwell Golf Park junior club champion, something that Duran had always known was going to happen. Every week on a Saturday afternoon, the twenty youngsters in Duran's junior program would compete in tournaments and the level reached, not just by Woods, was outstanding. In time, Duran's program could boast an alumni that included three US Boys Junior champions, three US Amateur men's national champions, and a women's US Amateur champion—not to mention many collegiate players and other players who would go on to become successful PGA club professionals. Put simply, Heartwell had provided the ideal grounding for young Tiger: challenging and competitive, educational and fun.

At Los Cerritos Elementary School, meanwhile, Woods had found some friends and had, for the most part, managed to forget about what did, or didn't, happen on his very first day there, although he still suffered from the occasional nightmare. In one recurring episode, for instance, he found himself playing golf in the Deep South and being pursued by someone trying to kill him.

Thankfully, he now had a few friends like Alfredo Arguello and Mike Gout who had his back. For those who got to know Woods, he seemed like a normal, everyday kid but one who, by dint of his golfing talent, always seemed to have television crews and cameras turning up at regular intervals to talk to him. Often, Tida, the proud mom, would call round Tiger's friends ahead of an TV appearance just so they could watch or, failing that, to tell them to set their new video recorders so they didn't miss him.

He had also found a kindred spirit on the junior circuit too. Three years older than Tiger, Notah Begay III was a Native American boy of Navajo, San Felipe, and Isleta heritage from Albuquerque, New Mexico, who, as another non-white golfer from another unwealthy family, had taken Tiger under his wing when they played at the same tournaments, telling him, "You'll never be alone again."

While Earl was working at McDonnell Douglas, it was Tida's job to be his eyes and ears when it came to their son's golf. She would take Tiger to all of his lessons and competitions and stand in the shadows with her scorecard, making sure that she never missed a shot, good or bad. But it would also prove to be some priceless time for a mother and a son to enjoy each other's company, before Earl Woods took over the role upon his retirement.

It was a bond deepened by Tiger's first trip to his mother's homeland when, aged nine, he visited Thailand with her. For a young Tiger, the trip was a sensory explosion in stark contrast to the manicured greens and suburban comforts of Cypress and California. Tida was in her element, immersing her son in her homeland's culture and rich traditions, and explaining the tenets of Buddhism. It was an experience designed to not only widen his worldview but also keep him grounded, reminding him that his identity stretched far beyond clubhouses and golf courses, and that this half of his heritage was every bit as key to his identity as his father's African-American lineage.

On the trip, Tida took with her a chart she had kept of Tiger's childhood development and showed it to a Buddhist monk they visited. What he said shocked Tida. "This kid is special, like God sent an angel to be born," the monk told Tida.

Later, when Tida phoned Earl to tell him what the monk had told her, he wasn't in the least bit surprised. "Tell me something I don't know," he said.

• • •

On his tenth birthday, Earl arranged a surprise for his son's special day: a round of golf at the Navy Club course where, as he had reached the designated age, nobody could or would say anything about him being on the premises. No more hiding in the bushes, waiting for his dad to call him out and hit a few shots. Just him, his dad, and a course that had given him more grief in his young life than any boy could ever deserve.

Occasionally, Tiger would also meet up with his siblings as Earl tried to maintain a relationship between his four children. Often, he would let the older kids take Tiger camping, where Tiger would tell Kevin, eighteen years older than him, about how his golf was coming along or how obsessed he had become with *Star Wars*. During one trip, Kevin found Tiger staring up into the high branches of some nearby trees.

"What are you looking at?" asked Kevin.

"Ewoks," replied Tiger.

Meanwhile, Rudy Duran was working diligently on how he could make Tiger even better. Each week, he would drive the three-and-a-half-hour journey south from his home up the coast in San Luis Obispo, just to take his lessons with Tiger Woods or to play a round with him. Sometimes, he would just drop by Teakwood Street to catch up with Earl and Tida and update them on their son's progress, even though Tiger had already filled them in comprehensively on all the things he had been working on that week.

One thing that always struck Rudy Duran was the way that Tiger never got down about his golf game, nor did he suffer the anger or frustration that most golfers invariably exhibit when playing the most maddening of sports. "I can't recall him ever saying that golf is a difficult game," he said. Even when Woods wasn't at his best, which wasn't often, Duran found a kid who seemed entirely centered and never more relaxed than when he was on the golf course playing the game he so clearly loved. During one round together at Mesa Verde Country Club in Costa Mesa, California, Duran watched on as Woods made a mess of the 424-yard par-4 tenth hole with its water hazards in front of the tee and all down the right-hand side of the fairway. After his tee shot found the water, Woods dropped another ball and then promptly tugged his next shot into the drink once more. After another couple of shots, Woods finally made it to the green where a miserable three-putt saw him heading to the next tee with a 10 on his scorecard.

Rudy Duran couldn't resist teasing his star student. "Ha!" he laughed. "The world-famous Tiger Woods just made a 10 on the tenth hole at age ten!"

What was remarkable, however, was that Tiger just laughed along with Duran, forgetting about the disaster that had just taken place almost as soon as it had happened. There was no club hurling, no cursing, and none of the simmering rage that can so often derail a player's round. "Even at a young age, Tiger's composure was astonishing," added Duran. "Most golfers would have been steaming mad or depressed. Tiger was neither."

Tiger sat at home, leafing through his dad's latest copy of *Golf Digest* when he came across an article on Jack Nicklaus, the greatest player the game of golf had ever witnessed. Ordinarily, Tiger wouldn't have bothered to read it—he seemed to be in every issue anyway—but this time, there was a list of all the milestones, achievements, and records of the man they called "the Golden Bear," and Tiger couldn't help but compare his progress before deciding, then and there, that he would try his hardest to eclipse everything Jack Nicklaus had ever done, including those record seventeen major titles. Happily, he could already tick off many of Nicklaus's landmarks, having already beaten some of them, sometimes by as many as a couple of years, like the first time he had broken 80 for a round, or his first hole in one.

The problem, however, was that now it was eighteen major titles, not seventeen. Yes, as young Tiger set himself to the toughest of all tasks, the magnitude of the task ahead of him only ever seemed to get that much bigger. The Golden Bear, far from being a relic of the past, continued to demonstrate his enduring prowess on the grandest of stages. The Masters in April, six years removed from his prior major triumph at the 1980 PGA Championship at Oak Hill in Rochester, New York, witnessed Nicklaus etch another indelible mark in the annals of golf. At the age of forty-six, four years short of a slot on the then Seniors Tour (now the Champions Tour), he slipped on the Green Jacket for an unprecedented sixth time, a feat that crowned him the oldest winner in the tournament's storied history. It was a victory that came a full twenty-three years after a youthful, blond-haired Nicklaus first entered Augusta's Butler Cabin as a winner and a testament to his extraordinary longevity and sustained pursuit of excellence.

Even amidst his burgeoning dreams of golfing supremacy, there was always a pragmatic awareness within the young Tiger. He possessed an innate understanding that his prodigious talent on the course would naturally pave the way for success, and with that success would inevitably come financial complexities. This foresight, this anxiety, may have been remarkably mature for a ten-year-old, but it prompted a pivotal conversation with his parents where he discussed how their lives might change once he became successful, as he inevitably would. He even announced his intention to pursue an accounting course when he went to college, clarifying his rationale with a wisdom far beyond his years: "So I can manage the people who manage my money."

That said, there was still a side to him other than focused golfer that would not only become more noticeable as time went on, but actually signal him as one who was self-obsessed and, at times, extremely unsporting. When Woods lost to Hawaii's Jaysen Manuia in the 1986 Optimist Junior World Championship, Manuia finished the game and, without so much as a handshake from Tiger Woods, decided to go and play with some friends instead. Woods, meanwhile, sulked and scurried away.

However, Tiger's ascent to the rarefied heights occupied by Jack Nicklaus demanded more than natural talent. In the mind of Earl Woods, it now required a recalibration of Project Tiger's backroom team. This meant a parting of ways with Rudy Duran, who had diligently nurtured Tiger's game since the age of four and was also heading off to a new job. The pursuit of a new mentor, a fresh voice to elevate Tiger's development to the next echelon, became paramount in Earl's vision for his son's future.

Inspired by Nicklaus's Masters triumph, Earl Woods initiated a change in direction. He contacted John Anselmo, the well-regarded head professional at Meadowlark Golf Course in Huntington Beach, a mere twenty-minute drive south from their Teakwood Street home. At sixty-five, a decade Earl's senior, Anselmo possessed a wealth of experience and held a distinguished reputation as one of California's premier golf instructors, despite never having really competed on the professional tours himself. He had even given Rudy Duran a few lessons over the years too.

As a young man in the navy, John Anselmo was stationed in San Diego during the concluding stages of World War II, coincidentally at the very same naval base where the legendary Sam Snead also served. During this time, Anselmo would often observe Snead's practice sessions and his rounds, absorbing every nuance of his swing and his approach, mentally cataloguing the insights that would refine his own understanding of the game.

An agreement was forged between Earl Woods and John Anselmo that mirrored the understanding the Woodses had with Rudy Duran. The exceptional talent that radiated from young Tiger Woods was obvious and undeniable, and Anselmo recognized the potential mutual benefits of any collaboration. But, more importantly, Earl Woods knew that too. That's why no money ever changed hands.

With the handshake agreement sealed, Anselmo returned to share the news with his son, Dan, himself a teaching professional. "I have this new kid named Tiger Woods," he exclaimed with palpable excitement. "He's a tour player trapped in a little boy's body. He just needs the physical growth to catch up."

John Anselmo wasn't a guru in the mold of later, more-famous swing doctors that Woods would employ. He was all about the fundamentals—a patient craftsman who believed in building a golf swing from the ground up, brick by meticulously placed brick. When the young Tiger was brought to Anselmo, the coach focused not on any radical overhaul or revolutionary techniques but on the purity of an already exemplary motion. He instilled rhythm and balance and a natural, athletic release that would serve as the immutable core of Tiger's swing for years to come.

In an era when many would have been tempted to sensationalize or overly complicate the instruction of such a talent, Anselmo remained steadfastly grounded. His teaching was about repetition, about feel, about understanding how the body worked in harmony with the club. There was no theatrical flair, no grand pronouncements; just diligent work on the driving range, refining the basic movements that would later be executed under unimaginable pressure.

In his initial sessions with Woods, like anyone else who witnessed him play, Anselmo was hugely impressed, but he still earmarked one aspect of Tiger's game that clearly required additional work. Sure, young Tiger could play most every shot in the book, but it was his insistence on hitting the ball as hard as he could—or "killing" it—that Anselmo felt might jeopardize his rounds from time to time. A little more composure and some work on improving his balance, he thought, might just make the best young player in America even better.

Meanwhile, Earl and Tiger hit the road, traversing the state so Tiger could show the rest of California what they were up against. Just as Tida had taken Tiger to Thailand, the long road trips were an opportunity for Earl and his son to spend quality time together, or, as was more often the case, for young Tiger to fill in the many gaps in his knowledge that had been bothering him. Together they sat, staring out to the road ahead, as Tiger threw question after question at his dad, not just about golf but about anything and everything that entered his little head. Maybe they would be lying in their beds in another motel somewhere. It didn't matter. If Tiger was puzzled by something, anything, then he wasn't afraid to ask his father about it.

"Dad, what's the male menopause?"

Nothing ever seemed to be off-limits, but just as Earl thought the two had exhausted a particular topic, Tiger had another one up his sleeve.

"Dad, what's the immigration policy of Australia?"

To his credit, Earl would endeavor to answer as best he could, but he would tire long before his inquisitive son ever did. Eventually, Earl decided the only thing he could think of to shut him up was to "put his butt in bed."

CHAPTER 5
BRAIN TRAINING

"You're working with a Leonardo. You have to let the eagle soar."
—Dr. Jay Brunza, Project Tiger's resident sports psychologist

It had been coming for some time, but now, finally, it had happened. On November 28, 1987, Tiger Woods—aged eleven years and eleven months—and his father, alongside Earl's friends Bill Thompson, Clark Canfield, and Rick Bird, played a round of golf at the Long Beach Navy Golf Course. Over the first nine holes, Tiger struggled, shooting a disappointing 39 on the way out, but once he reached the turn, he was an altogether different player. With four birdies on the back nine, including one at the last hole, the youngster came home in an impressive thirty-two shots for a final total of 71. "Made about a fifteen-footer, a little right to left," he recalled. "I gave it the fist pump walking off the green and everything."

The best Earl Woods could manage, however, was 72.

For the first time in their lives, Tiger Woods had beaten his father in a round of golf, and though neither of them knew at the time, Earl would never again defeat his son. Yes, Earl was irritated that he had lost, but it proved to be a turning point in his relationship with his son and Earl's attitude to the game of golf more generally. No longer did he feel compelled to try his absolute hardest to beat Tiger. Instead, the will to win gave way to a much greater appreciation of just what his son was capable of on a golf course. In other words, Earl learned to relax. Well, a little.

Tiger, however, didn't know the meaning of the word. When Earl asked why he didn't relax more when he was playing golf, Tiger told him the only way he could do that was by shooting even lower scores. Even in his downtime, Woods would be thinking about golf and how he could conquer the particular challenges on certain courses. He even entered *Golf Digest*'s first Armchair Architect Competition (although his dad did it for him as Tiger was too young to enter himself), where he designed his dream golf hole: a 610-yard U-shaped par-5 with a double dogleg and an island tee, island sand traps, and—as a nod to Sawgrass, perhaps—an island green too.

He didn't win.

Nevertheless, life was good for Tiger in 1987. He did experience some disappointment when he found out that the World Wrestling Federation bouts his father taped for him were fake ("I didn't realize," he said later. "I felt so stupid."), but otherwise, he was excelling at school, getting straight A's and awards for outstanding effort and participation. He even had his first interest from the opposite sex, despite his shyness and Coke-bottle-thick glasses. He was growing rapidly too. In less than two years, he had gone from four foot nine to five foot four, and while he was still as skinny as a 1-iron, his longer limbs, coupled with that exceptional clubhead speed, helped him propel the ball ever farther.

On the golf course, he became simply untouchable. Over a summer where the competitions came on an almost daily basis, Woods played thirty-six junior matches and tournaments and won each and every one of them. Many years later, in 2022, Woods would tell an interviewer that he felt his "life peaked" in the summer of 1987.

For all his ferocious natural talent, though, some elements of Tiger's game still needed a little careful attention. His coaches, first Rudy Duran and then John Anselmo, had taken care of his already sublime swing, ironing out some of the idiosyncrasies, but Earl Woods believed his son would benefit from some brain training as well—especially as he was about to enter his teens when his young mind would, inevitably, begin to wander.

When Tiger and his father turned up at the Navy Club to play a round with Earl's friend Eric Utegaard, he found that Eric had brought along a colleague to make up a four-ball. His name was Jay Brunza, a former naval officer but now a clinical psychologist and a single-figure golfer to boot. Brunza had worked in pediatric oncology, guiding young people through their cancer treatment and teaching them how to cope with pain and stress, and now Earl, sensing his son needed some new techniques as well as his own growing impetus desire to improve Tiger's focus, wanted to enlist him into Project Tiger.

Earl set up a meeting between Tiger and Brunza where the psychologist taught the youngster to regulate his breathing and steady his heart rate whenever he felt the pressure was on. He also suggested hypnosis as a means of focusing—and Tiger was more than happy to try it. To demonstrate just how effective it could be, Brunza hypnotized Tiger, had him stick his arm out straight, and then told him that it was immovable. Earl Woods grabbed his son's arm and tried—and failed—to pull it down. Earl was impressed.

Tom Sargent, who worked occasionally with young Tiger at Yorba Linda Country Club at the time, believed that Tiger was even capable of hypnotizing himself. "I don't know this for a fact, but I actually think Tiger can self-hypnotize," he said. "You look at some of the shots that he's produced over the years, at crunch times, and just think there has to be something there."

Later, Brunza told Earl Woods that he had never seen a child quite like Tiger in all his career. "You're working with a Leonardo," he said. "You have to let the eagle soar."

But in Tiger, Brunza also recognized a young man that was in almost complete control of his emotions, especially on the golf course. "Tiger shouldn't be portrayed as the Robo-golfer," he added. "He doesn't need motivation from anybody else. His is internal. I don't see him burning out because golf is pure pleasure for him."

But Earl Woods also had his own techniques he felt might benefit Tiger, learned and mastered from his time with the Green Berets when he interrogated prisoners. His plan was that Tiger would become a "cold-blooded assassin" on the golf course. He called it the Woods Finishing School.

As little more than a golf punching bag for his son when they played a round together, Earl now changed tactics. He began to employ all the dirty tricks he could think of while Tiger played or practiced. He would call him out and put him down. He would stand next to him, ensuring his shadow encroached on Tiger's line, and he would cough continually, blaming it on his long-standing cigarette addiction. Nothing was off-limits; shouting, hollering, pumping the rusty brake on their golf cart, or jangling the small change in his pocket—Earl threw everything at his son to try and distract him when he was playing his shot. "I tried to break him down mentally, tried to intimidate him verbally by saying, 'Water on the right, OB [out of bounds] on the left,' just before his downswing," Earl said. "He would look at me with the most evil look, but he wasn't permitted to say anything."

Tiger could see what his father was trying to do. "He would push me to breaking point, then back off, push me, then back off," Tiger explained later. "It was wild, but you got to think it helped."

Earl Woods is in no doubt that it did. "I wanted to make sure he would never run into anybody who was tougher mentally than he was," he later explained. "And we achieved that."

There can be no denying that, in this respect at least. Earl Woods's preparations to make his son the most mentally tough player on the golf course—that cold-blooded assassin he talked about—worked brilliantly as Tiger grew older, but, for now, he still suffered occasionally from bouts of nerves. At the Optimist Junior World Championships in San Diego, Woods, not unusually, had moved up an age category to play in the twelve-year-old category. In his first round of the day, he found himself playing against a boy who was six inches taller than him and weighing nearly two hundred pounds—almost double Woods's weight. Then his opponent drove the first green on a par-4 hole . . . and Tiger gulped.

Somehow, Woods managed to hold it together to win, but it was the first time Earl had seen anything like this in his son—and he didn't like it. Later, when he asked his son what was wrong, he told him that he had actually been intimidated by the size and power of his opponent.

"Did he par the hole?" asked Earl.

Tiger nodded.

"Did you par the hole?"

Tiger nodded again.

"And did you beat him?"

A final nod.

Earl had made his point, and Tiger, ever the learner, took it on board, lock, stock, and barrel. "Dad," he said, "I promise you no one will ever intimidate me again in my life."

Not just on the golf course but in his life.

It was exactly what Earl Woods wanted to hear.

Earl Woods was already counting the money. Increasingly, he knew that in Tiger he had a son—an asset—who would soon take care of all his financial worries and land him in the life of luxury he felt he warranted. The only issue was how long it was going to take and who among the many suitors in the sports marketing world was best placed to deliver the returns he felt his son's talent so richly deserved.

Among the many interested parties promising the world to Earl and Tiger was the biggest of them all, Mark McCormack's International Management Group (IMG). A talented golfer during his time at the College of William & Mary in Williamsburg, Virginia, McCormack also graduated from Yale Law School and had developed the idea that golfers needed representation, not just so their affairs were kept in order but so they could monetize their talents through equipment or apparel deals, alongside whatever winnings they made on tour. When Arnold Palmer signed with him in January 1959, his idea really took off, and soon he would be joined by Gary Player and Jack Nicklaus while the name of IMG became the go-to marketing agency for all sports and entertainment stars seeking to maximize their earnings potential on and off the golf course. "People say, 'Why don't you retire?' I say, 'Because I get to play golf with Arnold Palmer and Tiger Woods, tennis with Monica Seles, and I get to go to Wimbledon and Paul McCartney's wedding," he once said. "I do every day what most people retire to do. So why retire?"

Mark McCormack didn't just see a rare talent in Tiger; he saw the potential for a commercial juggernaut, a global icon waiting to be unleashed on a general public crying out for something new and different to emerge from the game of golf. What set Tiger apart, in McCormack's eyes, was his unique blend of charisma, his mixed heritage, and his crossover appeal. He ticked every box, he thought. "Tiger Woods is a once-in-a-century athlete who will change the world of golf," he once said.

The narrative wrote itself; the young phenomenon, trained by his dad and ready to take on a notoriously insular golf establishment. Yes, Tiger's was an appeal that wasn't limited just to golf fans. It could reach anyone who appreciated excellence, a captivating backstory, and that rarest of all commodities, genuine star power.

When Mark McCormack first heard about Tiger Woods, he had one of his most trusted agents, Hughes Norton, keep track of the youngster, periodically checking in with each other whenever Tiger cropped up on television or won yet another prestigious title. Never had McCormack been more convinced that golf had a new superstar-in-waiting.

Hailing from New England, Norton was a graduate of Yale's Phillips Exeter Academy and the Harvard Business School, and had been with the company since 1972. Vastly experienced and with a reputation as a granite negotiator, he had gained the nickname "Huge" at the company, not just for the salary and bonuses he had accrued but for some of the groundbreaking deals he sealed for IMG's clients as well.

Norton had already represented some of the biggest golfers in the professional game, including Tom Watson, Arnold Palmer, and the world's number one for over six years in the mid-1990s, the Australian Greg Norman. Some he loved, others less so. "Ultra-aggressive with no second gear," said Norton of Greg Norman. "He had little concern or tolerance for others, always convinced he was right. A classic narcissist."

It wasn't unusual for IMG to scout tennis prodigies in their early teens, but in the world of golf, the pathway tended to follow a tried and trusted route with potential recruits first going through college, playing NCAA and higher-profile amateur competitions, before graduating and turning professional. Besides, the agency already had some of the most successful golfers in the world on their books, and business was booming. Greg Norman was still represented, as was the back-to-back US Open winner and PGA Tour Player of the Year Curtis Strange. Then there was a stellar European contingent across the Atlantic that included Nick Faldo, Sandy Lyle, Bernhard Langer, and Ian Woosnam—players who would all win majors, and all of whom would win the Masters at some point in their successful careers.

But Tiger Woods wasn't just different or unusual—he was unique. It was why Mark McCormack got personally involved, too, often talking to Earl Woods as Tiger made his way through the junior ranks. Norton, meanwhile, had been keeping a discreet eye on Woods for years, compiling a dossier of all his achievements in junior golf in California and beyond. "I had just been reading about this kid who had been on *The Mike Douglas Show* when he was two years old and made a hole in one when he was six. I just thought, *Well, in a world of good prospects, this kid really seems to stand out*," he said.

And then some. Tiger Woods would play wherever and whenever he could. When Western High wasn't playing and he didn't have another tournament to win, he would practice or just go round with his father again. Given that Tiger was now closing in fast on a scratch handicap and had been beating Earl for some time, the only way his father could eke out some enjoyment, some personal benefit, out of an inevitable defeat was to engage in a few bets with Tiger. Typically, the pair would earmark a couple holes at the Navy

Course where the longest drive would win the money, the only stipulation being that the ball had to come to a halt in the fairway. It was a canny move from Earl. Though Tiger's tee shots would routinely sail sixty yards farther than his father's, they would blaze into the rough, proving one aspect of his golf game that was still prone to occasional inaccuracy. Earl's slow and steady approach, dropping his ball safely on the fairway time and time again, often saw him taking the money, much to his son's dismay.

Still, most weeks, he and Earl would return home with yet another trophy, sometimes two. As Tiger prepared to go back to school, 6704 Teakwood Street was overrun with the spoils of his victories. With Tiger by her side, Tida walked around their home counting all the trophies until she couldn't be bothered anymore. What Tida knew, though, was that it was far too many.

Joe Grohman, the new assistant professional at the Navy Club, was a regular visitor to Teakwood Street and had always been amazed by just how cluttered the house was with Tiger's awards and prizes. "When you go into their house, you walk in the hallway, and along both sides of the hallway are trophies. All the counters in the kitchen are trophies. All the shelves in the living room and on the walls," he recalled.

Eventually, Tiger conceded that living in a trophy cabinet wasn't conducive to a comfortable family life or, perhaps more importantly, having a happy mother. And so, with a heavy heart, he agreed to offload some of his trophies, giving them to friends like Joe Grohman, just so he could give his juniors a better prize than the ones the club itself had bought for their competitions. "They were the cheapest you could possibly order. I was embarrassed," said Grohman of the previous prizes.

Unknowingly, Grohman would be accepting 297 of Tiger's trophies.

"It took three Toyota truckloads to get all of them out of the house," said Grohman. "Some of these trophies were six feet tall. They were bigger than the kids I was giving them to."

Grohman still keeps a box of memories from his time playing with the young prodigy, including an invitation to Tiger's high school graduation, some treasured photographs, and a couple of those junior competition trophies that Woods won, engraved with his name, and which today would fetch a lot of money. Not that Grohman would ever dream of selling them. "This stuff belongs to Tiger," he said. "I would love for him to drive out here and come in and pick them up."

CHAPTER 6
SEVENTH-GRADE SCOUTING

"He is going to win more major championships than me and Arnold Palmer put together."
—Jack Nicklaus, all-time major championship record holder, 1997

While Tiger's relationship with his father seemed to go from strength to strength, Earl's relationship with Tida was showing cracks. Not dramatic, public fissures, but the ones developed and lengthened in the course of a long marriage. While she accepted she had a son with a rare gift, it was Earl's obsession with driving him forward that left her longing for something resembling a normal family life. But she was never going to get that with Earl, a man who had a marked tendency to spout nonsense, especially while building Tiger up. The more Tiger progressed, the more Earl took credit. The greater he played, the more he hogged the limelight. At times, Earl seemed to be in the media more than his son, reeling off all the stories everyone had heard before and making those silly pronouncements about the impact Tiger would have on the world, like being the new Mahatma Gandhi or saving humanity.

Tiger, meanwhile, said little or nothing, preferring to let his clubs do the talking.

Though Tiger Woods had been making enormous progress in junior golf, the fact was that, in Southern California at least, there still weren't many junior golf programs available. To their huge credit, Earl and Tida Woods had managed to locate and persuade a variety of coaches and experts to help with their son's golfing development, usually without any money changing hands as well. As a result, the progress of Project Tiger continued smoothly and seamlessly, with many triumphs and precious few setbacks along the way.

As one of the few golf professionals offering a junior program in the area, Tom Sargent came to know Tiger and his parents as their paths crossed regularly at his old club, Yorba Linda, where they held several of the region's bigger junior events. "I first ran into him when he was eight or nine, and even then he was playing in the competitions for eleven-year-olds . . . and winning them," he said. "Frankly, people weren't interested in coaching kids back then, but I'm glad I did."

Whenever there was a tournament at Yorba Linda, Earl Woods would drop Tiger off and then go and sit under a tree and smoke his cigarettes, leaving Tiger to emerge with the spoils. But as Tiger's reputation spread, Sargent's role as one of the peripheral members of Project Tiger became known too. Suddenly, he would have people in suits turning up at Yorba Linda, asking him to pass on business proposals to Earl Woods the next time he dropped by.

"They just started coming to me with these propositions because they didn't know how to get hold of Tiger or his parents," he said. "And at that point, I believe we were talking in the millions, even back then."

While Tiger's confidence on the golf course never tipped over into arrogance, his success still rubbed many people the wrong way. By the time he was thirteen, Tiger was 39–0 in Tom Sargent's events, but, inevitably, some parents took issue with him allowing Tiger to turn up and win each and every time. "You know, when somebody's on top, people take shots at you. Somebody wants to knock you off. That's normal," added Sargent, who is now head golf professional at Mesa Verde Country Club in California.

But while he was used to overly competitive parents whining, it was the nature of some of the complaints that really took him aback. "One of the notes I got was clearly racist," he recalled. "It was anonymous, but it was pretty obvious to me that the guy was one of the parents. So I just wrote it off as another idiot in the world. There's plenty of them."

It wouldn't be the last time Woods suffered racial discrimination. At some clubs, he was required to change his shoes in the parking lot because he was not allowed into the clubhouses. "The color of my skin dictated that," he said later. "You had to be twice as good to get half a chance . . . [so] I made practice so hard, hurt so much, because I want to make sure I was ready come game time."

At another event, Tiger had missed a simple putt and, irritated with himself, had thrown his putter in the air, failing to catch it on the way down. In the world of junior golf, there are two things guaranteed to get players in trouble: The first is swearing, which, in the years to come, would become one of Tiger's most noticeable traits as he became one of the most frequently fined players on the PGA Tour for profanity. The other is throwing your clubs, and while Woods's reaction was less of a hurl and more of a gentle toss, the two boys playing with Woods reported the incident, leading to Tiger's immediate disqualification. For Tida Woods, watching on, it was clear that it was racially motivated, not least because she knew the parents of the boys and the unsavory views they had already expressed. Still, she thought, if that was the only way they could find to beat her son, reprehensible though it was, then so be it.

The high regard in which Tom Sargent's junior program was held inevitably made him an ideal contact for the nation's college golf coaches, eager to land the next star recruit. One of those coaches was Wally Goodwin, coach of the golf team at Stanford University in Palo Alto. Prior to Stanford, Goodwin had coached at Northwestern University in Evanston, Illinois, and later started the Division I program at the University of Northern Colorado in Greeley, Colorado. Now, though, he had been tasked with turning around the fortunes of Stanford's struggling golf program.

"Wally called me up periodically to see what was going on down here and find out if there were any good players he should be looking at," recalled Sargent. "So I told him there's this one kid called Tiger Woods. He was only eleven at the time and not going to be in college for another six or seven years, but you really want to keep an eye on him."

Soon after, Dwaine Knight, golf coach for the University of Nevada, Las Vegas, was on the phone, too, and Sargent said the same thing. "I just told him, 'This kid's going to be something special.'"

As Tiger was at Orangeview Junior High School, there were no NCAA rules prohibiting college coaches from contacting potential recruits, so in the spring, Wally Goodwin decided to steal a march on his opposition and sent a letter to Tiger at Teakwood Street, outlining what his golf program could offer him on his way to one day turning professional as well as all the many advantages that a Stanford education could provide—something that was especially well-received by Tida Woods.

"Dear Tiger!" he wrote. "Here at Stanford, I am finding that it is never too early to get word out to you exceptional young men concerning what it will take a few years down the road in terms of application to Stanford," then added that what he, and his university, was looking for was "winners!"

Tiger, with the help of his father looking over his shoulder, wrote back, too, thanking Goodwin for his letter and expressing surprise that he and Stanford would be interested in a seventh grader like him. He also told Goodwin that his handicap was one that he was aiming to win his fourth Junior World title that summer and how he hoped to turn professional in the future. He signed it:

Sincerely,
Tiger Woods
5ft 5, 100lbs

It wasn't long, though, before Tiger's handicap was down to scratch. His work with John Anselmo was now paying the kind of dividends Earl had hoped for, even if he didn't pay for them. His tendency to blaze away off the tee was slowly giving way to a more mature approach where he could see the dangers ahead and play accordingly, rather than simply rely on his astonishing ability to recover from virtually any position his ball may have landed in.

That summer, at the Optimist Junior World Golf Championships at Torrey Pines, he recorded his fourth win in the event, having previously won the Under 10 division twice and the boys 11–12 division once, then he won the ages 13–14 category at a canter, defending the title he had won the year before. He also had another brush with one of the professional game's rising stars, twenty-three-year-old John Daly, an aspiring pro from Dardanelle, Arkansas.

The Insurance Youth Golf Classic, or the Big I, was an unusual event in that it paired twenty professional players with sixty junior golfers from around the United States. Woods would be playing with Daly, who was not so fresh from playing in the FedEx St. Jude Classic in Memphis, Tennessee. After David Ogrin had dropped out, Daly had taken a call at 11:30 p.m. the night before the event and accepted a place in the field, before setting off from his home in Blytheville at 3:00 a.m. to drive the 340 miles to the Texarkana Country Club, close to the border with Texas.

Nicknamed "the Wild Thing," and possessing a swing and a haircut unlike anything else in pro golf, Daly had dropped out of college at the University of Arkansas to turn professional and had already enjoyed several sponsors' exemptions to play in PGA Tour events. When Woods saw Daly's trademark overswing, where his clubhead went way beyond parallel at the top of his backswing and almost reached his left heel, Woods wasn't impressed, especially when he took it to the golf course. "He wasn't a smart player," he said. "He would take a driver and go over trees and would hit sand wedges to par-5s."

At the par-3 thirteenth hole, meanwhile, Daly's power proved too much for his golf ball, much to Tiger's astonishment. "It was like 210-yards, and I'm going to hit a 5-iron," Daly said in February 2025. "He's watching, and I was hitting an HT Maxfli. I hit this ball, and the rubber band came out of the ball, and it fizzed the whole way. It still got to the green. To this day, if anybody asks Tiger what the greatest shot you saw in golf, he'll say that."

With his parents watching, Woods reached the turn at 3-under-par, four shots ahead of his professional playing partner. Fearful of losing to a thirteen-year-old, Daly stepped on the gas, making birdie at four of the inward nine, while Woods carded three bogeys on his way to a level-par-72, leaving his pro partner to pinch the win. "That kid is great," said Daly in the wake of his face-saving victory. "Everybody was applauding him, and nobody applauded me. Of course, I didn't do much to applaud. I had heard a lot of good things about him, but he's better than I'd heard."

The round over, Daly made a point of seeking out Earl and Tida Woods before they left for the trip back to California. "Look," he told them. "I know he's going to make it, hopefully I will, too, but if you ever need anybody to look out for him, I will."

Tiger's performance at the Texarkana Country Club hadn't gone unnoticed by Hughes Norton, but by then, very few of his performances had passed him by. Now, as the head of the golf division at IMG, he decided to try his luck with Earl Woods. "I'd been tracking Tiger for about five years and figured it was high time I go pay him a visit," he said.

In September, Norton and two colleagues had been in Los Angeles for a meeting with the marketing team at the car manufacturer Mazda. While the trio had intended to fly straight back to IMG's headquarters in Cleveland, Ohio, Norton decided to take the opportunity to head down to Cypress and drop in on 6704 Teakwood Street, just to test the waters. When he called ahead, it seemed as though Earl Woods was almost anticipating his call. "Part of my job was to try to get there early, try to get there first, and put a stake in the ground with the Woods family," Norton explained. "So we sat down and told him about IMG. This is who we are; about Palmer, Player, and Nicklaus; and how we were the best in the world. But I wasn't pitching that day in his living room. I mean, [Tiger] was twelve years old, for God's sake!"

Hughes rang the doorbell and was greeted by "this big, burly guy with a really outgoing personality," recalled Norton.

"You could tell he liked being in charge."

As the pair chatted, Earl, now retired from his job at McDonnell Douglas, gave Norton the abridged version of Tiger's golf career to date, with the same old stories he had told a thousand times or more. "He was adamant that Tiger, this skinny kid with a goofy smile, was the savior of the world," explained Norton. "It was actually quite funny."

Norton's strategy made sense. After all, if Tiger went to college—and anything else simply wasn't an option for Tida Woods—it could be nine years before he turned professional, and anything could happen in that time frame, especially in the life of a teenage boy when other temptations would inevitably emerge. Norton was also concerned that, in the event of Tiger signing with him and IMG, it would be the first time in his career as a sports agent that he had ever represented anyone fully thirty years younger than him.

While Norton mentioned some of the names he represented, Earl Woods wasn't overly impressed, but then he never really was. None of them, not Greg Norman, not Arnold Palmer, nobody. All Earl wanted to talk about was Tiger and how his son, through his golf, was destined for a greatness far beyond the fairways and greens of the nation's golf courses. "This kid is gonna change the world," he told Norton, staring right into his eyes. "Not just the golf world, but the world."

When Tiger turned up, "all five-five and one hundred pounds of him," he showed Norton his room. The posters on his walls weren't of Michael Jordan, or even Michael Jackson. There was Jack Nicklaus above his bed, alongside Greg Norman, Seve Ballesteros, and clippings from various golf magazines, including the list of Nicklaus's achievements he had set his heart on trumping. Norton name-dropped that he used to represent Norman, and that he had met all of young Tiger's heroes many, many times.

"Cool," replied the youngster.

Norton also noticed there were no trophies either. "They're gone," Tiger said. "Mom made me give them all away."

After forty-five minutes, Norton bid farewell to the Woods family, but before he left, Earl Woods left him with one more prediction. "The first Black superstar in golf is going to make himself and someone else a whole lot of money," he said.

"That's why I'm here, Mr. Woods," replied Norton. "That's why I'm here."

Again, Earl Woods had focused on the racial aspect of his son's journey in golf, irrespective of whether Tiger agreed or, indeed, if it was accurate. For him, Tiger's success was part of a personal mission, an attempt to not only right the wrongs of the discrimination he had faced as a young baseball player and as a soldier, but to throw a hand grenade into the very heart of the game that was archaic and impenetrable in equal measure.

At least there was one person at the Navy Club who had his back, shielding him and Tiger from a lot of the discrimination they faced. Joe Grohman had moved to Southern California when he was seventeen and had tried for years to get a job as a golf professional, but without the relevant PGA qualifications, it had been nigh on impossible. He had called virtually every golf course in the state before, on his forty-second call and now aged twenty-four, the Navy Club in Los Alamitos said they might have a position for an operations clerk. And so, even if it wasn't his dream role, it was a job at a golf club, and with a wife and young child to support, it would do for now. "I just wanted to work at a golf course," he said.

Before long, Grohman moved into the club shop on a full-time basis and told his manager of the golf pro Jim Hickey, who had taken him under his wing when he was a military brat living at Plattsburgh Air Force Base in New York, helping him with his game as he played at the Barracks Golf Course and allowing him to play for free. Now, he said, he'd like to pay it forward and start helping the junior golfers at the Navy Club.

The issue, however, was that apart from a one-week school in the summer, there was no junior golf program at the Navy Club, largely because the average age of the members was sixty-three, and there were no juniors there. Apart from one, as Earl Woods told him when they first met. "All these retirees would be very standoffish, but when

I met Earl, he came in, shook my hand, and welcomed me to the course. And we immediately hit it off," said Grohman.

Earl would come to the club most days, dropping into the shop to buy cigarettes and chew the fat with Grohman. Earl had tried to quit smoking and managed eighteen months without lighting up, but when he went to his daughter's college graduation, he got stuck in his ex-wife's house with all her relatives and snapped, lighting up to relieve the stress.

Remarkably, though, Grohman hadn't even heard of Earl's son. "It was a completely different world back then. There was no cable TV as such, no internet, no cell phones. You couldn't just go on a website and find out what was going on," he added. "We had our *Southern California PGA* magazine that came out quarterly, and that was it really. That was how we found out about things in the local golf world."

It was only when Earl told Grohman to come and watch his son hitting some balls that he realized that the one and only junior at the Navy Club wasn't your average, everyday kid golfer.

"You've got to get him into junior golf," Grohman told Earl Woods excitedly.

"You've never heard of my son before, have you?" replied Earl, incredulous.

"No, I haven't," said Grohman. "Should I?"

Earl laughed before reeling off all of Tiger's many achievements, including the glut of international events and Junior World titles he had already won. Grohman was both impressed and embarrassed that he didn't know. "So there and then I found out Tiger was the best ranked junior golfer in the world." Grohman laughed. "And it was like the Second Coming, right? That's why I started calling the Navy Golf Course the 'Bethlehem of Golf.'"

But Earl Woods also told Grohman not just of the financial pressures of taking Tiger around the country to play but also how, when he was younger, Tiger was denied the opportunity to play at the Navy Course, with his tender age being cited as the principal reason. Grohman hadn't been long at the club, but having met certain members and the management, he suspected he knew the real reason, and it had nothing to do with how old Tiger was.

From that moment, Grohman pledged to do whatever he could to make things better for Tiger, Earl, and Tida. "I said to them, 'You're never going to pay for range balls. You're never going to pay for a cart. You're never going to pay for anything.' It had only been two and a half weeks since I'd started working there. I didn't know the landscape, the place, I didn't know the history. I just wanted to pay it forward. So that's what I did."

Whenever Tiger wanted five dollars' worth of balls for the practice range, Grohman would give him fifteen dollars' worth, or wave him onto the range or the golf course with a nod and a wink, and maybe throw him some keys to a golf cart too. If there was another member in the club shop, Tiger would give Grohman a twenty-dollar bill for his balls, only for Grohman to give him twenty dollars in change.

As the months passed, and Grohman and the Woods family grew closer, Earl and Joe would play a round of golf every Wednesday, and gradually, the extent of the treatment that he and Tiger had experienced at the Navy Club became evident, stiffening Grohman's resolve to help them in whichever way he could. Shocked by the comments he had overheard about Tiger and the double standards being applied by the club, he confided in Earl.

"I kept them protected. I kept them in a bubble. I didn't let them see all the frickin' darts that were being shot at them," he added. "I would tell Earl what was going on, but not Tiger. We didn't want Tiger to know any of this stuff because he was just too young, and he didn't need all these people frickin' talking all this shit about him."

The more Grohman played with Tiger, though, the more he realized that any lingering hope he may have harbored of one day making it to the PGA Tour himself had been dashed, not for any lack of ambition on his part, but simply because he had seen the future of golf, and it happened to be the skinny kid from down the road who was barely into his teens. "Unfortunately, my dreams of the tour were crushed pretty instantly, because I'm thinking if I can't even beat a thirteen-year-old kid, there's no way I've got a chance to get on the tour," he said.

What set Woods apart, Grohman believes, was his dedication to practice and an insatiable appetite for learning. "I remember him practicing his putting for my entire eight-hour shift one day. His work ethic was incredible for a kid. He was just so driven." The fact that Woods had spent his childhood surrounded by adults also meant Tiger was remarkably mature for his age. "I was twenty-four, and Tiger was thirteen, and he seemed more mature than me," Grohman added. "He just handled himself like an adult."

Whenever Tiger grew tired of beating all the other kids in the state, he would head back to the Navy Club with his dad and make up a four-ball with Earl's friends—and then beat them too. One of the regular victims was Bob Rogers. A close friend of Earl Woods, he remembers Tiger as a polite and mature youngster who was still more than capable at holding his own when it came to trash-talking on the course. "That was Tiger. He was such a competitive kid. I went home that day, and I told my wife I had played golf with a kid who could become one of the all-time greats," he recalled. "I tell people that I used to kick Tiger Woods's butt—until he turned twelve."

Still, seeing others being crushed at the Navy Club at least brought some comfort to Joe Grohman. "That made me feel better because it wasn't just me. He was beating the shit out of everybody." He laughed.

CHAPTER 7
TOURNAMENT TOUGH

Tiger Woods Made Me Look Like a Genius
—The title of a book by Don Crosby, Western High School's golf coach

Like every other golfer in Southern California, Don Crosby had heard all about young Tiger Woods. As a math teacher and the golf coach at Western High School in Anaheim, he had seen the youngster play at several local tournaments and also witnessed him practicing at the Navy Club in Los Alamitos, where some of his older students worked in the golf-cart barn in return for free play and use of the practice facilities. It also meant free golf for Crosby too. "It was like a private country club for Western High's team and me," he said.

Virtually every time Crosby visited the Navy Club, he found Tiger Woods was already there, working away on some aspect of his golf game. "Tiger was methodical. He hit shot after shot, club after club, through his whole bag. Then, if it was still light out, he started over," Crosby recalled. "[He was] like a Broadway performer—rehearse, rehearse, rehearse."

Then, miraculously, the stars aligned for Don Crosby and Western High School. As he coached his team, the Pioneers, one of his students mentioned to him in passing that Tiger Woods happened to live just around the corner from him in the same neighborhood in Cypress. His interest piqued, Crosby asked if it was the same Tiger Woods they had seen at the Navy Club, just in case there was another "Tiger Woods" living in the area who also happened to be a generational golf talent. "Yeah, Coach, *the* Tiger Woods," replied the kid.

"Well, he might just as well have told me Johnny Unitas, Mickey Mantle, and Michael Jordan were going to play for Western High," he said later. "This was a coach's dream."

The only issue that might affect Don Crosby's perfect recruit attending Western High School was a potential change in the school's catchment area. In the late eighties and early nineties, the entire school district had been experiencing declining enrollment, and the boundaries were often altered just to ensure that all the local schools remained of a similar size. Don Crosby's primary concern was that given recent changes, Teakwood Street might soon find itself in the area of another school, and that Tiger Woods—the kid earmarked as the savior of the Western High School golf team and, in Earl Woods's eyes at least, civilization itself—would end up representing somebody else.

Each year, just before the schools closed for the summer vacation, all the Western High's teachers would drop by the office of the principal Craig Haugen to talk about how the academic year had gone and what they might do in the one to come. For Don Crosby, however, it was less about what was happening in the math department and nearly always about guaranteeing that Tiger Woods became a Western High School student.

"I went into his office and pointed to this little square on the map on his wall and said, 'This little square over here, that's in Cypress, and that's where the future best golfer in the world lives.

So, if they start messing with our boundaries, you can give away anything, but hold on to that little square, the square that has the best golfer in the world.'

"Just make it happen," Crosby added. "You know the superintendent, and I don't."

Jeff Anderson, a student at Western High and a member of the golf team, had already heard rumors that Tiger Woods was heading to his school. His mother worked with the mother of Tiger's friend Bryon Bell at the same elementary school and word was getting around. "My mom was like, 'Hey, you're going to get a really good golfer coming in,' and I was like, 'Oh, that's great,'" he said. "Obviously, you don't think you're ever going to have the opportunity to be a high school teammate of someone like Tiger, but it really happened."

Whether it was some clever, hard-nosed negotiations from Haugen or just simple destiny, among the school boundaries becoming so convoluted ("They looked like snakes mating," said Crosby), Tiger Woods walked into Western High School on the first day of his freshman year, and all of Don Crosby's prayers had been answered.

When Woods started at Western High in the fall of 1990, his reputation, at least among the golf team, had preceded him. Now, the Pioneers had the best young player in the state, and maybe the country, on their team. As Jeff Anderson, one of Woods's teammates, explained, "There wasn't a young golfer locally who wasn't already in awe of Woods. We were all aware of him, and I think they all just wanted to be around him and just see how good he really was," he said. "When you saw him play, there were just jaws on the floor. He was on a different level. It was really special to watch him be around."

The Pioneers played their home games at Dad Miller Golf Course, five blocks away from Western High. Designed by Richard

Miller and opened in 1961, it was named after his father, Harold George "Dad" Miller, who, aged ninety-three, made a hole in one at the eleventh hole in 1970, becoming a Guinness World Record holder in the process as the oldest golfer to ever make an ace.

For the most part, the Pioneers golf team was a ragtag assembly of boys who couldn't really play any other sports, and the typical range of their scores, without counting Tiger's, ranged from the mid-high 70s through to the ones who hoped to break 100 on a good day. Mike Kruse, a boy in a man's body, was one of the better players but, in time, would realize he would only ever be playing second fiddle to Tiger. During one Easter break, the pair faced off in a long-drive contest during a break in a tournament at Rancho Canada Golf Club in Carmel. Two years older than Tiger, Kruse smoked what he thought was a winning drive of around 325 yards, only for Woods to smash his ball past the end of the range 350 yards away and into a river at the very end.

It was a similar story with Craig Black, a senior on Western High's varsity team. For years, he had worked on his golf game, but just as he thought he had the number one spot in the team sewn up, a skinny freshman called Tiger Woods turned up and ended that.

"I'll never be number one, will I?" Black asked Don Crosby.

Coach Crosby couldn't lie. "No, Craig, I don't think you will . . . Nobody's going to be number one here but Tiger for the next four years."

For Earl Woods, a man who came to the game of golf late in life, the swing of his son was a thing of rare beauty, an innate and natural movement that he could appreciate but never emulate. Sometimes, though, it seemed as if Tiger was just an asset Earl protected, knowing full well that, one day, the huge investment he had put in, financial and emotional (but mostly financial) would eventually reap huge dividends. It is why Earl and, in turn, Tida didn't want him to play any other sports where the chance of injury was so much greater than in golf. Woods, for example, was a talented runner and made the cross-country team at Western High, only to give it up when it started to interfere with the demands of his golf schedule. He was good on the track, too, a natural four-hundred-meter runner. Earl thought he looked like Jesse Owens when he ran, another pioneering Black athlete that Earl had been only too happy to teach his son about.

But Tiger, he said, appreciated the encouragement and discipline of concentrating solely on one sport, even if it curtailed his fun. Golf, his dad told him, was what he was born to do, and to waste his God-given talent would be verging on the unforgivable.

Though Earl maintained he wasn't pushing Tiger into golf at the expense of his childhood, nor to make him a professional golfer, the idea that he was merely facilitating his happiness was folly. Yes, the family had made significant sacrifices to make sure Tiger could play wherever and whenever he needed to, but that was their call, not his. Family vacations, replacing the old Mustang, they could all wait until Tiger hit the big time as Earl hoped and prayed that he would.

Tiger was in trouble with his mom again. As she gave away or donated more of his golf trophies, the more seemed to arrive each week to replace them. While she had come to terms with the fact that her home had now been converted into a 1,500-square-foot trophy cabinet, and possibly a museum, and that Earl was never going to turn his golf practice facility back into the garage it was intended to be, now Tiger had taken to working on his short game in the living room. Armed with his wedge, he would open up his stance and flip a golf ball up and over Earl's easy chair (as long as he wasn't there) and try to impart sufficient backspin so it stopped before it ran into the brick surround of the family fireplace. "It takes a lot of concentration, because there's a lot of pressure on me when I try that shot," he told the *Los Angeles Times* in August 1990. "If I miss, my mother will get after me, but it's good training for finesse and getting the right feel for delicate shots."

Keen to work on his wedge play, and with indoor golf now the subject of a banning order at Teakwood Street, Tiger devised a new short-game practice drill with the assistance of Coach Crosby. After school, they picked up their wedges and a handful of balls and headed to Western High's football field to play "field goal golf." Starting at one end of the field, they would attempt to hit their balls through the goalposts at the other end, getting closer and closer every time they were successful. Eventually, Woods got to within four feet of the goalposts and still managed to arc his ball up and over the posts before landing it just a few feet on the other side.

Tida's living room, for now at least, was safe, but while Woods enjoyed his ad hoc practice sessions with Coach Crosby, his relationship with his teammates remained cool and cordial at best. Writer James Dale worked with Don Crosby on his book *Tiger Woods Made Me Look Like a Genius: 5 Simple Ways to Take 10 Strokes Off Your Game*, published in 2000. He explains that while Woods wanted the team to do well, he was always a little distant from the rest of the boys.

"He got along well with the teammates, but Don never described a great deal of camaraderie," he recalled. "[Woods] was a quiet person. He kept to himself, and there wasn't anyone he really hung out with. Don described him as a solitary kind of person. Not unkind and not unpleasant, but not like a fun guy."

From the outset, Don Crosby knew that handling Tiger's schedule was critical, not least to protect his grades in class. Sitting down with Earl Woods, the pair agreed that if tournaments demanded more of Tiger's time, then all he had to do was speak up and he wouldn't have to play for Western High. "I gave him a free, no-guilt pass in advance," said Crosby. "[But] in four years, he took me up on it only a few times. To his credit, I don't recall him ever taking a day off when we absolutely had to have him to win."

In Don Crosby, Tiger had found a coach who maybe couldn't give him the technical instruction he might have needed—he had John Anselmo for that—but could provide the kind of positive, motivational input he occasionally required when Jay Brunza wasn't available. A little course management was always helpful, too, especially when Tiger just wanted to pull his driver out of his bag and teach his golf ball a lesson it would never forget.

It was Don Crosby, for instance, who accompanied Woods when he first met the man whose records he had kept in his sights since he was tiny: Jack Nicklaus. In the spring of 1990, Nicklaus was giving a clinic for the members at Bel-Air Country Club, the ultra-exclusive club in Los Angeles that boasted presidents, such as Ronald Reagan and Richard Nixon, and Hollywood A-listers, like Jack Nicholson and Clint Eastwood, as members. For Tiger Woods, a kid who had grown up with the sole aim of eclipsing everything that the world's greatest golfer had achieved, here was his chance not only to glean valuable information but also to show Nicklaus that his time as golf's GOAT was fast running out. Sure enough, Nicklaus summoned Woods and asked him to come forward and play a few shots for the assembled crowd. Tiger jumped at the chance, and when he arrowed his ball into the distance, there were gasps of amazement. Nicklaus smiled. "Tiger," he remarked, "when I grow up, I want to have a swing as pretty as yours."

Soon after, Woods also got to play with the world's number one player, Australia's Greg Norman. Arranged by IMG agent Hughes

Norton, the pair played nine holes at the new Old Marsh Golf Club in Palm Beach Gardens, Florida. As the two played, Norman was impressed by the talent of the "skinny little kid" next to him. Woods, on the other hand, headed back to Cypress that day thinking that if Norman was the best in the world, then it wouldn't be too long before he surpassed him.

That Woods was a cut above his teammates and contemporaries was apparent from the outset of his freshman year at Western High. In his first appearance for the Pioneers against Gahr High School, Woods played the nine holes in a level-par 34 shots, but later in the season, he was routinely shooting under-par. Come the end of the season, Woods's average score, after thirty-six nine-hole rounds for the Pioneers, was exactly level-par.

Outside of representing Western High, Woods continued to collect titles and trophies with a determination verging on gluttony in the spring and summer of 1991, swiftly replacing the ones he had given away. He won the Optimist International Junior World for a sixth time in San Diego and took titles in Los Angeles and Phoenix, Arizona. He won the California Interscholastic Federation, Southern Section Championship at Canyon Country Club in Palm Springs with a round of 68 and then claimed the CIF-SCGA Individual Championship at the Marbella Golf Country Club where, over the course of thirty-six holes in eight hours, he recorded rounds of 71 and 67—the latter featuring five birdies, four of which were on the back nine when most other players were exhausted, demoralized, or both. Woods finished a record ten strokes ahead of the runner-up, Joe Acosta of Redwood High School in Visalia, California, becoming the first player to win both the Southern Section and CIF-SCGA individual titles in a season. "I guess you could say I'm tournament tough," he suggested in the wake of his wins.

After a week off for his exams at Western High School, Woods was back on the road, intent on adding some far more prestigious titles to his already glittering résumé. For Earl and Tida, though, the expense incurred from taking Tiger around the country was beginning to bite. From the moment their son was born, the couple had agreed that Tida would stay at home and look after Tiger while Earl would be the breadwinner until he had reached his retirement, but increasingly, sacrifices were having to be made just to make ends meet and keep Tiger on track.

Summer meant tournament after tournament. Christmas meant Miami for the Junior Invitational Golf Tournament while Thanksgiving was spent at a competition in Tucson, Arizona. Easter, meanwhile, meant a trip to Texas for the Woodlands Tournament. By now, it was costing Earl and Tida around thirty thousand dollars each year just to keep the Tiger Tour on the road, and while many other competitors traveled alone, Earl had pledged that he would be with his son every step of the way. Such were the financial demands that forced Earl and Tida to take a home equity loan each year that would fund the many summer tournaments Tiger was playing in around the country. "Looking back now, sometimes I wonder how me made it," said Earl.

CHAPTER 8
KEEPING RECEIPTS

"It's not easy being Tiger Woods on the course. It's not easy being Tiger Woods off the course. In his defense, it's not easy being Tiger Woods."

—Tiger's golf coach 2004–2010, Hank Haney

Though Tiger Woods was a superstar in waiting, it wasn't the sport that made you cool at school. In fact, nobody bothered to watch the Pioneers golf team. "It was always basketball, baseball, and football. We didn't get a look in really," said Jeff Anderson, one of Coach Crosby's unsung heroes. For the most part, golf at Western High was a recreational pursuit for those who wanted to try something different. Slowly, though, a few more kids and some parents turned up, occasionally some spies from rival schools or even college coaches just to witness the unique talents of Tiger Woods. Then, there was the media interest. "Every once in a while, we'd have a TV crew that would come to one of our matches, or a newspaper reporter would visit, and that just wasn't heard of when it came to high school golf," added Anderson.

Often, the rest of the Pioneers team would find Tiger filling in another questionnaire sent from newspapers or magazines eager to get an insight into the life of the teenage golf phenomenon. Once,

Tiger was asked to write down which golfers he regarded as his heroes. His answer? None.

Self-belief had always been one of Tiger's strongest attributes, but, increasingly, it began to slip into bravado, even arrogance. Perhaps it was the inevitable result of a father forever telling him and anyone who would listen that there was nothing that could prevent Tiger from achieving the level of greatness a power far higher than even Earl Woods had designed for him, but now there were times that even a teenager Tiger seemed like he believed it to.

But then Tiger Woods, more than ever, was the news. He was named Southern California Amateur Player of the Year (for the second consecutive year) and *Golf Digest*'s Junior Amateur Player of the Year, and, increasingly, the country's biggest publications were now picking up on what he was doing. There was a profile in *People* magazine while *The New York Times*, for instance, warned the greatest of all time that there was a new kid on the block. "Fore! Nicklaus Beware of Teenager," screamed the headline, with Woods telling reporter Jaime Diaz that he wanted to be the best ever and become "the Michael Jordan of golf."

The adulation wasn't entirely universal. When Tiger headed to the Navy Club, taking his US Junior Amateur Championship trophy with him to show the members and to celebrate with a few of the other boys, the reception was far from welcoming. To mark the occasion, Tida Woods had prepared some food for the boys, but as she began setting up the plates in the lounge, the club manager appeared, instructing her that only food and drinks purchased in the club could be eaten there, and if she and Tiger wanted to eat theirs, they would have to do it outside. "Tida brought over a little tray of food, like macaroni salad and some chicken, and we were just going to sit there and have a tiny party. Instead, they made Tiger and the boys sit outside on a bench covered in bird shit," said Joe Grohman. "It was just ridiculous."

It wasn't long before Tiger was once more victim to the kind of needless officialdom that no other players at the Navy Club ever seemed to be subjected to. Unbeknownst to Joe Grohman, a club member had heard that Tiger was getting free or discounted rounds, a golf cart or range balls, and now the club manager (who Grohman doesn't want to name—"he has kids and a family") was intent on making the country's best young golfer pay his way.

Soon after, a letter dropped through the letterbox at Teakwood Street from the Navy Club's manager, instructing Tiger that, from now on, he would have to carry a valid receipt on him at all times to prove that he had paid for his golf and then to also produce it if and when requested. The next day at the Navy Club, Tiger showed Joe Grohman the letter he had received, so Grohman gave him a golf cart and sent him out to play for nothing. This time, though, he also gave him a receipt. Within minutes, though, the club manager was racing down the first fairway in pursuit of Woods, demanding he present his receipt. "It was like five or ten minutes later, and the manager runs out in the middle of the fairway and checks Tiger's receipt," said Grohman.

Clearly, it mattered not that the Navy Club had in their midst a generational talent that could have, theoretically at least, brought nothing but good news to their golf club and, for that matter, act as a useful recruiting tool for the navy too. Indeed, as Joe Grohman explained, the attitude of some staff and members was racist, pure and simple. "The people that were in control [at the Navy Club] just messed with him," he said.

It says much for Tiger's mindset that he was able to block out the discrimination he suffered at the Navy Club and continue with his irresistible march to golfing greatness. Of course, it also speaks to the years of training Earl had made his son undergo, too, even though he always denied doing so.

"I never had any intention of teaching Tiger anything about the rudiments of golf," he once said. "I didn't put him in the garage with me so that he could learn to play. I brought him with me for the company so we could be together." It was nothing to do with being a pushy parent, or Earl living vicariously through his talented son. "All it ever was," he said, "was some sort of mystical osmosis."

It had taken some protracted negotiations, but Joe Grohman had finally persuaded Tida Woods to let him take Tiger to the local park to play some basketball, but only if he promised that there would be no football involved. "So we're playing basketball, and there's a guy who's six foot three, another guy who's six foot four, and I'm like six foot two, and I'm the short one. Then there's Tiger who's like five foot seven and a hundred pounds," he explained. "And Tiger was good. He had a beautiful shot, and he was quick too."

But, as was usual now, the other players already knew who Tiger was and were keen to put the young star in his place. "They took too much joy just smashing him to the ground, and after he hit the ground a couple of times, I was like, 'Shit, this kid's going to get hurt.'"

Unbeknownst to Tida, though, Grohman had also brought a football with him, so the quartet decided to play a game of two on two instead. With Grohman dictating the plays, he fed Tiger the ball and watched as the fourteen-year-old flew repeatedly past his opponents, scoring touchdown after touchdown. But with the game becoming too one-sided, Grohman switched sides. "So I decided to cover Tiger, but every time I turned to run with him, he was already ten yards past me. He was like a rocket," he said.

As the teams went again, Grohman's friend threw another pass for Tiger, and as Woods raced past Grohman to catch it, all the time looking over his shoulder at the ball dropping out of the sky, Grohman froze. "Tiger's running at full speed. The ball's going through the air, and he's running right at a tree," recalled Grohman.

Sure enough, Woods ran straight into the tree and collapsed in a heap. "I'm looking at him, and he's not moving. I open his eyes, and I've never seen a guy knocked out like that before. His eyes are white," added Grohman. "I'm screaming, and I'm like, 'Oh my God! I think I killed Tiger Woods.'"

Grohman dropped to his knees and started slapping Tiger's cheeks. Finally, thankfully, Woods came to and, after a few minutes spent regaining his composure, spoke to Grohman. "You could have killed me."

While Grohman was relieved that it was nothing more than a concussion, the idea that he might have ended the life of the greatest golfing talent of his generation filled him with fear. In fact, almost as much fear as when he finally met up with Tida to break the news of what had happened.

Whether it was parental love, undue strictness, or a case of protecting their prized asset, the idea Tiger might jeopardize his future simply by doing what every other kid the world over was doing was simply unacceptable. Even if he grazed his knee playing soccer or tag football at school, as he did on many occasions, his parents would want to know why he had put himself in that position, usually because he had another important golf tournament to play soon. Friends recall Woods being terrified of revealing the cuts and bruises he had sustained playing sports at school to his parents, lest he threatened the career path that Earl Woods had set out for him so meticulously.

Inevitably, Tiger would rebel from time to time, throwing caution to the wind and playing other sports, in a bid just to feel normal and fit in, but it was clear he lived in fear of the repercussions from

Earl and Tida, who had put discipline at the very center of their parenting style.

Woods spent most lunchtimes at Western High in the room where the rest of the golf team hung out. Never happier than when he was talking about golf, and with golfers, Woods was a diligent student but awkward and uncomfortable whenever conversation strayed from the things he knew, which, to all intents and purposes, was golf and very little else. As for girls, well, they might as well have been an alien species.

At home, he was like any other teenage boy. He loved watching television, especially the World Wrestling Federation, which he taped on the family's new video recorder as Tida wouldn't let him stay up late to watch it. Envious of the immense strength of wrestlers like Randy Savage or the Ultimate Warrior, Tiger decided to try and beef up himself, but only in a way designed to improve his length off the tee, not throw "Rowdy" Roddy Piper over his shoulder or pin Hulk Hogan to the floor. Picking up a copy of *Golf Digest*, he noticed a coverline: "How to Get Your Golf Muscles in Shape This Winter." He found the feature "Winter Exercise for a Spring Payoff" by John Mahaffey inside, twelve pages after yet another huge profile of Jack Nicklaus called "The Aging of a Champion," and set to work.

Like every other teenage boy in history, though, Tiger Woods had an appetite that was insatiable and a diet that was wholly incompatible with any effective exercise regime. When his head wasn't in the fridge, he would take the money he had won in putting contests and head straight to McDonald's or Taco Bell, preferring fast food to any of the more exotic delights that Tida was cooking up at home. Indeed, when Tiger Woods won the Masters in 1997, at the age of twenty-one, he returned the following year where, as the reigning champion, he could select what was to be served at the traditional Champions Dinner that takes place prior to the tournament starting. His selection? Cheeseburgers and French fries.

By now, the various elements of Project Tiger were working in harmony, and Woods was reaping the rewards on the golf course. What Earl Woods hadn't banked on, however, was the idea that Tiger himself might want to play a more active role in his own affairs. When he reached his fifteenth birthday, Tiger sat down with his father and, displaying a rare maturity, told him that he wanted to start taking greater control of his career and learn how to manage the people on his team and, of course, the money he was going to make. Soon, when they were on the road together, Tiger would sign the pair into their lodgings and then decided what and where they were going to eat in the evening. He would arrange their schedule and carry out all his equipment checks. By sixteen, Woods had assumed responsibility for almost everything, from travel and accommodation arrangements to hiring caddies and reserving practice times. His father called it a "role reversal" in which he "became the child and [Tiger] became the parent."

On the golf course and off the golf course, Tiger Woods's maturity was always evident, even when he started working with Rudy Duran when he was four years old. Disciplined on the practice range and conscientious at school—he made the honor roll each year—Earl attributed his son's sensibleness to his mother and the cultural influence of her Asian background. "Tida always preached humility, determination, respect, spirituality, honesty, and diligence in her daily interaction with Tiger," he said.

When you look through his father's 1998 book, *Playing Through: Straight Talk on Hard Work, Big Dreams, and Adventures with Tiger*, written in the wake of Tiger's remarkable victory at the 1997 Masters, you will find many cute photographs of Tiger as a child: with his parents, with his dogs, or lifting some trophy or other on the golf course, usually next to an adult. There aren't any with friends, apart from a couple near the end when he has flown the nest and is a student at Stanford University, away from the scrutiny of Teakwood Street and his parents.

For those that knew Tiger growing up, it's not surprising. After all, Woods's childhood was anything but normal, not least because it wasn't even his. Golf was all he ever knew, and he did what he was told, lest he incur the wrath of his father or the disapproval of his mother. Did he miss out on a childhood? Joe Grohman thinks he did. "He was either at school, at a tournament, or at the course. He didn't have any [close] friends," he said. "If he did, they were just school friends, but they never came to the course."

Another school friend, speaking on condition of anonymity, said, "He couldn't go to parties. Tiger never went out. I think the one time he did go out was when we went to prom."

CHAPTER 9
A NATIONAL CHAMPION

"I heard the Lord saying it was time to stop playing."
—Brad Zwetschke, in the wake of his defeat to Tiger Woods in 1994

Tiger was sweating. As his golf took him around the state and beyond, very occasionally his schoolwork would slip, much to the displeasure of Tida Woods. Now, a biology project set by his teachers two months earlier, where students were required to collect and present a variety of bugs, was due in the next day, and Tiger, who had been busy collecting junior golf titles and trophies instead, had forgotten about it entirely. He hadn't told his mother either.

Panicking, Woods called his childhood friend Alfredo Arguello, who, along with Dennis Bergal, had been diligently collecting bugs for their own projects.

"I need help," Tiger pleaded.

When Arguello asked how many bugs Woods had, Tiger told him he had just five that he had found in his own backyard, even though students had been asked to collect at least twenty-five. Worse still, Woods had just thrown them all in one of his father's old tobacco boxes. Arguello tutted before heading to his freezer and giving Woods a selection of his before helping with how he presented them. The following day, Woods handed his bug collection in as required, receiving a mark of 95 percent compared to Arguello's 100 percent.

While his mother was none the wiser about how close Tiger had sailed to the wind with his biology project, it was a clear indication of just how much time Tiger was now dedicating to golf and how easily his schoolwork could slip and take second place if the circumstances arose. Joe Grohman, the professional at the Navy Club, recalled just how difficult it was trying to stop him from playing. "He would play till he couldn't anymore. I remember one night we were out there, and it's already dark. I can't even see my ball anymore, and yet he just wanted to carry on. I felt so guilty telling him we've got to go in."

Aside from his divine talent, Tiger's work ethic was what seemed to set him apart from his contemporaries. After his lessons with John Anselmo, he would head straight to the Navy Club and talk through everything that he had been working on with Grohman. "He'd come back and tell me what he learned and brief me every time. He just loved to talk about swing theory. He would come into the shop and show me, getting into all these positions. It was amazing to watch that enthusiasm," said Grohman. "You know, if Tiger wasn't the best golfer in the world, he would be the best golf instructor in the world."

Some days, Woods would hit hundreds of balls, working on ironing out some issue with his swing, or developing a new shot that might prove useful should the need arise. "You don't make the sniper team without shooting a lot of bullets," added Grohman.

Besides, Tiger needed as much practice as he could get as he had a new and ambitious target in sight. In March 1991, Woods, aged just fifteen years, one month, and sixteen days old, and still weighing only 138-pounds, attempted to qualify for the Nissan Los Angeles Open, the PGA Tour event due in town the following week and a competition that had been won by all of the game's greats, including Ben Hogan, Arnold Palmer, and Charlie Sifford, who took the title in a playoff in 1969.

Qualifying took place on the South Course at Los Serranos Country Club, thirty miles away from Cypress in Chino, where Woods found himself in a field of 132 golfers with just two places up for grabs for the tournament itself, which was to be hosted at the exclusive Riviera Country Club in Pacific Palisades. With his dad on his bag, Tiger started poorly. In the first four holes, his tee shots hit one tree and two cart paths, jeopardizing the safety of the crowds of curious onlookers as he tried too hard to impress. Just as everyone was beginning to think it was a step too far for Tiger, however, he found some form. Two birdies at the sixth and seventh holes put him back in contention while an outrageous chip-in from forty yards at the long eighth gave him an unlikely eagle.

At the penultimate hole, Earl Woods had learned that journeyman pro Mac O'Grady stood at 8-under-par, with another player already in the clubhouse at 7-under-par. With Tiger on 6-under, it meant he needed at least a birdie on the final hole to stand any chance of making the field at Riviera. But Tiger being Tiger, well, he wanted an eagle to remove any doubt.

The eighteenth hole at Los Serranos is a long par-5 with a pond ahead of the putting surface, and Woods thought he had given himself the best chance of reaching the green in two when his tee shot found the fairway. But no. When he got to his ball, with around 250 yards left just to clear the pond and another thirty or so to make the green, he found it sat on a downslope with precious little grass underneath it. Undeterred by the tightest of lies, Woods pulled a fairway wood out of his bag.

All or nothing.

It would be his worst shot of an otherwise exceptional round. As soon as he hit his ball, he knew where it was headed, and, sure enough, it took one bounce before dropping into the pond. The best Woods could do was a bogey—his only one of the day—and a round of 69, three adrift of Mac O'Grady's total.

Distraught, Tiger jumped in the passenger seat in his father's Mustang and headed back to Teakwood Street with his head in his hands. Earl Woods, behind the wheel, sat silently, concentrating on the road ahead, fuming that his son hadn't erred on the side of caution when he still had a chance of making the top two qualifying spots. But this was a different Tiger. Since he started working with Jay Brunza, the pair had discussed how Tiger might better handle the disappointment of a poor performance, instructing him to let any bad shot go and regain focus for the hole ahead. Even Earl had had to intervene at the Orange Bowl Junior Classic in Miami when Tiger had missed a short putt and then sulked for the rest of the round, blowing his chance of victory in the process, lecturing his son about how perseverance, and not quitting, was the only way to play.

Still, Tiger (and Earl) needn't have worried. Impressed by how close the teenager had come, the tournament organizers from the LA Open would be in touch again before the year was out.

The 1991 Western High School yearbook is a sight to behold. From a boy's startled expression, as though he had just been caught in a compromising position, to a girl looking like she has just stepped off the set of *Little House on the Prairie*, it is amusing and surprising in equal measure. Four rows down on page 215 is Eldrick Woods (the school was still using his given name in official publications, even when the rest of the world called him Tiger by now). Aged fourteen, it is almost impossible to imagine this kid with his teeth clenched, an uncomfortable grimace, and his collars up, becoming the most famous sports personality on the planet long before the decade was even out.

Of course, not many doubted that Woods would go on to a successful career in professional golf, but precious few could ever have imagined the new levels he would reach. At the Navy Club, though, Tiger Woods had one fan in Joe Grohman who always knew that the youngster was destined for greatness in whatever he decided to do. But, more than that, he found a youngster who was both humble and helpful. Whenever Tiger appeared in golf magazines, he never really mentioned it to Grohman, assuming it was no big deal. When time allowed, Tiger would also drop in on some of Grohman's junior group lessons and help out, bringing some of his more famous trophies along for the kids to see.

"Here's the number one junior golfer in the world, talking to my junior golf class. Who gets to do that?" Grohman said. "I was just tickled pink when he would do that. I don't know if the kids understood what was happening, but it was just like, 'This was the coolest thing I've ever seen.' You know, the number one junior golfer in the world at my course and talking to my junior kids. Incredible."

That year, Woods went on to win his sixth Optimist Junior World title, becoming the youngest-ever winner of the 15–17 age division. He also took the California Interscholastic Federation, Southern Section's individual championship, a couple of AJGA events at the PING Phoenix Junior, and the Edgewood Tahoe Junior Classic as well as the Los Angeles City Junior Championship and the Orange Bowl Junior title.

As each summer went by and Tiger's true potential began to dawn on Earl and everyone who came across him, so too did Earl's expenditure increase exponentially. But even now, with his son still only fifteen, Earl knew his investment would prove to be the best deal he would ever make. If he needed proof, it came in late July when Tiger teed it up at the United States Junior Amateur Golf Championship at Arnold Palmer's Bay Hill Club & Lodge in Orlando, Florida, also home to the Invitational, one of the more prestigious stops on the PGA Tour.

From the moment he struck his opening tee shot at the opening par-4 hole, Woods seemed focused, determined, and wholly intent on victory. In the first thirty-six holes of medal play, he recorded a 4-under-par total of 140 to comfortably lead the standings. As the competition went into match play, he showed no sign of letting up as he won four of the first five holes and had three birdies and eight pars.

By the time he reached the semifinals, Woods's imperious golf had the crowds flocking to watch him, much to the chagrin of his opponent Kevin Mihailoff, a seventeen-year-old from Naples, Florida, who had just made the national top-twenty junior rankings. Like Woods, Mihailoff had breezed through the opening rounds on his way to the final four and felt confident of making it through once more. "I knew Tiger was a great player, but I wasn't intimidated going into the match at all," he recalled. "What was intimidating was being on the first tee at Bay Hill and seeing hundreds of people on both sides of the fairway knowing that if I slice it or hook it, I could hit somebody!

"It definitely was nerve-racking because I'd never been in front of a gallery before."

While Mihailoff knew all about Woods, he didn't expect him to be quite so aloof. "He was very intense, and I remember he never really said 'good shot' to me or anything to that effect," he said. "And he had his sports psychologist [Jay Brunza] caddying for him, which was a little weird to me. I just had a local one from Bay Hill."

But Tiger did what Tiger nearly always did. He dispatched Mihailoff with almost indecent haste, winning 5 and 4, to advance to the final. "No excuses. It was definitely the worst I played out of all the matches in the tournament." Mihailoff laughed.

Waiting for him in the final was seventeen-year-old Brad Zwetschke from Kankakee, Illinois. Though he had heard all about Woods, he had never played against him. "I started playing national tournaments when I was thirteen or fourteen, and *Golfweek* had all the national rankings, so I knew going into that tournament that he was number one in the country," he recalled. "There was definitely a real buzz around him."

Zwetschke had arrived at Bay Hill in some of the best form of his young life, confident of not only doing well in the tournament but also bagging himself a college scholarship in the process. Like so many others who played against Woods, especially in his midteens onward, Zwetschke found a player completely focused on winning. Yes, he was cordial on the first tee, but once the match was underway, it was all about taking care of business. "What set him apart, as with all the other athletes that reach the pinnacle of their sport, was his drive and his ability to focus when it mattered most," he said.

Zwetschke began impressively, too, racing into a three-hole lead after six holes. Then Tiger flicked the switch, winning the next five holes, and by the time they reached the sixteenth, Woods was one hole up and closing in on victory. At the 220-yard par-3 seventeenth hole, Zwetschke hit his tee shot to ten feet while Woods put his within four feet. Remarkably, though, both players missed their birdie putts. "I just thought that it was game over," recalled Zwetschke.

Presuming the worst, Zwetschke stood on the eighteenth tee but watched as Woods yanked his tee shot out of bounds. "I stood there thinking, *I'm back in it. We've got a game on*," said Zwetschke, who won that final hole to take the game into a sudden death playoff.

But his joy was short-lived.

After a delay for rain, the pair resumed battle, and when Zwetschke missed a four-foot putt to take the game into another hole, despite a terrific recovery shot from the greenside bunker, Tiger Woods, at the age of fifteen, had become the youngest winner of the US Junior Amateur Championship in its forty-four-year existence. Just as important, to Earl Woods at least, was that Tiger was also the first Black winner in the event's history. "You will forever be a part of history," he told his son.

Years later, Woods recalled the rollercoaster ride of his first national amateur title. "I was choking my guts out," he said. "I thought I was going to faint. I bent down to mark my ball and could feel my eyeballs beating."

For Zwetschke, it had been a crushing blow but, thirty-four years later, one he could look back on with pride, not regret. "It was heartbreaking, and when you're in the middle of it, you're just trying to do the best that you can to win. But in hindsight, after all that he's accomplished and all that he's done throughout his career, it's nice to be a part of that.

"I suppose it had to start somewhere, and it started with me, I guess."

What is interesting is that both Brad Zwetschke and Kevin Mihailoff never really pursued a career in professional golf. Both men went to college and played—Zwetschke for North Carolina State, University of Illinois, and then Eastern Illinois University; Mihailoff for University of Florida—and both flirted with the pro ranks. But now, over three decades on from their meeting with Woods, Zwetschke is now a chaplain in the US Army ("I heard the Lord saying it was time to stop playing"), and Mihailoff is a charter boat captain taking fishing trips around the Florida Everglades. In fact, Brad Zwetschke hardly plays at all these days. Occasionally, he is asked to make up a four-ball, but for the most part, he just hits a few balls in his backyard first thing in the morning or when the sun is going down. "It's my therapy," he joked.

For many of Tiger's "victims," it can seem that with defeat to Woods comes a demoralizing reckoning—the result, perhaps, of some crushing realization that maybe you're not as good as you thought you were after all. More than that, and compared to Tiger Woods, at least, you never will be.

CHAPTER 10
YOUNG LOVE

"Hockey is a sport for white men. Basketball is a sport for Black men. Golf is a sport for white men dressed like Black pimps."

—Tiger Woods, date unknown

Dina Gravell didn't have a clue who Tiger Woods was. Yes, she knew of him, that he was one of the smarter kids at Western High School. But apart from that, they seemed to have little in common other than the advanced accounting class they shared. Gravell, with her blonde hair and blue eyes, had caught Tiger's attention, and despite the age difference—he was still a sophomore, she was a junior—the two grew close. Just before Tiger's sixteenth birthday, the pair were talking near the sports field when Woods happened to mention that he played golf, and contrary to what she thought, it wasn't a game for old folks waiting to die. Besides, he added, he was pretty good at it as well.

What made their fledgling relationship even more engaging was that Gravell knew nothing about Woods playing golf on TV before he was even three years old, the appearance on *That's Incredible!*, or the profiles in *Golf Digest* and *People* magazine. The US Junior Amateur victory and six Junior World Golf Championship titles had passed her by too. All she saw was a sweet, shy boy who was fun to talk to and who her parents would approve of. "We were first boyfriend and girlfriend in all sense of the word," she said in 2009. "We would wait for my parents to go to bed and then make out on the sofa in front of the television for hours."

But it was only when Gravell was invited round to meet Tiger's parents that she finally learned of the extent of his golfing prowess, first by all the trophies and awards pinned to the walls and cluttering the place up, then because of Earl's insistence that he give her a complete breakdown of everything his son had achieved in the game, even though she had no idea of what any of it really meant.

Occasionally, Tiger would stay over at Gravell's for longer than expected and have Joe Grohman at the Navy Club provide an alibi for him. When Earl and Tida found out, however, they hit the roof—Earl because he was missing out on valuable golf practice, and Tida because he should have been doing his schoolwork.

For some time, Earl and Tida had been worried about Tiger's teenage years, a period where, inevitably, new distractions would emerge, but in Dina Gravell, Tiger had found someone whose schooling was just as important as his, and that ticked Tida's boxes. Earl was less convinced. If Gravell didn't know or realize just how important Tiger's golf was in his and his family's life, then that, as far as he was concerned, was a genuine concern.

He needn't have worried, at least not for a while. With love in his life and a spring in his step, Tiger Woods found yet another gear, winning four more American Junior Golf Association titles (the PING Phoenix Junior, the Nabisco Mission Hills Desert Junior, the Pro-Gear San Antonio Shootout, and the Insurance Youth Golf Classic). He also mounted a successful defense of his US Junior Amateur title, coming from two down with six to play against Mark Wilson in the eighteen-hole final Wollaston Golf

Club in Milton, Massachusetts, to become the first player to win back-to-back titles since the event was first played in 1948. "I think it was tougher than last year," said Woods later. "He kept the ball on the fairway and didn't make any mistakes."

Come the end of the season, Tiger Woods had amassed more awards and trophies than two or three Teakwood Street houses could ever accommodate. *Golf Digest* named him their Amateur Player of the Year, as did *Golfweek. Golf World*, meanwhile, went one further, proclaiming him their Player of the Year.

On September 1, 1992, the day that college coaches were officially allowed to contact high school juniors with their recruitment pitches, the letters started arriving at Teakwood Street, offering the youngster the moon. While most knew that Woods was likely to go to either Stanford or the University of Nevada, Las Vegas, it didn't stop other coaches from trying their luck. In the hypercompetitive world of college athletics, landing a recruit as prized as Tiger Woods wouldn't just define a coach's career but transform the fortunes of any university golf team.

Mike Moraghan, golf coach at the University of Virginia, was one of them. He had watched Woods that summer lay waste to every opponent and golf course he faced. "Like every other coach in the country, I'd been pursuing Tiger Woods, the best junior golfer in history," he said. "It was widely known that he was a good student who would go to Stanford. But man, he was so good, I had to at least try to get him interested in Virginia."

That summer, Moraghan charted Tiger's progress, watching many of his rounds just to see if he really was the player everyone was saying he was. "The kid was phenomenal," he added. "Of the eight rounds I witnessed, he had no bogeys in four of them, including a 66 in the second round of the US Amateur at Muirfield Village, a masterpiece of four birdies, one eagle, and thirteen tap-in pars."

When he watched the third round of the seventy-two-hole Insurance Youth Classic at Pinehurst No. 7 in North Carolina, an event Tiger won by nine shots, Moraghan saw a player in control of every facet of his golf game, despite being hit with everything that Mother Nature could throw at him. "The third round there was brutal, with constant rain and wind that pushed the average score to around 77. But Tiger was in the middle of every fairway, hit every green in regulation, and shot 69 with fifteen pars and three birdies to build an insurmountable lead," he said.

In October 1991, the phone rang at Teakwood Street. Earl Woods answered, expecting it to be another college golf coach trying their luck. But on the other end of the line was Greg McLaughlin, tournament director at the Nissan Los Angeles Open, the annual PGA Tour event hosted at the Riviera Country Club in Pacific Palisades, seventeen miles west of the city. He had a proposal he wanted to discuss. "Mr. Woods," he said, "we would like to offer Tiger a sponsor's exemption to play in our tournament next February."

Earl paused, assuming it was a prank call, but soon realized it wasn't when McLaughlin talked through the details.

"Sir," Earl replied, "my son would be honored to play in the Los Angeles Open."

As he hung up, Earl raced to find Tiger lying on his bed, flicking through a copy of *Golf Digest.* But when he told his son about the invitation, Tiger didn't even look up from his magazine. "Cool," was all he said, before muttering something about having to miss his advanced geometry classes.

When McLaughlin made his offer, Tiger Woods was fifteen years old and would just turn sixteen when the tournament began in February 1992, making him the youngest player in the event's seventy-five-year history. For his part, Earl had no qualms that his son would be able to handle the pressure of being in the spotlight at his first taste of a bona fide PGA Tour event. Nor did Greg McLaughlin. "I knew he was special. You just saw it," he told the press, adding that he "just had a notion that he was going to be a big star."

More concerning, however, was some of the public's reaction to Woods's appearance at the competition. In the days leading up to the event, McLaughlin arrived at the tournament office each morning to find messages on the answer machine, variously calling Woods a "n*****" or abusing him for asking a minority player to participate in the competition. Worse still were the death threats, prompting the tournament director to beef up security around Woods and the club more generally. While McLaughlin had discussed the threats with Earl Woods and outlined the additional security measures in place, Earl decided to keep them from his son, only telling him once the tournament was over.

While Tiger's appearance at the tournament was a PR masterstroke by Greg McLaughlin, guaranteeing larger crowds and huge media coverage, it wasn't universally popular, with some of the 143 professional players taking exception to the hoopla surrounding this skinny teenager from Cypress. Mark Carnevale, the 1992 PGA Tour Rookie of the Year, was one.

"There was resentment at the attention he was getting, probably more than anything," he said. "Some of the guys were like, 'Who the hell is this guy, and why is he playing in this event?' You could sense there was some of that."

After finishing his practice round with his friend Doug Martin, Bob Friend sat down in the players' area to enjoy some lunch. As the two men dined, a tournament official walked past their table, handing them a piece of paper with the tee times and pairings for the first and second rounds. As a rookie pro just a few weeks into his first year on the PGA Tour, Friend, then twenty-eight, wasn't expecting to be paired with any of the bigger names in the game, but when he saw who he would be playing with, his heart sank. "I looked at my sheet, and I'm like, 'Oh God, I've got this kid! This is going to be a zoo,'" he recalled. "I knew all about Tiger Woods—we all did—but my concern was how the circus following him was going to affect my game. I was playing for my livelihood, after all, and I was concerned that his followers might not have the highest golf IQ."

Sure enough, Friend soon realized just what a phenomenon Tiger Woods was. As he waited on the elevated tee box at the par-5 opening hole, alongside the third player in the group, Georgia's Dicky Thompson, the two professionals couldn't believe their eyes. Beyond the tournament officials, a phalanx of cameramen, friends and family, Rudy Duran, Tiger's girlfriend Gravell, and his mother and father were thousands upon thousands of curious fans lining the first fairway, eager to see just what all the fuss was about. Even Slammin' Sammy Snead, the man Woods had played with when he was six, was watching intently. "He looks like he's going to be a real force on tour," Snead said.

Joe Grohman, meanwhile, was charged with making sure Tida could see her son in action. "I had Tida on my arm," he said. "The people watching Tiger were five deep, six deep, ten deep in some places. And I'd say, 'I'm coming through. Tiger's my man,' and the seas would part. We'd get right to the front row on every hole."

At times it seemed as though everyone who knew Tiger was there. Not only had his Western High golf coach Don Crosby called in sick to attend ("I just hoped that I didn't get on TV," he said) but a bunch of Tiger's classmates and teammates had also developed sudden ailments preventing them from attending that morning's geometry class. Jeff Anderson was one. "There was a group of us following him around that day. It was very cool. A high school kid playing in a PGA Tour event—and he went to our school," he said.

What Anderson also remembers is what Woods told him prior to the tournament.

"He wanted to win," he added. "He wasn't just going there because he had an exemption. He wanted to go there and win. He really believed that, and he had that drive and that motivation. It was just so cool to witness it."

If Woods was nervous—and nobody would have blamed him if he was—he didn't show it. Instead, the sixteen-year-old, dressed in a stripy polo shirt and Chinos, pulled his driver out of his bag and, a couple of wiggles later, split the fairway nearly three hundred yards in the distance. Years later, Woods would recall that opening tee shot at Riviera. "I've never felt a golf club that heavy in my life," he said. "I teed it up fine, but as I took the club back, I've never felt a club weigh so much."

Bob Friend was certainly impressed. "He did not appear to be nervous, but he had a lot of moxie, especially for a sixteen-year-old," he said. "And as a PGA Tour professional, you get to see the prettiest golf swings in the world, and you can discern whether somebody has the required skills or not. But you listen too. You listen to the contact they make and the ball's flight. Tiger was maybe five foot nine or five foot ten and couldn't have weighed more than 135 pounds soaking wet, but he produced this penetrating ball flight. And he compressed it too. It sounded like rifle fire. He was producing PGA Tour sounding shots."

When he saw Woods crash his drive down the first fairway, Coach Don Crosby, watching from behind the ropes, knew instantly that his young charge had what it took to make it in the pro game. "The great ones get better when you turn up the heat. Tiger definitely takes his game up a notch when he's on the spot," he said.

"The bigger the troop that follows him up the fairway, the louder the cheers he hears from another hole, the more hushed the crowd around the green, the greater the tension in the air, the more chance there is that Tiger Woods is going to reach in his bag for a club and pull out a rabbit."

But while Friend had been struck by the prodigious talent of young Tiger, he was less enamored with the circus that followed him around. While the crowd was unusually enthusiastic with cries of "you the kid!" ringing out regularly, it was the behavior of the media that took him by surprise, especially those journalists, cameramen, and photographers that didn't typically cover golf tournaments. "The crowd was super polite. The marshals were great. We had no issues with that whatsoever. It was the people just inside the ropes, the media, that really made it very, quite trying," said Friend. "It was the people that were from non-golf magazines who had zero clue how to behave on a golf course."

On the seventh green, for example, Friend was lining up a putt from the fringe when a photographer, oblivious to what he was doing, stood directly in front of his ball, just to get a shot of Tiger leaning on his putter on the other side of the putting surface. "My caddie couldn't believe it. He was like, 'Dude! Dude! Get out of the way!'" he added. "But that was the sort of stuff we had to deal with for two days. It had zero to do with Tiger, but it had everything to do with him, you know?"

Tiger ended his first round with a 1-over-par 72, eight shots adrift of the leaders. The following day when, again, the crowds flocked to see him in huge numbers, Woods couldn't replicate the promise of his opening round, and a 75 saw the sophomore miss the cut by five strokes. Woods, however, still declared the experience to have been "the best two days of my life." (For the record, it was Fred Couples that won the 1992 Nissan Los Angeles Open, beating

Davis Love III in a playoff. But nobody was really talking about that.)

With the tournament over, Earl Woods took his son to one side and told him how proud he was of the way he had played and the manner in which he had handled himself throughout the event. Then he told him about the death threats.

"Hmm," Tiger replied. "Sixteen years old and I've already had my first death threat."

After the love-in of Los Angeles, Tiger returned to Cypress and to the other life he led where nobody ever really clamored to talk to him or want his photograph, as his friend and teammate Jeff Anderson explained. "Everyone was starting to understand who he was, but he wasn't treated any different. He was just one of the guys," he said. "He still wanted to go to the football games. He still wanted to go to the basketball games. He just wanted to be a normal teenager, doing normal teenage boy stuff."

That was largely down to Western High's Principal Craig Haugen, who found himself in the extraordinary position of overseeing the education of a bona fide prodigy, but he also ensured that Tiger, for all his unique gifts, experienced something akin to a normal high school life. For Haugen, it meant little more than protecting Woods from any media interest and allowing him to be as normal a teenager as possible in a stable and supportive environment.

That also meant teeing it up for Don Crosby's Western High School golf team where he remained the dominant force, not just on the team but in high school golf in Southern California more generally. By now, there was very little Coach Crosby could teach Tiger about golf. Here, after all, was a sixteen-year-old with the golf world at his feet who had proved himself more than capable of coping with the demands of the professional ranks—perhaps not so much on the golf course yet, where he had already identified what aspects of his game required improvement, but most noticeably off it, where he handled his burgeoning celebrity with a rare maturity. But Crosby recognized that, in high school golf at least, Woods was coasting, especially in those home games at Dad Miller. So he cut a deal with Chuck McAuley, owner of nearby Los Coyotes Country Club, so the team could use the course for free. McCauley had watched Tiger play in the Lee Hamill Junior Tournament that he hosted and was only too keen to have a potential superstar grace his golf course on a more regular basis.

It was a different story at Los Coyotes though. Significantly longer and undeniably more testing than Dad Miller, it saw Woods's round average rise from 1-over-par in his freshman year to 9-over-par in his sophomore season. Often, Tiger would ask Coach Crosby when they would be back at Dad Miller, knowing full well that every time he played there, he would inevitably be 3- or 4-under-par for his nine holes, thereby improving his average.

For the other players on the Pioneers, Woods was still shooting the kind of scores they could only dream of. "There were so many times where he's played nine holes, and he's gone around in 33, 34. And those were his bad days," said Jeff Anderson. "I saw him shoot 28 over nine holes. I saw him shoot 29 with a bogey. It was just a different level."

Crosby's hunch that a more challenging home track might improve Tiger's game may not have pleased the rest of the Pioneers team, but it had the desired effect on his star student. Tiger adjusted, and by the time he finished the season, Woods had won his second California Interscholastic Federation title, shooting a 4-under round of 68 at Big Canyon Country Club and set his sights on finishing his high school golf career with an average that was under-par.

Tiger might have been socially awkward, but on the golf course and around the other golfers on the Pioneers, he always felt relaxed, even mischievous. After a two-day competition at Rancho Canada near Monterey where Woods set the all-time tournament record, eclipsing the long-standing mark by a staggering six strokes, the team jumped in Crosby's motorhome to head home, but after some persuasive words from Tiger, the coach decided to take the famous Seventeen-Mile Drive, a route that took the young golfers past the ultraexclusive Cypress Point Golf Club.

Cypress Point is Everest for the golf addict. Set on the spectacular Monterey Peninsula, it only ever has 250 members, whose identities are fiercely protected. It is impossible to play the course without first being invited by one of those select few. But Tiger knew all about Cypress Point and wasn't going to pass up the opportunity to try and play it.

Persuading Coach Crosby to pull over near the fifteenth tee, Tiger and the team grabbed their clubs, hopped off the bus, and leapt over the course's security fence. The plan was to play fifteen, sixteen, and seventeen before jumping back in the motorhome, which he would then park near the eighteen tee.

Initially, it worked like a dream. The boys played the short par-3 fifteenth hole and managed to complete the world-famous sixteenth, but when they got to the seventeenth, there was a course official waiting to escort them off the premises.

Meanwhile, Don Crosby was waiting down the road by the eighteenth, wondering where the boys had got to. Eventually, they appeared walking up the road, clubs slung on their back and their tails between their legs. "I wonder if anyone at Cypress realized they had the distinction of kicking Tiger Woods off their golf course," recalled Crosby.

CHAPTER 11

DECISION TIME

"Certain players, you look at them once and see something. As soon as I saw Tiger Woods swing, I thought, 'Man, this young guy has got it. "It" being something indescribable.'"

—Gary Player, nine-time major championship winner

ESPN was in town to record a piece on the young man they were calling "the world's best junior golfer, namely Eldrick 'Tiger' Woods." It was all the usual stuff they had come to expect from a media profile of Woods, from the childhood TV appearances to shots of the Teakwood Street sideboards groaning under the weight of his many trophies.

Most of the piece takes place on the golf course, with Tiger demonstrating his skills or goofing around with the camera, while some of his Pioneers teammates explain how strange it is to be playing with a schoolmate who often has to stop to sign autographs. "I'm a normal teenager," said Woods. "It's just that I do one thing better than the average teenager, and that's play golf."

His personal coach John Anselmo made an appearance too. Standing behind the green with Tiger a hundred yards back down the fairway, he's asked how his student is from this kind of distance, at which point Tiger's wedge shot drops pin-high on the green in front of them, before spinning sideways and stopping eighteen inches from the hole. "How is he from that distance?" said Anselmo. "You just saw."

Inevitably, Earl Woods appeared, too, explaining that what Tiger has isn't a love of the game of golf. "It transcends love," he said. "He's addicted to greatness. He's addicted to being the best that has ever played the game."

When talk turned to where Tiger intends to go to college and if Woods keeps his counsel, it is his father who put his foot down. "All of you reporters who think Tiger is going to so-and-so, your sources are dead wrong," he said, before repeating himself. "Dead wrong."

Though he had the pick of any college in the country, it had actually been a straight choice between Stanford and the University of Nevada, Las Vegas (UNLV), and those reporters' sources weren't "dead wrong" at all. Both college golf coaches—Wally Goodwin at Stanford and Dwaine Knight at UNLV—had long been monitoring Woods's progress, with Goodwin first on the scene in the spring of 1989, mooting the idea of him one day joining his team.

Initially, Tiger and Earl Woods preferred UNLV. The three-hundred-plus days of sun a year suited him, as did the variety of golf courses in the area. The drive was shorter than going to Stanford, and UNLV, unlike Stanford, also had the business (accounting) major that Woods favored.

Dwaine Knight had really pulled out all the stops to land Tiger for UNLV. He had kept in touch with the family for five years, been to Tiger's house, and had shown him around Las Vegas several times. On one visit, he had arranged accommodations for Tiger at the city's plush Mirage Hotel and hosted a grand reception at the school president's house.

He also gave the teenager a tour of some of the golf courses in the area, including one of Tiger's favorites, and the most expensive course in the United States, Shadow Creek. As the pair walked the seventeenth hole, a golf cart pulled up next to him. There, sitting behind the wheel, was the actress Elizabeth Taylor. If the encounter with Hollywood royalty was designed to seduce Tiger, it failed miserably. "He had no clue who she was," Knight said.

But after Coach Wally Goodwin turned up at Teakwood Street with a pizza, and Tiger visited the campus in Palo Alto, Woods eventually opted for Stanford, majoring in economics with an emphasis on accounting.

Goodwin and Earl Woods kept in regular contact, exchanging phone calls regularly and talking through any concerns Tiger, and Earl, may have had about committing to Stanford, rather than any other college. As Tiger returned to Western High for his senior year, he and his father once again summoned the Stanford University golf coach for dinner at Teakwood Street. Woods and Goodwin had established a rapport over the years, ever since they exchanged letters when Tiger was in his early teens. Now, Tiger wanted to tell the good news, although not before he had a little fun with Goodwin.

"Hey, Coach, I've got something to show you," said Tiger as they sat in the living room. Woods reached under his chair, revealed a University of Nevada, Las Vegas hat and put it on his head.

"Hey, you little twerp!" replied Goodwin, failing to see the funny side. "You wouldn't have asked me to come down here if you were going to go to Vegas. I can't understand why you'd want to go there anyway. You wouldn't have me down for dinner for that. You'd have your father call on the phone."

"Relax, Coach." Tiger laughed before pulling out an Arizona State cap instead.

"I have to get back to Stanford," Goodwin replied, the joke wearing thin.

It was then that Tiger stopped him and placed a Stanford cap on his head. "Coach," he said. "I'm with you."

Pledging a vow of silence until Tiger announced his decision publicly, Wally Goodwin skipped back to his car and drove the 350 miles back to Palo Alto, all the time wearing the biggest and widest grin his face had ever managed to muster.

Soon after, on the morning of Wednesday, November 10, 1993, Western High School did something it had never done in all of its near-forty-year existence. With speculation reaching fever pitch about which college Woods would choose, they decided to hold a press conference, inviting local press and even reporters from national titles like *Sports Illustrated* and *Golf Digest* and broadcasters including ESPN.

At a little after 10:00 a.m., Tiger Woods, still seven weeks shy of his eighteenth birthday, flanked by his parents, Earl and Tida, sat down in the school gymnasium and did the cap gag that he had played on Wally Goodwin again, placing two hats in front of him on the table, one from University of Nevada, Las Vegas, the other from Stanford.

To prolong the suspense, Woods smiled as he shuffled the hats around like a magician playing a card trick before picking up the UNLV one, to the surprise of everyone watching, and then promptly throwing it under the table and then placing the Stanford cap front and center. "I figured, 'What's more important, school or golf?' My entire life has always been school first, golf second, so why change now?" he told his press conference.

It was a line almost certainly written by his mother. While his GPA was better than 3.7, Woods was never really taken with the idea of more studying, not when everybody at Stanford was even smarter than him and there were so many more golf trophies to win.

The following day, the *Los Angeles Times* reported on how Woods had made up his mind, writing: "The choice between Stanford and Nevada, Las Vegas would seem to be simple, but Eldrick (Tiger) Woods still agonized over it.

"Woods, a Western High honors student who happens to be one of the best junior golfers in the nation, made such a strong effort to keep an open mind that he says the pressure made him physically ill. So it was with relief Wednesday that Woods announced he will attend Stanford."

"Now I can tell people where I'm going to college," Woods said.

The UNLV assistant golf coach J.T. Higgins, meanwhile, was left to reflect on what might have been. "[Tiger] was in," he said. "At the end of the day, just like so many coaches will tell you, it came down to mom. [Kultida] had her heart set on her son going to Stanford for his whole life—that's where she wanted him to go. She wasn't gonna let him go to Vegas.

"Earl loved us, and I think Tiger loved it in Vegas."

Besides, Stanford was only too happy to do anything it could to help accommodate Woods, even if that meant inventing a new, tailor-made major more to his liking. "The dean, the athletic director, and the business director said, 'We'll work with you. We'll create you a major,'" Woods explained. "I said, 'Okay.'"

If Tiger still doubted his right to be at one of America's most prestigious colleges, he needed only to remind himself that Stanford, one of the most selective universities in the world where fewer than 4 percent of applicants receive an admission offer (and fewer still actually attend), hadn't just given him a full-ride scholarship but were now designing a major *just for him*.

Meanwhile in Palo Alto, Assistant Sports Information Director Steve Raczynski braced himself for the inevitable deluge of media requests about the university's newest freshman. Sure enough, as soon as news broke of Tiger's decision, his phone rang off the hook. "We took a little poll in the office, asking what athlete has entered Stanford with more interest," he said. "We had John McEnroe, who advanced to the Wimbledon semifinals the summer before college; swimmer Janet Evans, who won Olympic gold medals before coming here; and quarterback John Elway. None of them was in Tiger's category."

When the annals of golf are written, the name of Paul Page will be lucky to merit a footnote. It's no slight on the Englishman. He was, after all, the English Boys' Champion, a Walker Cup player in 1993, and made it on to the European Tour (now the DP World Tour). But he was also the last ever player to beat Tiger Woods as an amateur in a national championship.

In 1993 at the US Amateur Championship, staged on the Cypress Creek course at the Champions Golf Club in Houston, Texas, Page was twenty-one and fresh from a runners-up place in the British Amateur Championship at Royal Portrush in Northern Ireland. Having booked his place in the second round of match play, Page took his place on the practice range, sandwiched between the Irishman Pádraig Harrington and the Texan Justin Leonard. "It was quite a lineup," said Page, who now runs his own golf academy in Kent, England.

As the players hit drivers on the range, their golf balls bouncing and rolling into the fence 285 yards in the distance, Leonard turned to Page. "You're playing Tiger, right?"

Page nodded, although in the pre-internet age of the early 1990s and coming from the other side of the Atlantic Ocean, he had no real idea who his opponent was.

"Who is he?" he asked.

Leonard lifted his golf club, using it to point to the skinny teenager, four places down on the range. "So I turned round, and Tiger was there with what I thought was a driver, and he's clearing the fence at the end of the range—and the fence is ten meters high." He laughed. "I was like, 'Jesus, that is off the charts.'"

Then Page did a double take. "Turns out it wasn't a driver," he added. "It was a 3-wood."

It would be a tight encounter. Though he was outdriving Page by sixty or seventy yards on most of the longer holes, Woods was erratic, too, gifting several holes to his English opponent. By the time they reached the seventeenth, Page was one hole to the good and holding his own. When the pair teed off, Page found the fairway while Woods, wayward again, found the trees. The second shots were equally unconvincing, with Page finding a greenside bunker, leaving himself an up and down to win.

But just as the pair reached their balls, a thunderstorm swept across Houston, forcing the pair to leave their balls and the golf course. It would be five hours before they returned to conclude their game where, given the sodden nature of the sand trap, Page was permitted to place his ball in the bunker. What happened next was the kind of thing that Woods had done, and would do, to so many opponents over the years. Page played what he called "the best bunker shot I've ever hit," spinning the ball fully sixty feet to gimme range to seal a 2-and-1 victory.

The match over, Woods whipped off his straw hat and thanked Page for the match, wishing him well for the rest of the tournament. In return, Page simply shook Woods's hand, and realizing that a seventeen-year-old could and should have beaten him, predicted great things for his opponent. "I just said to him, 'You are going to be a great player,'" he said. "And I wasn't wrong."

After the match, Page returned to the players' locker room, and as he sat down to change his shoes, in walked a stern-faced Earl Woods. Expecting a word of congratulation or at least some token conversation about the match, Page smiled at him but got nothing in return. "For Christ's sake, any normal man would have said, 'Good luck in the next round, son,' even if he didn't mean it," he recalled, "but he didn't even say anything. He just walked off. He didn't give me the time of day. He wasn't pleasant at all.

"He probably saw me as a blip on his son's progression—and he'd be right."

In 2006, in an interview with *Golf Digest*, Earl Woods spoke about how gracious a loser Tiger was on those admittedly rare occasions when other players got the better of him. "Listen to Tiger when he loses," he said. "He acknowledges that the other guy was the better golfer that day. The one thing he doesn't say is that the other guy was better overall."

Only that wasn't true. On too many occasions in his junior and amateur career, Woods had been guilty of the kind of disrespect to opponents that is frowned upon in a game that prides itself on sportsmanship. Remarkably, though, Woods—and his father—never seemed to get called out for it, let alone reprimanded.

While a "blip" like this was part and parcel of any young golfer's journey through the game, it had irritated his father, even though there was no shame in a junior player losing in a men's event. Racking his brains to find some answers, Earl Woods decided it was high time Tiger moved on when it came to coaching, not least as John Anselmo had been diagnosed with colon cancer and, inevitably, had to cut back on his regular lessons with Earl's son.

Tiger's relationship with Anselmo was, by its very nature, a transitional one. As Tiger grew, as his game evolved, and as the stakes escalated, different expertise was required, but there was little doubt that Anselmo had helped Tiger understand the simple, timeless truths of the golf swing, acting as the calm, steady hand needed at a time when Tiger's potential called for nurturing, not exploiting.

A few months earlier, IMG agent Hughes Norton had spoken with Earl Woods about going to see Butch Harmon, the club professional at Lochinvar Golf Club, just twelve miles east of the Champions Club, and suggested he let him run the rule over Tiger's game. The son of the 1948 Masters winner, Claude Harmon, Butch Harmon was already a revered figure in golf tuition by the mid-1990s, a swing whisperer with a reputation for taking exceptional talent and making them even better. In the early 1990s, Harmon had reworked Greg Norman's swing, helping the Australian out of a slump and on to his second major title victory when he added the 1993 British Open at Royal St. George's to the one he won on Turnberry Ailsa Course eight years earlier.

One of four brothers, all of whom had played professionally, Butch Harmon might not have matched his father's success—he only ever won one minor tournament in 1971—but he had inherited his sense of humor. As a player on tour, for instance, he had called his father to tell him about another missed cut. "But, according to the newspaper, you're leading the tournament," said Claude Harmon.

"I finished dead last," replied Butch.

"Wait a minute," said his father. "I'm holding the paper upside down."

A meeting was convened, and, fresh from his defeat to Paul Page, Tiger and Earl drove the short distance out to see Harmon at Lochinvar where Woods, wearing his sneakers, hit a bunch of balls for him on the range. For Harmon, there would be no issue with Tiger's ability or, perhaps more importantly, his willingness to learn. Instead, it was Earl Woods, the man that had nurtured Tiger's talent almost from birth, that Harmon considered to be the main blocker to a successful working relationship. Put simply, Harmon was worried that Earl Woods would dispute or override anything he didn't like about Harmon's methods, and if this new approach was going to work, then Earl needed to let go a little—or a lot. "If you don't think you can turn him over to me, it is probably not a good thing," Harmon told the senior Woods.

Eventually, the two men, both Vietnam veterans, found common ground. "I'll make a deal with you," Earl Woods told Harmon. "I won't try and be his golf coach if you don't try and be his dad."

From the outset, Harmon could see the potential in his new student and was so confident Woods had what it took to make it in the game that he even refused to invoice Earl for his tuition until such time Tiger turned professional. "When I first saw Tiger swing a club, standing there was a tremendous amount of natural, raw talent," Harmon said. "He was like a trophy that needed to be polished."

Harmon was also struck by how little Tiger actually thought about game or course management when he was playing it. "I just hit the ball as hard as I can, go and find it, and hit it again," Woods told him, a simple strategy which, on the face of it, had served him very well up to this point.

A new year, but it was just another week and another trophy. This time, Dial High School Athlete Scholars of the United States awards had been in touch to say Tiger had won and how he needed to go to Washington, DC, to collect his award. While it was the first Tiger had heard of it, Coach Don Crosby knew it was coming. After all, he had nominated his star player, sending off all manner of stats and results as well as his GPA and all the other awards and distinctions he had amassed in the last year. Soon after, Tiger and his parents, along with Coach Don Crosby and his wife, Faith, attended a black-tie banquet at the Washington Hilton where Woods, alongside standout volleyball and basketball player Kristen Folkl of St. Louis, Missori, received their awards.

The truth was Western High School knew they had a special student on their roll call, and, consequently, they couldn't do enough to accommodate Tiger's ceaseless pursuit of golfing glory, as long as he pledged to get all of his schoolwork done promptly. At home in Orange County, he routinely drew crowds on the rare occasions when his hectic schedule now allowed him to tee it up for Coach Crosby's Pioneers. It wasn't just the United States where an appearance from Woods was guaranteed to garner greater interest. On a school team trip to Canada to play a tournament at Olympic View Golf Course on Vancouver Island, Woods, again, was the star of the show.

"By the last day of the match, we'd built up quite a crowd watching us. 'Us' being another way of saying 'Tiger,'" said Don Crosby. "At the last hole, it was kind of a miniature version of the end of the US Open, with a ring of fans five deep around the green as we came up the fairway."

The truth was Tiger's name was fast spreading across not just North America but the world. In February, he had been given a sponsor's exemption to play in the Johnnie Walker Asian Classic in Phuket, Thailand. A prestigious stop on the then European Tour, it was a tournament featuring a stellar cast including Nick Faldo, Greg Norman, and 1992 Masters winner and possessor of the silkiest swing in golf, Fred Couples. What made the trip even more special for Woods was that he could really explore and enjoy the Thai and Asian side of his heritage once more, without his father there to push his African American background to the fore. Indeed, as soon as he landed in Bangkok, it seemed as though the Thai people had already adopted him as one of their own. Even local media was using his face to promote the tournament. Tiger responded by wearing a heavy gold chain with a replica of a gold Buddha around his neck. He played well, too, making the cut for the first time in a professional event and finishing in a tie for 34th in a field of 156.

The trip to Thailand, however, had confused Tiger a little. Back in the United States, he spoke about not just how he was received around the world, but how he was perceived too. "Being Black is just looked at differently. And in this country, I'm just looked at as being Black," he added. "When I go to Thailand, I'm considered Thai. It's very interesting. And when I go to Japan, I'm considered Asian. I don't know why it is, but it just is."

In the years after he had turned professional, Tiger would often take the opportunity to play in Thailand and the Johnnie Walker Classic whenever the chance presented itself, winning the event a couple of times as well. Not only did it please his mother to see him enjoying her homeland, but as it wasn't a PGA Tour event, it meant Tiger could also command the kind of hefty, seven-figure appearance fee that no other player in the game could expect.

And that pleased him, and his father, even more.

CHAPTER 12
A NEW DOMINANCE

"When you've got the son of a bitch down, stomp on him."

—Earl Woods's match play advice to his son

Tiger Woods was smart, but Dennis Bergal was smarter. Maybe not academically but clever enough to recognize an opportunity when one presented itself. As Tiger's time at Western High School drew to a close, and he prepared to graduate, Tiger and his fellow seniors browsed their yearbooks, and there he was, voted "Most Likely to Succeed."

As Woods flicked through the pages, Bergal, who had known him since their time together at Los Cerritos Elementary, approached him, carrying his own copy. "Hey, Tiger, can you sign my yearbook?" he asked.

"Sure," replied Tiger. "What do you want me to put?"

"Nothing," said Bergal. "Don't put anything. Just sign your name and nothing else."

Woods was puzzled, not least as they had known each other for so long, but agreed nonetheless. Then Bergal explained himself. "I hear you're going to be famous one day, and I just want your autograph because I'm going to sell this for a lot of money," he added.

When their prom came around, Woods dug out the same tuxedo he had worn to the Dial High Awards in Washington, DC, earlier in the year and attended with his girlfriend Dina Gravell, along with friends Alfredo Arguello, Mike Gout, and Bryon Bell and their dates.

Like everyone else at Western High who had heard all about Woods's exploits on the golf course, it seemed predestined that he would go on to become one of the school's most decorated alumni, maybe even eclipsing the likes of the LA Dodgers pitcher Andy Messersmith who had graduated back in 1963.

By the time he left Western High, boasting a GPA of 3.7, Woods had already been approached by a steady stream of talent agents and management companies, eager to sell him—or rather, Earl Woods—their vision for his professional career and all the lucrative opportunities that would present themselves. Tiger couldn't care less about the money, but Earl could. Superagencies like William Morris sent a proposal, as did Leigh Steinberg, the Los Angeles sports agent and rumored inspiration for *Jerry Maguire*. But it was Hughes Norton and IMG that were in the driver's seat—and it wasn't just the company's reputation that had piqued Earl Woods's interest.

On his way home from work one day, Hughes Norton had a brain wave. Throughout his many discussions with Earl Woods over the years, it had always struck him just how difficult the family had found it financially with taking Tiger to tournaments across the country. Even with Earl's two pensions—one from the military, another from his long service at McDonnell Douglas—the Woods family was still making sacrifices.

Norton's idea, given the money worries Earl and Tida Woods were suffering in supporting their son, was to use Earl Woods's expertise and now-retired availability in scouting talented players on the college circuit when he accompanied Tiger around the country. It made sense on many levels. Not only would the twenty-five thousand dollars a year (plus expenses) ease Earl's money worries, but it might just unearth another gem in IMG's quest to dominate player representation. More than that, though, it would go a long way to convincing Earl that IMG was where Tiger's future career lay when he decided the time was right to take to the professional ranks.

"I ended up hiring his dad." Norton laughed.

The only issue was whether the deal contravened the United States Golf Association strict rules on amateur status, but after IMG boss Mark McCormack spoke with USGA president, and former Stanford University golf star, Frank "Sandy" Tatum, it was waved through on the strict condition that any job offer that Earl received or accepted from IMG would have nothing to do with Tiger's decision to sign with the agency.

For two years, Earl Woods diligently prepared his scouting reports for Hughes Norton, despite knowing that, in reality, none of the players he was watching could, or would, ever compare to the ability and potential of his own son. Indeed, not a single recommendation from Earl Woods to Norton ever made the grade in professional golf, and, years later, Norton declared Earl to be the "worst talent scout in history."

But it didn't matter. After all, Earl's hiring, no matter how important he might have thought it was or how conscientiously he carried out his duties, was never about finding the next Tiger Woods. It was, despite what the USGA might have demanded, all about landing IMG *the* Tiger Woods.

Back at the Navy Club, though, Joe Grohman suspected that moves were already afoot for Tiger to turn professional in the not-too-distant future. "There was definitely something going on," he recalled. "Earl magically had a trunk full of brand-new Titleist balls all the time, and he'd throw me a dozen here and there. I never discussed with him what position he was in. I didn't even want to speculate. But I think what they did was they tried to groom the parents to get to the kid."

Still, with no high school to worry about and Stanford still several months away, Woods had nothing but golf to concentrate on in the summer of 1994, and ahead of him was a schedule guaranteed to test him both physically and mentally. But if Woods was worried about the challenges awaiting him, it didn't show. In mid-July, he accepted an invitation from John Bodenhamer, the director of the Pacific Northwest Golf Association, to play in their amateur championship. He headed to Vancouver, Washington, to play in the Pacific Northwest Golf Association Amateur Championship at Royal Oaks Country Club (ROCC) and breezed through to the final where he faced Oregon Amateur champion Ted Snavely in what turned out to be an awful mismatch.

In the final over thirty-six holes, Woods was 13-under-par through twenty-six holes and needed just thirty putts before he closed out the match for a scarcely believable 11-and-10 win and his first victory in a nonjunior event. Later, Woods called it "the best round of my life," and nobody who witnessed the evisceration could really mount any disagreement, largely because everyone was left speechless.

For Earl Woods, it was almost the perfect performance. Ruthless and efficient, Tiger had listened to the advice his father had given him and shown no mercy as he dispatched Snavely with almost indecent haste. "When you've got the son of a bitch down," he told his son, "stomp on him."

One of the tournament referees that week was Steve Bowen. When he oversaw Tiger's quarter-final match, he had assumed that

Woods was on his way home as he stood two down with three holes to play. But when Woods took the game to extra holes, suddenly the youngster changed tactics. "The first extra hole was at the first at Royal Oaks, which was 368 yards with a fairly tight dogleg right," explained Bowen. "All week Tiger had been taking a 4-iron off the tee to the corner of the dogleg and then hitting a wedge into the green, but in the playoff, he took out his iron again and then backed away. I remember the conversation he had with his caddie as he swapped it for his driver. He just said, 'Let's end this,' and then hit a perfect cut around the corner to about fifty yards from the green. He then proceeded to hit his pitch shot to six inches, and the match was over! He should have lost that match but ended up winning."

For Steve Bowen and the other PNGA officials in attendance, the dominance of Woods that week in Vancouver left them in no doubt about what the world of golf had in store in the years to come. "What impressed me the most about his game was not his length but his superior short game. Most of the young players at that time could really hit the ball with distance, but Tiger was amazing with his touch around the greens," added Bowen. "But we all felt he was destined to be great! Little did we know how understated that would turn out to be."

That summer, Tiger Woods found yet another gear, impossible though it may have seemed at times. When he won the California Amateur Championship to take his fourth AJGA title of the summer, he set a new course record of 62 at the Hacienda Club in La Habra Heights, lowering the record by four shots and setting a new low for any round in an SCGA event.

The tidal wave of triumphs continued at the Western Amateur, the third oldest amateur event in golf. Held at the Robert Trent Jones–designed Point O'Woods Golf & Country Club in Benton Harbor, Michigan, it dated back to 1899, and its roll call of winners included everyone from the 1913 US Open champion Francis Ouimet to Ben Crenshaw, Curtis Strange, Hal Sutton, Phil Mickelson, and, inevitably, Jack Nicklaus.

In the round-of-sixteen match against Chris Tidland, an All-American from Oklahoma State University, Woods nearly fell victim to a kind of improbable comeback he had so often inflicted on others. With just six holes to play, Woods was set fair with a four-up lead and easing his way to a place in the semifinals. Suddenly, Tidland caught alight. With birdies at thirteen, fourteen, fifteen, sixteen, and seventeen, he then chipped in from sixty feet at the last hole for another, leaving Woods having to make a massive, snaking putt of thirty-five feet to take the match into extra holes. Which, of course, he did. "I shot thirty-three on the backside and still got killed," Woods said later. "That doesn't happen that often."

At the second extra hole, meanwhile, Tidland made yet another birdie—his seventh in just eight holes—leaving Tiger with a twenty-foot putt for an eagle and the win. When his putt dropped, the sense of relief, rather than jubilation, was tangible. For once, Woods had been pushed further than he might have expected, but with the pressure on, he had passed this latest test with flying colors.

"It was probably one of the greatest matches of all time in our tournament or any tournament," said Gary Holaway, director of communications for the Western Golf Association. "For someone to birdie the last six holes and still not win is incredible."

Tidland's OSU teammate Alan Bratton watched the match unfold, incredulous that his close friend hadn't been able to win. "Chris birdied seven of the last eight holes and still lost his match," he recalled. "So that tells you how difficult it is to beat Tiger Woods, whether it's in stroke play or match play. He was behind by significant amounts in many, many matches back then, and yet he's nearly always turned it around. Tiger just did whatever he had to do to win. Bottom line is he's just freaking good."

The close call about Chris Tidland seemed to shake Woods into action for the rest of the tournament, however, when he never really looked in danger of losing. In the final, Woods came up against another All-American (and future Ryder Cup player), Nevada, Las Vegas's Chris Riley, defeating him 2 and 1 for his third consecutive victory at national amateur level.

As Tiger and Earl headed to the Chicago's O'Hare Airport to get their flight back to California and the next day's qualifying for the US Amateur, he smiled when his father told him that not even Bobby Jones, a player who won four US Opens and five US Amateurs, won the Western Amateur. For Tiger, though, it was just another of Jack Nicklaus's achievements ticked off in his quest to reel in the Golden Bear.

But Tiger nearly didn't make qualifying. Stuck in heavy traffic on the two-hour drive to O'Hare International, the pair missed their flight. When they tried to book one of the two remaining flights that evening, they then discovered they were sold out. Placed on standby, Earl and Tiger waited and waited until their names were finally called for the last flight home. "I prayed, and my prayers were answered," Earl said. "Thank God we got on that damn airplane."

They eventually arrived back at Teakwood Street at 1:00 a.m. on Monday morning, and Tiger finally fell asleep at 2:30 a.m. Three hours later, he was up again and on the way to Western Hills Golf and Country Club in Chino Hills, half an hour away, to meet his 8:00 a.m. tee time. Whether it was the boundless energy of youth or simply digging ever deeper, Woods shot an astonishing seven-under round of 65 in the morning, followed by a 73 in the afternoon in what were his ninth and tenth rounds of golf in just six days.

Still, it was more than sufficient to earn his spot at the US Amateur. "I was dead," Woods said. "I had no energy left. I went around in the afternoon and tried to hang in there. I didn't really concentrate. I couldn't."

The sheer amount of golf that Tiger was playing, and the huge distances involved, inevitably took its toll on Woods's golf game. While his results suggested otherwise, the fatigue of tournament after tournament had reminded him just what he needed to do to be better, if that were possible. Dissatisfied with his driving and irritated by what he perceived as his inconsistent iron play, he believed that it was only his miraculous short game on and around the greens that was keeping his scores low. "I'm just getting up and down and salvaging rounds," he sighed.

While Woods seemed fine to the wider world, it was hard to escape the idea that Tiger was being driven above and beyond his physical limits. To all intents and purposes, it appeared as though as long as Tiger was winning, as he was in the summer of 1994, then Earl Woods had no problem with him keeping the kind of hectic schedule that might, ultimately, be detrimental to his health and, in turn, his golf game. After all, he was working with Butch Harmon now, and his new coach could surely iron out any issues that Tiger felt were troubling him.

It was, nevertheless, a testament to the mental fortitude of Tiger that he rarely revealed any concerns about his ceaseless schedule. Certainly, it seemed to make little or no difference when he arrived at TPC Sawgrass in Ponte Vedra Beach, Florida, for his third crack at the US Men's Amateur Championship.

Designed by Pete Dye, the Darth Vader of golf course architecture, and home to golf's unofficial fifth major, the Players' Championship, it features one of the most notorious and stress-inducing holes in golf—the infamous par-3 seventeenth island hole.

"If the players aren't complaining about my golf courses, then I haven't done my job," Pete Dye once said.

Having tried his hand twice before in the men's championship and been defeated by Tim Herron in 1992 and Paul Page in 1993, Woods was older and wiser going into his latest attempt to become the youngest-ever winner of the US Amateur as well as the first African American to do so.

Almost as soon as he arrived, though, he was all too aware of the latter. As he practiced hitting some gentle pitch shots on the range, a voice echoed out from behind a nearby fence, calling him the N-word repeatedly. With a sigh and a shake of the head, Woods carried on with his drill, determined to use the insults as motivation for an even better performance.

In the first round, Woods defeated Vaughn Moise, who, as a PGA Tour rules official, would later oversee Woods when he played professionally ("I don't think he ever gave me a good ruling after that," Woods would joke). He thrashed Michael Flynn of Texas Christian University 6 and 5 and then pipped Buddy Alexander, the University of Florida golf coach who had unsuccessfully tried to recruit him, at the final hole of their third-round match that afternoon. Three down with five to play, Alexander, the 1986 US Amateur champion, had the chance to win but three-putted from twenty-eight feet on the final green, handing victory to his teenage opponent. "I've never lost a match like that," he said. "I didn't hit a good shot after the twelfth hole. I just played lousy."

After the scare against Alexander, Woods eased ominously into the final, defeating thirty-five-year-old Tim Jackson of Germantown, Tennessee, 5 and 4. In the semifinals, he won 5 and 3 against three-time Kent All-American Eric Frishette.

Awaiting Woods in the final was Trip Kuehne, one of three siblings, alongside Hank and Kelli, from a Texan family renowned for their golfing heritage. The pair had known each other for several years and played successfully together as a team in the AJGA Canon Cup, where they had also caddied for each other when they played their singles matches in the event. Indeed, when Earl and Tida Woods first let Tiger attend a tournament unaccompanied at the AJGA tournament at Las Colinas in Irving, Texas, he stayed at Trip Kuehne's house in nearby Dallas.

A two-time All-American at Oklahoma State University, Kuehne was three-and-half-years older than Woods and, despite Woods's impressive march to the final, was still favorite to win, not least as nobody young as Tiger Woods had even won the US Amateur title. "I knew Tiger well, and I knew the way he played, but I wasn't intimidated by him at all," he said. "I was playing some good golf and figured I would win."

Winning, as far as Kuehne planned, meant getting off to a fast start in the thirty-six-hole match and closing it out as early as possible. In other words, not giving Woods the kind of opportunity to mount the kind of irrepressible comeback that he seemed to relish so much. The gameplan so nearly worked too. Kuehne got off to an ideal start, his exemplary putting yielding seven birdies in the first thirteen holes and giving him a commanding four-hole lead after the first eighteen holes.

The afternoon round began in much the same fashion. Kuehne birdied the second (twentieth hole) of the match to extend his lead. "But I never made a birdie after that," said Kuehne. Instead, Woods, dressed in baggy shorts, a pink-and-white striped shirt, and with a wide-brimmed straw hat sitting on his head, clawed his way back into the game, largely because Trip Kuehne let him when he bogeyed the twenty-fifth and twenty-seventh holes. Woods's birdie at the twenty-nineth hole, meanwhile, reduced the deficit still further. When he won the thirty-second hole, Kuehne's lead had been cut to just one hole with four to play.

Despite his comeback, Woods was still noticeably wayward off the tee, and whenever his ball did stray or he failed to execute a shot in quite the way he had intended, caddie Jay Brunza was there with whispered affirmations, keeping Woods on an even keel and ensuring he regained focus as quickly as possible. In that respect, it wasn't Brunza's job to read putts like the other rake rats. If anything, it was to read Tiger himself.

For Trip Kuehne, meanwhile, it was one of the only hopes that now had the potential to keep him in a match he had been winning so comfortably. "He was the best putter, best chipper, best diver, best iron player, best clutch player, best mental game, so the only thing that was somewhat missing that wasn't the best at the time was the driver," he explained. "He was just the total package, and my question was, if he ever really figured out how to become one of the best drivers in the golf world, nobody was going to be able to beat him."

Woods's inability to find the fairways also meant the two barely spoke to each other as they made their way around. "He was so far in the woods on a bunch of those holes that there really wasn't any good conversation walking down the fairway because, for the most part, he was one way, and I was the other," added Kuehne.

It was Woods's knack of salvaging something from a poor tee shot that kept his chances alive in the match. At the famous island hole par-3 seventeenth, his high, soft cut wedge flew 139 yards over the flag at the back right of the green, seemingly destined for the water. But when it caught the apron, the spin took effect, and, miraculously, the ball clung on to dry land by a few inches. Woods took full advantage of his good fortune, holing a tricky right to left fifteen-footer from the fringe to take a one-hole lead into the final hole.

At the thirty-sixth, Tiger Woods completed the most remarkable of all his comeback wins when Kuehne missed his par putt, leaving Woods the comfort of lagging his birdie putt up to the hole and accepting the inevitable concession from his opponent. For Kuehne, the disappointment of closing out victory dissipated over the years as Woods went on to a career unparalleled in the professional game. Indeed, he has since realized that he was bested by a generational talent.

"When I look back on what Tiger has been able to do, it's the ability for him to create shots and hit incredible shots when he really needed to," he said. "His drive, his vision, his will to win, and his will to be the best superseded everything."

At eighteen years, seven months, and twenty-nine days, though, Tiger Woods had become the youngest-ever winner of the US Amateur title and the Havemeyer Trophy, eclipsing a record that dated back to 1909 when Yale sophomore Robert Gardner, aged nineteen years and five months, triumphed. More important, to Earl Woods at least, was that he was also the first African American winner of the event. As he was congratulated by Kuehne and by his caddie and sports psychologist Jay Brunza, Earl Woods, with his shades and TaylorMade cap, appeared on the green and engulfed his son in a never-ending bear hug.

After Earl Woods had finally released his son from his vicelike grasp, ESPN reporter Bob Rosburg asked Woods if he had ever been six down in a match before. "I've never been six down and won. I've been six down and lost." He laughed before being presented with the Havemeyer Trophy.

The celebrations continued when Tiger returned home. Tida Woods laid on a surprise party for her son and his friends while Cypress decided to honor him with the key to the city, holding a presentation at Cypress Golf Club. Tiger gave them one of the Top Flite XL golf balls he had used at TPC Sawgrass in return.

Producers from TV chat shows like *Letterman* and *The Tonight Show with Jay Leno* called the house, their invitations politely declined. The Reverend Jesse Jackson phoned him. He even got a letter from President Bill Clinton, commending him on his "outstanding achievement" and his "personal dedication to excellence and wishing him every success when he went to Stanford." Tida couldn't get it framed and on the wall quick enough.

But not everybody was so generous. When Tiger Woods left a message at the Navy Club, asking the manager if he would like to display the Havemeyer Trophy at the clubhouse, the manager didn't even return his call. It was the final straw for Woods, as Joe Grohman explained. "That was Tiger's last shot . . . and this motherfucker didn't even get back to him," he recalled. "He's like a month away from going to Stanford, and he's a superstar. And they sent him off with a kick in the pants."

For Earl Woods, the Navy Club's overt racism was a stark and depressing example of the prejudice he had long cautioned Tiger about in his years growing up on the golf courses of the United States. Instead of succumbing to bitterness, though, Earl used the injustice to make Tiger, and himself, even stronger whenever they faced it. It also strengthened and validated his conviction that the systemic disadvantages Tiger faced in golf and beyond meant that his journey in the game was always going to be harder than any kid who played at a country club every weekend. It was why Earl was always on hand to identify and address any mistreatment his son encountered and to call it out for what it was. And, if circumstances required, to embellish it a little too.

CHAPTER 13
DEPARTURE

"I love that kid, man. What he has done in golf is amazing."

—John Daly, 1991 PGA Champion and 1995 British Open winner

With yet another hug for his dad and a couple more kisses on the cheek for his mom, Tiger Woods jumped into his navy Toyota Supra, complete with a new bass speaker in the back, and set off for Stanford, leaving behind his computer, his TV, his Nintendo console, and some loose change on his bedside table. He would never return to 6704 Teakwood Street.

Earl and Tida knew this day had been coming and knew, in all likelihood, he would never come back home. "You know, he's gone," Earl told his wife. "He will never be a resident of this house again in his entire life."

"What do you mean?" asked Tida.

"Well, he'll only ever be a visitor from now on," replied Earl.

While Earl joked that he was finally free from the responsibility of looking after Tiger and his golf career, his departure from Teakwood Street was the beginning of the end of his relationship with Tida Woods. When Tiger was there, there was always a joint focus for the pair of them, but with their son 340 miles away in

Palo Alto, the extent of just how far they had drifted apart became all too apparent. It wouldn't be long before they were not only living separate lives but living in separate homes too.

Woods arrived at Stanford a couple of days before his classes started on September 28, 1994, and unpacked his belongings in room 8 of the college's Stern Hall dormitory. Built in 1948, Stern Hall was named after college benefactor Lucie Stern, or "Aunt Lucy," whose generosity toward Stanford led her to be known as "Palo Alto's fairy godmother." Her generosity, especially after her husband Louis's death, manifested not just in named buildings but in opening her home to students and offering loans to those students in need. But by 1994, the condition of Stern Hall was so poor that it suggested Aunt Lucy perhaps hadn't donated enough. Stern, for example, was the only dormitory at Stanford that had never been renovated. It didn't even have cable television.

It wasn't long before his roommate, a Scandinavian engineering student called Bjorn Johnson, walked in to greet him. "He was unbelievable," Woods said later. "He never studied and just kept getting A's. I am like, 'How do you do this?' He's obviously brilliant."

But then everyone was brilliant at Stanford. There were gifted and talented people everywhere: The kid who built his own computers. The one with the photographic memory. The next Olympic gold medalist. Even Fred Savage, who found fame as Kevin Arnold in the hit TV show *The Wonder Years*, was a freshman. "Everybody is extraordinary at Stanford," Tiger told his father. "I'm not anything special there. And when everybody's special, nobody is."

Woods would meet his new golf teammates in the first week when they convened at Coach Goodwin's golf office. There, waiting for all of them, were their own new Stanford golf bags with their names written in cursive font on them.

When Eri Crum saw his, he instinctively looked to see whose bag was next to his and saw the name "Tiger Woods" sitting next to his. "There were four golf bags with the names of the four new freshman—me, Jake Poe, Ryan Chavez, and Tiger Woods," he recalled. "I definitely felt a sense of pride and gratitude for the chance to play with Tiger and the team."

It would perhaps be the first and the last time that any of the Cardinal golf recruits would ever feel remotely equal to Woods. "Tiger was well-known in the golfing community ever since he won the US Junior Amateur at fifteen," added Eri Crum. "When he won the US Amateur the summer before his freshman year, I remember watching him on TV, thinking, *I can't believe I am going to have the opportunity to play with this guy!*"

Having played junior golf with Woods, Notah Begay, who had also made it to Stanford on a scholarship, suggested to Tiger he join him and teammate Casey Martin for a round at nearby Sharon Heights Golf Club. "Notah had prepped me about what to expect, but I didn't realize just how good Tiger was," said Martin, who is now the golf coach at the University of Oregon. "Sharon Heights was a tight, narrow golf course, and they had just punched the greens, but it didn't matter. He didn't miss a shot. He hit every green on the golf course. He hit eighteen greens, you know. You're putting on punched greens, but he still shot 68."

As the trio left Sharon Heights, Woods jumped in his Toyota Supra while Martin and Begay clambered into Martin's car. "We looked at each other and just started laughing. We just said, 'What did we just watch today?'" recalled Martin. "We were All-Americans, we were NCAA champions, and yet this guy was next level, and we got to see it firsthand. He was so much better than we were. We were truly humbled.

"I was like, 'I think Tiger's a Top 20 or Top 10 player in the world, and he's a freshman in college.' I just couldn't fathom that there would be twenty guys in the world better than this guy."

For an experienced player like Casey Martin, the arrival of Tiger Woods at Stanford was a double-edged sword. On one hand, it was the recruiting coup of the century for the Cardinal, but, conversely, it came with the depressing realization that even if you were an All-American with an NCAA title under your belt, there was still someone who was much, much better. "I played with Phil Mickelson a handful of times, and I played with Stewart Cink and Justin Leonard, all future major winners, and it just wasn't comparable," added Martin. "Tiger was so much better, cleaner, more powerful, more dynamic than all those guys. Those guys were great, don't get me wrong, yet this guy was just significantly different."

Having won the NCAA team championship in 1994, Cardinal golf coach Wally Goodwin had persuaded Casey Martin and Notah Begay to take another year at college (or "redshirt") as they weren't going to graduate on time. For one, the pair needed the extra time to complete their studies, but it was also part of Goodwin's master-plan to create a Stanford men's golf team that would be the envy of every college across the nation. "We were both All-Americans, and yet we were redshirting in the middle of our season," explains Martin. "Sure, part of it was because we were missing a lot of school, but the main reason was, 'Let's wait for Tiger and make a run.' So the plan was to basically put a team together for that one year that would be kind of an all-star team."

Indeed, Woods wasted no time in demonstrating just how superior he was to his teammates, winning the first tournament he played when he shot 68, 72, and 68 to win the William H. Tucker Invitational at the University of New Mexico's south championship course in September. Of the first four events he played, meanwhile, he won two.

As the reigning US Amateur champion, Woods was now known to most anybody with an interest in the game of golf—and sometimes those at Stanford who couldn't care less. When the phone rang at Stern Hall one day, Tiger's roommate answered it, telling Woods that there was a man with an Australian accent on the line for him. When Tiger picked up the receiver, he discovered it was the world number one, Greg Norman, inviting him to play a few holes when he had the time.

When the Cardinal golf team was on the road, his teammates soon learned the extent of his celebrity as well. When they were traveling to a tournament in their university-branded golf van, Coach Goodwin had hit sixty miles per hour when an old car, seemingly on its last legs, spluttered alongside it. As the team looked over, the car window rolled down, and a man appeared. "Is Tiger in there?" he shouted. The team nodded, and when the vehicles stopped at some traffic lights, the motorist stretched out of the window and handed them a piece of paper, asking for Tiger's autograph. Team player Conrad Ray took it, signed, "Much love, Tiger Woods," and handed it back, and the happy autograph hunter was none the wiser.

Not everybody was quite so keen to meet him. Just weeks into his new life at Stanford, Woods received an anonymous letter at Stern Hall. "You can take the n***** out of the jungle, but you can't take the jungle out of the n*****" it read. Woods sighed, pinned it to his wall, and redoubled his determination to become even better.

Woods had barely unpacked his bags, however, before he was on a plane to Paris, France, as one of a four-strong team representing the United States in the biennial World Amateur Team Championship to compete for the Eisenhower Trophy. At eighteen, Woods was the youngest of the American quartet that also included renowned amateur Allen Doyle, forty-six, and John Harris, the forty-one-year-old 1993 US Amateur champion. The final member of the team, meanwhile, was twenty-two-year-old Todd Demsey, the 1993 NCAA champion from Arizona State University.

Like every other college golfer, Demsey knew all about Tiger Woods but wasn't convinced that all the hype surrounding his teammate was entirely justified. "I'll be honest, I was a little skeptical," he said. "[Tiger] talked and acted like he was the best player ever to play the game. He wasn't overly arrogant—you could just tell that he thought he was the best player there by far. I don't know if there was a doubt in his mind."

As was increasingly common, Tiger's reputation had preceded him by the time the United States team arrived at Le Golf National near Versailles on the outskirts of Paris. The sports newspaper *L'Équipe* led with the headline "Tiger La Terreur" while, at his practice sessions, banks of spectators had gathered by the range to watch him. "There were huge crowds watching him hit long iron after long iron for hours," recalled Todd Demsey. "It was cold and windy, but there [were] just hundreds of people watching him hit 3-irons."

When practice was finally done, Woods and Demsey skipped the fancy French cuisine on offer for dinner in search of something more familiar. "Me and Tiger would always go to McDonald's afterward," he said. "Stick with what you know."

For the older, more experienced members of the US team, the very presence of Woods injected a fresh new impetus into proceedings. "When you get to my age, and you've played a lot of golf, you've seen a lot of guys who were supposed to be can't-miss kids, so I think everybody was a little skeptical at first," said Allen Doyle. "But I thought he was great, and being around those younger kids made me feel a little younger."

It also inspired the United States team to a comfortable and convincing victory in the forty-five-team competition as they finished eleven shots clear of the silver medalists, Great Britain and Ireland. For once, Woods wasn't the star of the show, even though the galleries following him dwarfed those watching other players. Instead, it was Allen Doyle, who cantered to the individual title, four shots clear of his nearest rivals over his four rounds and seven clear of Woods in sixth position. Tiger, however, was more than happy with his week's work. "I loved it," he told the media.

Woods returned to Stanford in the second week of October, hooking up once more with his new teammates on the golf team. Woods was happy to see the familiar face of Notah Begay again. Begay, like all the students on the team, was keen to cut him down to size. When Woods arrived at a team meeting wearing his thick glasses, Begay immediately christened him "Urkel," after the nerdy high school kid on the TV show *Family Matters*.

When they weren't studying or playing golf, Woods and Begay watched football games, went to the movies, or played video games at Chuck E. Cheese. As members of the Sigma Chi fraternity, they were regulars at the frat parties and would often be seen trying to impress coeds with their questionable dance moves, occasionally jumping on top of the DJ's tall speakers so that their gyrations could be seen by more onlookers. Woods also earned the nickname "Dynamite," simply because one of his signature dance moves looked like a demolition expert detonating some TNT. "On the dance floor, it looked like he was blowing up a house, or pumping up a bike," said Eri Crum.

What Woods soon realized was that at Stanford, nobody gave a damn about his ethnicity. While the media—and, to an extent, his father—seemed obsessed by his race and what it meant in the wider picture of a sport noted for exclusion and discrimination, life at college was blissfully different. Indeed, the only issues Woods ever had was when he was on the road with the Cardinal, especially in the Deep South. In late October, Woods and the Stanford team headed to Birmingham, Alabama, for the Jerry Pate Invitational and to a golf club that had become a byword for racial discrimination: Shoal Creek.

Just four years earlier, in 1990, Shoal Creek had nearly lost the right to stage the seventy-second PGA Championship because of its long-standing policy of refusing membership to African Americans. As the tournament drew closer, the club's founder, Hal Thompson, cited its acceptance of women and Jewish members as evidence of its inclusivity but told one reporter from the *Birmingham Post-Herald* newspaper that "we don't discriminate in every other area . . . except Blacks," before adding, "that's just not done in Birmingham."

Even in the hermetically sealed world of a sport that had long maintained discriminatory practices designed to exclude minorities or women, Thompson's remarks sparked fury. Civil rights organizations were appalled while the Reverend Joseph Lowery, who founded the Southern Christian Leadership Conference with the Reverend Martin Luther King Jr., organized pickets at Shoal Creek and threatened them with bussing protesters in from across the country to join the protest.

As the furor escalated, key tournament sponsors including IBM and Toyota pulled TV advertising, costing the event broadcasters, ABC, an estimated $2 million in revenue.

As the controversy engulfed their flagship event, PGA of America President Pat Rielly was faced with a dilemma—allow Shoal Creek to continue as host or force their hand. But he knew what he had to do. "Shoal Creek was easy for me," Rielly told *Golfweek* magazine in 2015. "I knew what I was going to do. If they didn't do what they did, we weren't going to be there. The game is bigger than the PGA. The game is everything."

With Hal Thompson refusing to alter his club's membership policy, Rielly called his bluff, sounding out other golf clubs, including Jack Nicklaus's Muirfield Village and TPC Sawgrass in Ponte Vedra Beach, Florida, to see if they could step in and replace Shoal Creek as hosts but, eventually, just two weeks before the tournament was due to start, Thompson capitulated and offered an honorary, fee-free membership to a local Black businessman, Louis J. Willie, even though he hadn't even played golf for twenty years.

The crisis averted, the PGA Championship went ahead as planned, won by Australia's Wayne Grady, but the crisis had been a watershed moment for golf, and even when Tiger Woods arrived as a Stanford freshman, four years on, it was still a contentious issue.

Now, it was African Americans taking issue with Woods deciding to play Shoal Creek rather than boycott it. What confounded Don Crosby was that on his team was a Navajo Indian in Notah Begay, a Chinese American in Jerry Chang, and a Japanese American in Will Yanagisawa. "And here they are picking on Tiger," he said. "It was ludicrous."

For Tiger, however, the decision to play reinforced his belief that he should always let his golf clubs do his talking and that winning at Shoal Creek would constitute more of a statement than any public pronouncement he could make or interview he might grant on the subject. As he had said repeatedly: "I don't want to be the best Black golfer. I want to be the best golfer."

True to his word, he did just that, winning the event with rounds of 71, 68, and 67. Even Hal Thompson congratulated him. "You're a great player," he told Woods. "I'm proud of you. You're superb."

That's not to say that there weren't problems for Woods on campus. On Wednesday, November 31, 1994, just after 11:00 p.m., Woods was walking back to his room after a celebrity dinner in San Francisco with the reigning Superbowl champions, the 49ers. He had parked his car and was about to head over to Stern Hall when he was grabbed from behind and felt a knife pressed against his throat. The assailant punched Woods to the ground with the handle of the knife, making off with his Casio wristwatch and a five-thousand-dollar gold chain that Tiger's mother had given him.

The experience was frightening, but Tiger didn't really want to make a thing of it. But Earl had other ideas. Before long, the biggest newspapers in the country were running with the story. "Woods Not Seriously Injured in Robbery on Stanford Campus" reported the *Los Angeles Times*. *The New York Times* ran with "Golfer Woods Is Mugged." For Earl Woods, the idea that Tiger was getting nationwide coverage, even in these unfortunate circumstances, was further evidence that his master plan—to let the legend grow—was working.

Tida Woods wasn't impressed. She was growing tired of what she perceived as her husband's exploitation of their son's vulnerability and his endless attempts to cast him as some kind of modern-day Jackie Robinson, albeit in golf spikes and chinos. She had even given him a new nickname: Old Man Bullshit.

Later, in 2008, Earl Woods spoke to *Golf Digest* writer Matthew Rudy. In a wide-ranging conversation, they touched on everything from jazz ("one of the last creative arts we have") and hip-hop ("Don't put any of that stuff on my sound system") to Tiger's relationship with his half-siblings and his attitude toward drugs and alcohol. He swerved the question about sex though.

But it was only when Rudy asked him about his parenting style that Earl Woods sounded defensive. "My purpose in raising Tiger was not to raise a golfer," he insisted. "I wanted to raise a good person."

But by the mid-1990s, Tida Woods had had enough. Stuck in a decaying marriage, she was tired of his outlandish claims about their son's impact on the world. She had moved into her own place in Tustin, leaving Earl in the home they once shared in Cypress, slumped in his red leather recliner, smoking and gradually turning the house into a shrine to the couple's only child together.

Even the high chair that Tiger had climbed out of to hit his first golf shot in the garage was still in the very same place it had been on that special day. Tida Woods had tried to throw it out on several occasions, but Earl had always rescued it. "You can't throw it away," he told her. "That's going to be in a Hall of Fame someday."

Earl had even removed two doors—one with Tiger's growth chart on it, and another displaying his favorite *Star Wars* poster—putting them in storage so that when the house finally became a museum, as it obviously would, visitors—or pilgrims—could see exactly how Eldrick "Tiger" Woods lived in those years before he conquered golf and/or saved the human race.

"I have prepared this house," Earl Woods would later explain, "so that it can be converted into a national historical monument one day. It is built to last, because I am certain that one day, the birthplace of Tiger Woods is going to become widely acknowledged."

This is what drove Tida crazy. Proclamations that went far beyond unconditional paternal love and tipped into some alternative reality where their little boy wasn't just really good at golf but, in all likelihood, the Second Coming.

The trouble was that Earl simply couldn't help himself when it came to his favorite child. There was the time he declared that Tiger "will do more than any other man in history to change the course of humanity." When his son met Nelson Mandela in South Africa in 1998, Earl ventured it was the first time Tiger had "met a human being who was equal to him." Every time Tida challenged her husband, imploring him to dial down his messianic fervor, Earl repeated the mantra she'd heard more times than she cared to remember: "Let the legend grow . . ."

CHAPTER 14
GEORGIA ON HIS MIND

"Fantasyland and Disney World wrapped into one."
—Tiger Woods, on his first taste of Augusta National and the Masters

Tiger wasn't overly impressed by Magnolia Lane. For most of his young life, he had heard the fables, fairy tales, and folklore about Augusta National. But now he was here, and it wasn't exactly what he was expecting. In fact, it was "much shorter" than he had ever really imagined it.

Woods arrived from Stanford having just completed his exams and took up residence for the week in the Crow's Nest, the clubhouse dormitory reserved for amateurs playing at the Masters. There, he found the friendly face of the player he had beaten in the final of the 1994 US Amateur just seven months earlier, Trip Kuehne, also unpacking his things. "We had such a great time," recalled Kuehne. "It was tons of fun."

Accessed through a door marked telephone and up a steep staircase, the Crow's Nest is situated on the second floor of the clubhouse, above the Champions Locker Room and the library, and measures just thirty feet by forty feet. As well as a compact sitting room, there are three smaller rooms with one single bed each and another with twin beds. For a freshman like Woods, by now accustomed to the cramped conditions of student accommodations, it was more than adequate. Besides, if it was good enough for Jack Nicklaus, it was good enough for him.

With time to kill, before they could get on the golf course and play a practice round, Woods and Kuehne went exploring, all the while risking the wrath of the men of the Masters. "We snuck into the Champions Locker Room. We weren't supposed to do it, but we did." Kuehne laughed. "When you used to walk up the stairs to go to the Crow's Nest, where all the amateurs stayed, all you had to do was walk through one door. And there they were, all these great names on the lockers. We just looked at them and kind of dreamed about what it would be like to have your name in this locker room. Almost the immortality of being a Masters champion.

"Tiger did it, of course, and I did not."

That week, Tiger had also been asked by *Golfweek* and *Golf World* to write a diary of his time at Augusta National, and he was happy to oblige, although the NCAA would later declare them to be a "promotion of a commercial publication," earning Woods a one-match suspension from the Cardinal team.

Earl Woods had other things to worry about. After too many years of smoking cigarettes, eating the wrong things, and a waistline expanding exponentially, Earl Woods had decided that maybe he wasn't the right man to carry Tiger's bag over Augusta's energy-sapping slopes after all, much as he would have liked to. So they found someone else to do the job—Tommy Bennett.

The golf writer Lawrence Donegan said it best in his book *Four-Iron in the Soul*, his hilarious account of life on the then European Tour as a trainee caddie for the journeyman Scottish professional Ross Drummond. "The first thing to understand about caddying is that it's not brain surgery," he wrote. "It is more complicated than that." It's true. A good caddie is worth much more than the 10 percent of a player's purse. They can cajole and console, advise and motivate. They can be a companion, a comedian, or even a counsellor. Look at any of the legends of the game and you will see a great caddie alongside them. Arnold Palmer had Ernest "Creamy" Carolan, Jack Nicklaus had Angelo Argea, and Tom Watson had Bruce Edwards. In that respect, the caddie is just as valuable, if not more so, than any of the clubs sitting in the bag.

Earl Woods felt the same too. "To a golfer at Tiger's level, a good caddie is as important as a good wife," he once said.

In Tommy Bennett, young Tiger Woods had, inadvertently, stumbled across the ideal candidate for his week at Augusta National.

Born and raised by his grandmother in a one-bedroom house in Augusta's Sand Hills neighborhood, Bennett had first caddied at Augusta National in 1959 when, as a skinny ten-year-old, he managed just five holes before giving up and going home. In 1965, though, after five years earning three bucks a round for members, Bennett made his Masters debut carrying the bag of talented amateur Downing Gray where, in their first two rounds, they were paired with the seven-time major winner Gene Sarazen. He had also tasted some success at Augusta, alongside the Kentuckian Jodie Mudd when he finished in a tie for seventh in 1991.

Like most every other Black caddie working at Augusta National, Bennett, too, had a nickname—"Burnt Biscuits," the result of a childhood accident where he badly burned his left leg trying to steal some biscuits that were baking on the stove.

Now, Earl Woods wanted him on Tiger's bag, although, initially at least, Bennett wasn't exactly keen, setting his sights instead on bagging twenty-five-year-old Dicky Pride, the young professional from Tuscaloosa, Alabama, who had already won the St. Jude Classic in 1994. But when Pride rejected Bennett's advances, and with his options for the week fast running out, Burnt Biscuits shook hands with Earl. "[But] I didn't want no damn amateur," Bennett said. "I wanted that Green Jacket."

On the morning of Monday, April 3, Bennett met with Tiger on the practice range at Augusta National, shaking hands before Woods, wearing his Stanford cap, went back to crushing balls into the distance and over the fence the organizers had raised at the end of range three years earlier when John Daly, the longest hitter on tour, made his debut at Augusta. Thankfully, the giant pines behind the fence still provided ample protection for the traffic passing on Washington Road.

That morning, Woods played his first full round at the course that would become a second home for him in the years to come, playing eighteen holes with England's two-time Masters winner and former world number one Nick Faldo, and the new British amateur champion, twenty-two-year-old Lee James.

It wasn't James's first encounter with Woods. Six months earlier, James had been a member of the Great Britain and Ireland team that finished a distant second to the United States at the Eisenhower Trophy at Versailles in France, and he watched as Woods and his three teammates peered down on him and his team from the top of the podium at the presentation ceremony.

For James, who had grown up watching Faldo dominate European and then world golf, playing with him at Augusta was a pinch-me moment, but it was the performance, and presence, of Woods that day that left an indelible mark. "Even though it was the pre-internet age, and there was no social media or viral videos, we all knew about Tiger, so his reputation was certainly spreading," he recalled.

From the very first hole, James realized just how impressive Woods was and the vast potential he possessed. "The thing that really stood out was his length. Nick and I were probably about the same off the tee, but Tiger was absolutely ridiculous," he said.

Woods's strategy at the fifteenth hole, Firethorn, was a case in point. While James and Faldo's tee shots found the fairway at the difficult par-5, Woods blazed his drive fully seventy yards past them, and while the Englishmen both used 3-irons to reach the green, Tiger eased his ball onto the putting surface with a 9-iron, before making the four-foot putt for an eagle. "He was a different league when it came to distance," added James. "It was like he was playing a different game to the rest of us. It was just silly."

Nick Faldo put it more succinctly. "He's just a very talented kid," he said.

Tommy Bennett, meanwhile, was quickly reassessing his chances of a successful week caddying and, like so many others who had seen Woods play up close, was left gobsmacked by the unique sound and trajectory of his ball striking. "Tiger swings so pure, and that ball doesn't want to come down," he observed. "Sometimes I felt like there just wasn't enough golf course out there for him."

Traditionally, the players would stop near the oak tree adjacent to the clubhouse at the end of their practice rounds to talk to the assembled media. It was one of those unwritten rules; one of the innumerable and sometimes maddening customs that people and patrons are just expected to know, and heaven help them if they didn't. But while everyone from Nicklaus to Norman stopped to talk, Woods simply strolled straight past the entire press corps, ignoring their pleas for an interview.

Woods's reputation had clearly preceded him. Oddsmakers were already offering just one hundred to one on the youngster actually winning the Green Jacket. Tiger said, "They're crazy," adding that five hundred thousand to one was probably more accurate. Prior to the tournament starting on Thursday, meanwhile, some of the biggest names in the game including Greg Norman, Fred Couples, Nick Price, and Raymond Floyd were lining up to play practice rounds with Woods. He also won five bucks in a money match with Trip Kuehne and got to play with three-time winner Gary Player in Wednesday's informal Par 3 Contest.

"Certain players, you look at them once, and you see something," Player said. "The first time I saw Jack Nicklaus or Arnold Palmer or Ben Hogan or Sam Snead or Lee Trevino, I saw something special. As soon as I saw Tiger Woods swing today, I thought, *Man, this young guy has got it*. It is something indescribable. It's the way he puts his hands on the club, the way he stands over the ball. It's agility, it's speed. It is what a great horse has."

For the opening round, Woods was paired with Spain's José María Olazábal, who had taken the Green Jacket and his maiden major title twelve months earlier with a hard-fought two-shot win over American Tom Lehman. As Tiger gathered his thoughts in the locker room, a message came from reception. A telegram had arrived for him. It was from Charlie Sifford. "Go out there, good luck, don't get caught up in the hype," it read. "Just take care of business and have fun."

For Sifford, the Black player denied the opportunity to play in the Masters, Tiger Woods may have been a source of immense pride becoming just the fourth Black man and the first Black amateur to play in the Masters. But Tiger was also a painful reminder of a not-so-distant past when men like him were deemed good enough only to carry the bags of the players.

As Woods and Bennett made their way to the first tee, past hundreds of patrons lining the way, the caddie double-checked he had everything his player needed for his round but was surprised to find just three golf balls lying in the pocket of his black leather golf bag. When he queried the wisdom of taking to Augusta

National, with all of its notorious hazards and danger at every turn, with so few balls, Woods laughed and smiled. "That's all I need."

For Olazábal, so long billed as the next Seve Ballesteros, it had been his first taste returning as a major champion and, with it, all of the additional interest and responsibilities being a Green Jacket winner entails. Hardly surprising, then, that he hadn't given much thought to whom he might be playing with when he finally began the defense of his title. "To be totally honest, I knew very little about Tiger Woods before arriving at the Masters in 1995," he said. "But when some of the pros realized I was playing with him, they all said that he was a very special player."

It wouldn't be long before Olazábal became properly acquainted with Tiger's unique talent. At 1:11 p.m. on April 6, 1995, Tiger Woods took his very first shot in a major championship, and his quest to reel in Jack Nicklaus and his seemingly unassailable tally of eighteen major victories was underway.

As Woods pulled out his steel-shafted Cobra driver and addressed his ball, José María Olazábal stood behind him, noticing that his playing partner was aiming directly at the bunker to the right of the first fairway, about three hundred yards in the distance. "I was looking at him thinking, *Surely he cannot carry the bunker*, but he hit it straight on that line and flew right over it," he added. "I couldn't believe my eyes!"

Yet it wasn't the perfect start, despite the astonishing opening tee shot. While his wedge into the green found the notoriously slippery putting surface, his approach finished thirty feet from the hole, leaving him a difficult opportunity of a birdie. In fact, it wasn't just difficult; it would prove impossible. Whether it was adrenaline or impetuosity, Woods gave his putt a little too much and then watched aghast as it rolled past the hole and off the other side of the green and a farther twenty-five feet from the cup.

In his book *The 1997 Masters: My Story*, Woods described the shot as "one of the most embarrassing moments that I can ever remember," adding that it was a "great start to my Augusta career. Hit the green in regulation, and then hit my first putt off the green."

Woods shook his head, bewildered by just how poor his putt had been.

Tommy Bennett stepped in. "Listen, we all get nervous," he told Woods. "We've got a long week here. Just chip it back up there and make the putt."

Woods duly chipped back onto the green but failed to make his par putt, and while his Masters career had begun with a bogey, Bennett's timely intervention had the desired effect. A birdie at the par-5 second put the teenager back on track, and he would end his opening round with a respectable level-par score of 72—six shots adrift of his playing partner and coleader José María Olazábal.

Certainly, the reigning champion was impressed by how Woods had handled himself in the spotlight of his Masters debut. "What struck me straight away was the huge self-belief he had for a nineteen-year-old," said Olazábal. "He seemed totally comfortable."

Burnt Biscuits felt the same. "The kid was so mentally strong," said Bennett. "He was just in another zone."

Woods followed up his opening round with another level-par round of 72, and his total of 144 ensured he made the cut, which, as he knew only too well, was something Jack Nicklaus failed to do in his first Masters appearance in 1959. Remarkably, it was the first cut Woods had made in the eight professional tournaments he had played in, and as the only one of the five amateurs in the field to survive into the weekend, he was guaranteed to be the tournament's leading amateur come the end of play on Sunday evening.

For Woods's Stanford teammate Dave Garcia, the fact he had finally made a cut in a pro event, and at the Masters of all places, was a pivotal moment in Tiger's amateur career. "We had been saying, 'How hard is it to make it on a PGA Tour? We're playing side by side with this guy [Tiger] every day, and we see how much better he is than us, and yet he can't even make a cut on a PGA Tour?' So, yeah, that was enormous," he said.

His place in the weekend field assured, Woods headed to the local public course Forest Hills, four miles south of Augusta National, where he put on a swing clinic for local youngsters and spent some time with Tommy Bennett's caddie friends who couldn't find a bag for the week. Later, Earl Woods said it was his son's way of honoring the Black caddies that had graced Augusta National over the years. "It's a Black thing," he told reporters. "We are acknowledging that we know who came before Tiger and that they suffered humiliation and that we realize the debt. It's a way of saying thank-you and a promise to carry the baton."

Saturday brought disappointment. While his opening rounds had given him belief in his ability to play at the highest level—on one of the most taxing golf courses, at that—Tiger was still nine shots adrift of the leaders, and the last thing he needed was his worst round of the week, and a 5-over-par 77 left the nineteen-year-old now fifteen strokes distant from the fifty-four-hole coleaders, the Californian Brian Henninger and the 1984 champion Ben Crenshaw.

Sunday's final round brought better fortune for Woods as he carded three birdies and three bogeys for a level-par round of 72, but it was clear that the demands of Augusta, both physical and mental, were taking their toll. He finished in a tie for forty-first alongside three major winners: Mark Calcavecchia, Jeff Sluman, and Payne Stewart, and three shots clear of two-time Masters champion Seve Ballesteros and the man who would go on to win that year's Open Championship and the 1991 PGA Champion,

John Daly. Tiger had also led the driving distances across the entire field, averaging a scarcely believable 311.1 yards—over twenty yards farther than the PGA Tour's longest driver, John Daly, and nearly sixty yards more than the PGA Tour average for the year.

Tiger liked the exalted company he found himself in, and with his final round over and his father's mile-wide smile etched permanently across his face, Woods headed to the Butler Cabin to receive the Silver Cup, presented to the Masters' leading amateur. Had he renounced his amateur status, he would have won $8,567—big money for a poverty-stricken student. But for now, he contented himself with another trophy to clutter the Teakwood Street sideboard.

Built in 1964 and named after Augusta member and one-time playing partner of Dwight Eisenhower, the Butler Cabin is one of twelve such properties on the Augusta National estate, and when the Masters isn't being played, it is used by members and their guests as an accommodation. For Masters week, though, it serves two purposes. First, as a home to the American TV broadcasters. Second, and more recognizably, it's where the winner receives the coveted Green Jacket from the previous year's champion and where the leading amateur also collects their award. Typically, both presentations occur at the same time, but in 1995, Tiger's ceremony, with CBS anchor Jim Nantz and the Augusta National Vice Chairman Joe Ford in attendance, had to be conducted on its own, as Woods had to fly back to California for college the following morning.

"We had to tape this interview in advance as you want to get back for class tomorrow morning at Stanford," Nantz explained.

"I don't want to get back," Tiger interjected. "I have to get back."

During the interview, Nantz quizzed Woods on college and whether he would see out his course at Stanford or be tempted to turn professional sooner. "I'm going to go all four. It's a tough business out there," replied Woods, smiling. "Right now, I'm only nineteen years old. I feel it's right for me to live it up a little. You're only young once, and college is such a great atmosphere, and I really love it there."

The truth was everybody on Team Tiger knew he wouldn't see out his time at Stanford, not when there were moments like this to be had, not once a year but each and every week on the PGA Tour. And not when there was much, much more than $8,567 to be made.

As he departed Augusta National, Woods sought out Tommy Bennett, the caddie who didn't even want to work with him, to thank him for his efforts. Bennett wished him well, telling Tiger he fully expected him to return to the Masters and win one day.

Back in Stern Hall, and having made his 9:00 a.m. history class, Tiger Woods sat at his desk, put pen to paper, composing a letter to Augusta National Chairman Jack Stephens and the club's members and thanking them for letting him play in their tournament. Describing the experience as "Fantasyland and Disney World wrapped into one," he said the tournament was where he "left my youth behind and became a man," adding that it was "the most wonderful week of his life."

Well, at least until he turned up a couple of years later.

Back in Teakwood Street, there was another letter waiting for Tiger, sent originally to Augusta National but forwarded straight to the Woods house in Cypress. As she did with all of the increasing volume of fan mail Tiger was receiving, his mother, Tida, opened it. It read, simply: "Just what we don't need, another n***** in sports."

CHAPTER 15
LIVING THE LIFE

"I think Tiger Woods can possibly be the biggest thing in golf in the last fifty years."

—Tom Watson, eight-time major winner and Stanford's most famous golfing alumnus

Amidst the rising tide of his golf career at Stanford, Tiger Woods's personal life took a dramatic turn with the abrupt end of his four-year relationship with his first true love, Dina Gravell. Gravell had been one of the few people outside his immediate family whom Tiger genuinely trusted, making their sudden split even more difficult, especially for her.

The catalyst for the break-up came at the 1995 US Intercollegiate Golf Tournament Invitational in Palo Alto when Tiger's parents pointedly ignored her as they all arrived to support Tiger. Gravell thought nothing of it, assuming Earl and Tida had been arguing. But on the second day of the tournament, Woods was forced to withdraw with a shoulder injury, and while he went to the hospital for an MRI scan, Gravell headed back to her parent's hotel to await news of the extent of his injury. Five hours later, and with no update, the phone in her room rang. It was reception. There was a delivery for her. It was a case with all of her belongings that she had left in Tiger's room the previous day.

There was also a letter. Gravell opened it. "Dina," it read. "The reason for writing this letter is to inform you [that] my parents and myself never want to talk or hear from you again . . . Reflecting back over this relationship, I feel used and manipulated by you and your family . . . I hope the rest of your life runs well for you. I know this is sudden and a surprise, but it is, in my opinion, much warranted. Sincerely, Tiger."

Then he added a postscript: "PS Please mail my necklace I gave you to me when you get back home. Don't show up at the tournament tomorrow because you are just not welcomed."

With him in Palo Alto and her back at community college in Anaheim, the idea of maintaining a long-distance love had waned and trying to make it work was only going to be a distraction to his golf career. For Gravell, it was clear that the split had been driven by Earl and Tida, potentially as a power play to remove her from Tiger's tight-knit inner circle. The letter itself was unnecessarily cruel and for all the world looked like it had been dictated to Woods by his parents before he had put pen to paper. Gravell was taken aback. Yes, it hadn't been easy for the couple, but for it to end so abruptly and so brutally had rocked her. Later, she would describe how she felt "punched in the stomach" by the way the relationship ended, but it was clear by the tone of the letter and the reference to "my parents" as to who had made the decision to end it.

In 2002, in an interview with Lawrence Donegan of the UK newspaper *The Observer*, Earl Woods reflected on young Tiger's love life, a topic that, within a decade, would dominate the headlines globally. "He had one girlfriend in school and one in college. I didn't think the one at school was a bad idea. What I thought was a bad idea was what her family had in mind," he said. "They had determined that Tiger was going to make a lot of money. They were meaning to make the relationship a permanent relationship. I could see this, but Tiger couldn't. As a parent, I could do one of two things: I could forbid him to see her, or I could counsel him and then wait for him to grow and determine what was right for himself. I chose the latter. And that's what happened to that relationship."

The key word here, of course, is "counsel." While it implies offering fatherly advice and handing autonomy to their son, it is clear that it was anything but. And a twin-pronged attack from Earl and Tida Woods would have left their son in no doubt about what they thought of Gravell and the prospects, or lack thereof, for their relationship. It is also revealing in that it demonstrates just how ruthless and calculating Tiger Woods could be, even in the preprofessional days when there was no money at stake yet. Here, after all, was a nineteen-year-old ready and willing to cast aside someone close to him, someone he professed to love, without compassion and without any regret. It wouldn't be the first time that Tiger Woods behaved in such a callous manner.

Soon, though, he would have a new girlfriend—a fellow undergraduate with her eyes set on a career in law called Irene Folstrom. She soon realized just how famous Tiger was becoming whenever they went out to eat. "Our favorite restaurant was a Chinese joint in Mountain View," she recalled. "The guys there must have been golf fans because they always gave us free desserts, which was a big deal to us."

In any other era, though, the idea that a Stanford golfer could play at the Masters, and emerge as the leading amateur, would have been a cause for celebration not just in the golf office but across the university itself. But it was different with Tiger Woods. With his record, it was almost expected that all of these major milestones would be passed without fuss or complication, and while Woods himself tried to maintain the image of just another regular guy on campus, his fame, even in a place like Stanford that was littered with future stars, continued to flourish.

"Tiger was definitely a celebrity in college," his teammate Casey Martin recalled. "I remember walking to a class with him, and he was signing autographs walking through campus, which, for golfers, is unheard of, right? When Michael Jordan was in college, he wasn't really Michael Jordan yet, but Tiger really was that guy, even in college."

At Stanford, it had seemed as though Woods was finally beginning to enjoy, and even exploit, the recognition he was receiving. No longer was he the happy-go-lucky kid simply intent on beating anyone who teed it up against him. Now, he was reveling in his newfound freedom, away from Cypress and the hawkish attention of his parents.

One old friend who visited him at Stanford was shocked not just by how popular and well-known he already was but how people went out of their way to do his bidding. Whenever Woods wanted a night out, they would call ahead to their chosen venue, and later, when they arrived, the table—usually in the corner—would be roped off and reserved. Woods would then enter with a couple of friends leading the way ahead of him and another pair bringing up the rear.

All eyes would be on Woods, men and women. Rarely would he buy a drink, not least because he didn't yet have anywhere near as much money as his wealthy friends, but whatever he wanted, he invariably got. Yes, he was still broke, but the riches that would certainly arrive when he turned professional were now tantalizingly close, and everyone knew it. Money, of course, breeds money, and Woods's friend group reflected that. Now, there were people whose parents were multimillionaires who ran hugely successful businesses or owned hotels in Las Vegas. And Woods, the kid who relied on free range balls at the Navy Club just a few years earlier, felt he had arrived.

Even when it came to his family, as his half-sister and clothes washer Royce had discovered, Woods knew he could use his status and the guarantee of the fortunes he would surely make to get things done for him.

It wasn't just Palo Alto where Tiger's celebrity status preceded him. Whenever the Cardinal played away, there was always a hubbub surrounding Woods. "Even then, with no social media, we were getting on airplanes, and people knew exactly who we were because you could hear them talking," added Casey Martin.

At times, as teammate Dave Garcia explained, what was only a golf game turned out to be a zoo. "The media was crazy around him," he said. "We would fly to a tournament, and somehow people would find out. This was before the internet, and yet there would still be lines of people outside just as soon as we'd get off the plane wanting his autograph or a photograph."

For Coach Wally Goodwin, who, perhaps like Coach Crosby at Western High, had long since realized that there was little he could actually teach Tiger Woods about playing golf, especially as Woods was now working with Butch Harmon, it now became necessary for him to try as best he could to protect his young player from the ever-increasing and sometimes overzealous demands of fans and media alike. Often, Goodwin would have to intervene as spectators engulfed Woods on the golf course, making it impossible for him to even swing his club.

"The coach's job turned more into managing the external world surrounding Tiger versus trying to teach him how to play better golf," added Dave Garcia. "He was kind of a security guard a lot of the time."

Casey Martin agreed. "There were some big-time challenges for our coach to prep for when a guy like Tiger showed up, just from all the hangers-on and all these people that wanted to be part of it."

When a golfing supernova like Tiger Woods arrives on the collegiate scene, one might expect him to fall under the tutelage of some hypertechnical, swing-guru savant—all analytics, spin rates, and launch angles. But at Stanford, Tiger found Wally Goodwin, a man who, to the casual observer, might have seemed as out of place as a 5-iron in a boardroom. Yet their relationship became a crucial, often understated, chapter in the making of the greatest golfer of his generation.

Goodwin wasn't the typical sleek, modern coach. He was more of an old-school cowboy, a straight talker with a twinkle in his eye and a firm belief in character over clubhead speed. He had a knack for nurturing talent, but more importantly, he nurtured young men. And when an eighteen-year-old Woods, already burdened by unprecedented hype, showed up on his roster, Goodwin didn't try to reinvent the wheel. He simply set about providing the kind of grounding and common sense that only a seasoned veteran, immune to the dazzle of celebrity, could offer.

Tiger, for all his otherworldly talent, was still a kid finding his way in a new environment. He arrived with a swing meticulously crafted by his father, Earl, but Goodwin understood that college golf wasn't just about hitting bombs and draining putts; it was about teamwork, about managing expectations, about life lessons learned on and off the course. Goodwin's subtle genius lay in knowing when to push, when to pull back, and when to just let Tiger be Tiger, all while ensuring he remained part of a collective.

Yes, Goodwin would instill a sense of normalcy in Woods, a reminder that even a chosen one had responsibilities to his teammates, to his university, and to himself beyond the next birdie. He wasn't afraid to challenge Tiger—not on his swing, perhaps, but on his approach, his focus, his attitude. He treated Woods like any other promising college golfer, albeit one who happened to draw crowds worthy of a US Open.

But it was a relationship built on mutual respect. Goodwin admired Tiger's relentless drive and inner fire, while Tiger, perhaps surprisingly, appreciated Goodwin's understated wisdom and no-nonsense demeanor. Goodwin, in his own humble way, often downplayed his influence, preferring to credit the players. But the truth is, he provided the stable, principled environment that allowed Woods to thrive, to grow, and to maintain a semblance of normalcy before the world truly came calling. Their bond, though rarely splashed across headlines like some of Tiger's other relationships, was a quiet testament to a coach who understood that shaping a champion involved far more than just golf clubs and Green Jackets. It was about shaping the man.

At the NCAA Regionals in May 1995, Stanford traveled to Notah Begay's hometown of Albuquerque, New Mexico, with their strongest possible line-up of Woods, Begay, Casey Martin, Jerry Chang, and Will Yanagisawa confident of another strong showing. On their first night, Begay decided to take the team to his favorite barbeque restaurant in town where Woods and Martin both ordered the same dish. Later that night, Coach Goodwin held a team meeting, before his players headed off to bed around 10:00 p.m.

Casey Martin, who was sharing a room with Tiger Woods, takes up the story. "I remember waking up probably about one in the morning, thinking, *Oh no, this is not good.* It was like my body was revolting," he said. "So I go to the bathroom, trying not to wake

Tiger up, and start throwing up. But he hears me and says, 'Dude, I got it too.' And we were like, 'What is going on?'"

The pair continued to be sick throughout the night, taking turns in the bathroom. At 4:30 a.m., and with no sign of the vomiting abating, Casey Martin called Coach Goodwin in his room and asked for him to come over. "Coach," he gasped. "I'm dying."

Goodwin threw on some clothes and hurried round to Martin and Woods's room, only to find Martin lying in bed doubled up in agony and Woods in the bathroom with his head down the toilet. Then the panic set in. For Stanford to have any chance of advancing, four of their five rounds had to be counted, but with two players waylaid by food poisoning and incapacitated, it looked as though the Cardinal's chance of a shot at the title were fading fast. Somebody had to play, or Stanford was out.

Next, Notah Begay wandered in. "One of you guys has got to go, so you decide who it's going to be," he said, without a shred of sympathy.

"I'm going to die if I try to play today," said Martin, puffing his cheeks out.

With no other option, Woods reluctantly volunteered, just as he made another emergency trip to the bathroom again. "I'll try and give it a go," he said.

While Martin sank back into his bed, groaning, Woods took to the University of New Mexico's Championship Golf Course and somehow managed to shoot a round of 72, in between regular bouts of on-course vomiting. At the long par-3 seventeenth hole, for instance, Woods was just about to play his tee shot when he backed off, walked to the side of the tee box, and threw up before wiping his mouth, knocking his ball on the green, and two-putting for his par. The round over, both Woods and Martin were taken to the local emergency room, placed on IV drips, and spent a couple of hours being rehydrated.

In late April, meanwhile, Tiger Woods finally made his home debut for Stanford University at the US Intercollegiate tournament. Ahead of the competition, Tom Watson, the eight-time major winner and Stanford's most famous golfing alumnus, spoke to the media about the impact Woods might have on the game, saying: "I think Tiger Woods can possibly be the biggest thing in golf in the last fifty years."

No pressure, then.

Ordinarily, Stanford's men's golf team would be lucky to get a crowd over one or two hundred at best, but now there were 2,500 fans packed in to see Stanford's star man in action. Certainly, the unprecedented galleries that had showed up at Stanford's golf course for Saturday's second round astonished Cardinal's Coach Wally Goodwin. "It's almost unfathomable," he said. "Nicklaus was a great player, but he wasn't as good as Tiger when he was in school, wasn't nearly as charismatic. I've been to the last six or seven NCAA tournaments, and it wasn't even close. These crowds were larger. They were huge crowds. They're here to see Tiger play."

But the huge galleries would be disappointed. After a first round 73 on Friday, Woods started his second round on Saturday, but soreness in his right shoulder forced his withdrawal midway through. His playing partner that day was Arizona State University's Todd Demsey, the 1993 NCAA individual champion who went on to win the individual event that weekend. "It got really crazy. There were probably five hundred people or more following our group alone, which, at the time, seemed pretty huge for a college tournament," he said. "I didn't quite understand it, to be honest."

For Goodwin, meanwhile, it was becoming increasingly clear that security would now have to be improved whenever Woods teed it up for his team. "I knew we weren't prepared because nobody believed the crowds would be that big," he said later. "This sends a warning to all the schools we're playing next year. If you're hosting a tournament with Tiger Woods in it, you had better be prepared."

Wally Goodwin had also realized that being part of Project Tiger, unwittingly or otherwise, often came saddled with as many minuses as it did plusses. At his office at Stanford, he was fielding over fifty telephone calls a day from media representatives desperate to talk to Tiger Woods. At the Thunderbird Intercollegiate event at Arizona State University, meanwhile, Goodwin became increasingly exasperated at the media frenzy pursuing his famous freshman. Now, reporters suddenly wanted interviews with all the other Cardinal players, just so they could ask about Tiger. When one journalist asked for two minutes with Notah Begay, Goodwin combusted. "Just two minutes," he snapped. "Everybody wants two minutes. And two minutes times ten is twenty minutes."

Coach Wally Goodwin, despite the immense talent Tiger Woods brought to the Stanford golf team, found himself increasingly battling the unprecedented craze swirling around his star player. By the time the NCAA Championships rolled around at Ohio State University's mammoth Scarlet Course in Columbus at the end of May, the atmosphere was as charged as he had ever witnessed.

Organizers braced for record crowds, a testament to Woods's burgeoning celebrity, and the major broadcaster ESPN even decided to cover the event, a groundbreaking move for college golf. The palpable anticipation centered almost entirely on Woods, with most observers fully expecting him to dominate.

However, the narrative of the tournament took an unexpected turn. While all eyes were fixed on Tiger Woods, literally, it was Chip Spratlin, a seasoned senior from Auburn University in Alabama, who ultimately captured the coveted individual title. This surprising outcome momentarily shifted the spotlight, leaving many to ponder the intense hype surrounding Woods before the collective attention pivoted dramatically to the nail-biting conclusion of the team event, where every stroke mattered.

Though Spratlin wasn't paired with Woods, the pair had been previously. Earlier in the season, they had played together at the Jerry Pate Invitational at Shoal Creek in Alabama, where Auburn's team—the Tigers—and Stanford faced up. "I just remember watching him coming down the last hole, and he made this thirty-footer up and over the hill on the green and gave one of those big fist pumps, like he did back in those days," said Spratlin.

They had also played a round together at the Carpet Capital Collegiate Classic at the Farm Golf Club in Dalton, Georgia. "It was a shotgun start early in the morning, and it was cold. Our first hole was a par-5 with a carry over the water to reach the green, and Tiger missed the fairway with his tee shot, and I just assumed he would have to lay up," recalled Spratlin. "I was standing behind him, and he pulls out a 4- or 5-iron, and he launches the ball straight up in the air with about a fifteen-yard slice. It landed about twenty feet behind the pin, and then he goes ahead and makes it for [an] eagle.

"That was the very first hole I ever played with Tiger, and I already saw a shot that I just did not have in my bag, you know? I just thought, *This is going to be a long day.*"

At another event, played on ASU's Karsten course in Tempe, Arizona, the pair played a round with one of Auburn's most recognizable alumni walking round with them: the NBA superstar Charles Barkley. "I know he was out there watching Tiger, even though he liked to support Auburn," said Spratlin.

It was a round where Woods was anything but impressive. With a twenty-five-miles-per-hour wind whipping the golf course, Woods was "hitting it all over the place," but there was one moment where, Spratlin believes, Woods let his reputation do the talking.

At the par-3 sixteenth hole, the pair were faced with a shot of 248 yards straight into a strong headwind just to make the putting surface. Thinking he might not be able to get there, Spratlin grabbed his driver, but as he put his ball on his tee peg, he noticed Woods out of the corner of his eye leaning on his 2-iron. "Not a fairway wood, a 2-iron. And it's my shot, right? So I've got all these people around watching, and I'm thinking, *There's no way I can get there with an iron,*" he continued. "Of course, the temptation is to go for an iron, too, but I just knew I couldn't get anything there except [with] the driver. It was very clever on his part."

After rounds of 73, 72, and 70, Woods seemed irritable and edgy in the final crucial round. On his twelfth hole (the course's third), he hooked his tee shot wildly into the trees, and while that wasn't unusual, his response was. After a poor recovery that came up short, he thudded his iron into the ground. Moments later, after his short wedge shot dropped into a greenside bunker, he smashed his club into his golf bag, damaging it beyond repair and prompting a visit from some stern-faced NCAA tournament officials who informed him that if they had to warn him for his behavior in the rest of the round, he would be subject to a two-stroke penalty.

As the individual title slipped slowly from his grasp, Woods displayed commendable composure, quickly refocusing his formidable mental strength on his team's pursuit of glory. *Chip Spratlin could take the win*, thought Tiger, *but we're not leaving here empty-handed.* Still, Spratlin's victory remains an enduring point of pride and a story he's more than happy to recount, even decades later.

"'I want you to meet Chip. He won the '95 NCAA championship, and he beat Tiger Woods!'" Spratlin recounted with a chuckle. "It's how everybody introduces me everywhere I go." And while his name might be a footnote in the storied life of the world's greatest golfer, for Chip Spratlin, the man who took down Tiger, it's something he wouldn't swap for the world.

Though Woods would come up short in his first tilt at emulating Jack Nicklaus's achievement of winning the NCAA individual title, the Stanford Cardinal were still in with a genuine chance of landing the team event prize. As the Stanford players reached the final hole, three of them, including Woods, all had birdie putts that would, if made, secure their successful defense of their NCAA team title. But when seniors Notah Begay and Casey Martin both missed short putts for the win, it left Woods, coming up behind them at 1-under-par for the day and 2-under-par for the tournament, with a twenty-five-foot birdie putt of his own to win it for the Cardinal.

It was one of those moments that Woods always seemed to find himself in and one, for the most part, where he nearly always seemed to emerge as the victor. For once, though, it just didn't happen. With hundreds of spectators around the green, Woods lined up his putt, taking longer than usual, and then watched as his ball weaved its way to the hole before brushing the right edge and staying above ground.

Stanford was now tied with Oklahoma State University at the top of the final leaderboard, both with a total score of 1,156. And for the first time in the ninety-eight-year history of NCAA tournament golf, the Division I men's golf championship would be decided by a sudden-death playoff, to be conducted on the par-4 eighteenth hole.

The odds, initially at least, seemed to favor Stanford, especially as they had Tiger Woods in their ranks that, all too often, felt like being one up on the tee. OSU's Alan Bratton was a fifth-year senior but also a four-time All-American and the corecipient of the 1994 Jack Nicklaus Award for the nation's top collegiate golfer. Bratton had already played with Woods in collegiate events before the

NCAA Championships in 1995 as well as at the Western Amateur prior to Woods starting at Stanford. "I was much older [than Woods], but I could tell the young kid was going to blow right on by me," he explained. "I wasn't too worried about trying to beat Tiger Woods. I was just trying to get as good as I could get, which was nowhere near as good as him."

With a full complement of five players to choose their four scores from, the Cardinal had the luxury of discounting one of their scores while OSU had already bid farewell to one of their players, the Swede Leif Westerberg, as he had to leave early to board a flight to the United Kingdom to play in the British Amateur Championship. "We really had no room to maneuver," added Bratton.

Despite their status as pretournament favorites, Stanford were powerless to prevent OSU from ending the playoff at the earliest opportunity. While Woods and his teammates recorded four pars and a bogey for the hole, Oklahoma State snatched the title from the defending champions thanks to birdies from Kris Cox and Alan Bratton and two pars from Trip Kuehne and Chris Tidland.

For Woods, a player so accustomed to winning, and winning well, the idea of defeat might have been anathema to him, but the fact that he would be partly responsible for the team losing, when everyone expected otherwise, was irritating in the extreme. For now, the NCAA titles, both team and individual, would have to wait for another season.

For the rest of the team, who had played so brilliantly, winning the title the year before Woods arrived on the scene, there was a sense that having Tiger in their ranks wasn't always conducive to better performances. Certainly, there was a sense of frustration among some of the Cardinal lineup. "Being in the spotlight as we are every day has put a lot of pressure on us," Casey Martin told the press in the wake of the loss. "It's been a great experience, having

Tiger, but it's also been tough and has probably hurt our performance somewhat."

Dave Garcia, who played with Woods in the following season, agreed. "I remember we'd be in a practice round, and word would get out that Tiger Woods is on course, and by the fifth hole, there's like a hundred people or more just following us around. And you're just going, 'Oh my God! It's a practice round!'" he recalled. "It was fun and exciting, but sometimes it was a little scary because anyone could just walk up to him and say anything or do anything."

Today, however, Casey Martin views it a little differently. "We were the defending national champions, and the team was intact coming back. We had four of the five starters from the year before, and then we added Tiger. It was just a loaded team," he said. "We were winning by a lot, and we were the number-one-ranked team for most of the year.

"But we faded at the end."

At the end of his first year as Cardinal, Woods's record was undeniably impressive, but the sense that there was more to come was palpable, especially as the team had failed to defend their NCAA title, and Woods himself couldn't land the individual award. With three wins under his belt, he had a scoring average of 71.37 and boasted nine rounds in the 60s and 25 at par or better. Yes, his season had been impacted by taking time out to play in more high-profile events, like the Masters, but there had also been persistent injuries that needed attention. In December 1994, during his first semester at Stanford, for instance, Woods had surgery to remove two benign tumors and scar tissue from his left knee, keeping him out of action for several weeks.

While his debut at the Masters had cemented his reputation as the game's most promising youngster, an even sterner test awaited at the next major Woods was now entitled to play in, thanks to his

US Amateur Championship victory: the US Open at Shinnecock Hills on Long Island, New York. One of the oldest golf courses in the United States, Shinnecock Hills is a course steeped in history. In July 1896, it played host to the second-ever US Open when Scottish-born émigré James Foulis finished three strokes ahead of the defending champion, Horace Rawlins. Though it had to wait another ninety years to stage another, when Raymond Floyd became the oldest ever-winner of the US Open, aged 43 years and 284 days, it has since remained a regular host on the tournament's roster of venues.

While Woods didn't expect to win, nor did anyone else expect him to, with each amateur victory came an exponential increase in the media attention toward him. Irritatingly for him, however, was that it was less likely to be about the quality of the golf he was playing and more about his background and backstory. While Earl Woods had long made an issue of Tiger's Black heritage and the messianic status he would almost certainly assume in time, Woods himself was less keen on promoting his father's preferred narrative. For one, he was nineteen, a freshman at Stanford, and just wanted to play golf. But more importantly because, in Tiger's eyes, it entirely disregarded his mother's ethnicity and, in that sense at least, just wasn't accurate.

With Earl's verbosity and hyperbolic outbursts causing ever-increasing degrees of awkwardness or embarrassment for Tiger, his son took it upon himself to address the inaccuracies in some of the reporting of his background, leaving a printed statement on the desks in the media tent at Shinnecock Hills in a bid to fend off the stream of maddening questions that kept being directed at him.

"The purpose of this statement," it read, "is to explain my heritage for the benefit of members of the media, who may be seeing me play for the first time. It is the final and only comment I will make regarding the issue. My parents have taught me always to be proud of my ethnic background. Please rest assured that is, and will be, the case. Past, present, and future. The various media have portrayed me as an African American, sometimes Asian. In fact, I am both. . . . That is who I am and what I am. Now, with your cooperation, I hope I can just be a golfer and a human being."

Two years later, in the wake of his seismic win at the 1997 Masters, Woods would appear on *The Oprah Winfrey Show* where the host asked about his ethnic makeup. In reply, Woods offered that he preferred to call himself "Cablinasian," a portmanteau term he himself had coined that used the first syllables of all the ethnicities that made him who he is (Caucasian, Black, American Indian, and Asian). "It's just who I am. Whoever you see in front of you," he said.

That a teenage amateur felt compelled to act as Woods did at Shinnecock Hills was both understandable and depressing. Rather than quell any questions about it, it had the polar opposite effect, provoking more questions than it did provide answers. When Tiger was growing up, his talent flourishing, Earl had often warned him of the struggles he would encounter trying to make his way in the game, purely because of the color of his skin, and Woods had seen just what he had meant, even at places like the Navy Club that were, theoretically at least, more welcoming than others. The bottom line was that golf—perhaps the most white, middle-class, and conservative sport in existence—was still, two decades after Lee Elder had finally broken the color barrier and played at the Masters, somehow struggling to get its head around the idea of a mixed-race player among their ranks who, if Earl Woods was to be believed, was about to turn their cozy world on its head.

Tiger's second major championship appearance didn't go as well as his first showing two months earlier. Like most US Open courses, Shinnecock's set-up was typically brutal and unforgiving. It was here, in 1986, that Jack Nicklaus had lost the second and final ball he would ever lose in tournament play when it disappeared into the knee-deep bluestem grass off the tenth fairway, never to be seen again.

Woods, too, would suffer. Playing with Zimbabwe's Nick Price and the defending champion, South Africa's Ernie Els, he made his par on the opening hole but then dropped shots on each of the next four. He did rally, but a round of 74, 4-over-par, left him eight shots adrift of the leaders.

Worse was to come. Though Woods's game was often beyond reproach, perhaps his only real weakness was his propensity for a wayward tee shot. While that wasn't ordinarily a huge problem on most courses he played, not least because of his extraordinary powers of recovery, at Shinnecock Hills, it could ruin a round or, as Woods discovered, end your entire tournament. On the five-hundred-yard par-4 third hole, Woods opted for a 1-iron off the tee rather than his driver, but he pulled it left into the kind of dense rough that had done in Nicklaus. Though he found his ball, the best Woods could do was get a wedge on it and try to put it back in play, but as he drove down on his ball, something tweaked in his wrist. Woods persevered but the pain worsened. Another drive on the fifth hole also leaked left into the thick round, and the same thing happened again. By the sixth hole, Woods, now unable to grip his clubs properly, couldn't continue, and after speaking to his playing partners and the rules official, withdrew from the tournament. "I'm kind of bummed out by the fact I'm not playing," he said. "This is what happens when you hit it into the long grass. You're supposed to stay out of it."

A month later, his wrist rested and better, Woods headed across the Atlantic to Scotland, to play first in the Scottish Open at Carnoustie, where he started with a first round 69 and ended with a 78 for a tie for forty-seventh place, then on to St. Andrew's for his first experience of playing at the spiritual home of golf.

Wearing a Titleist sweater with "The Home of Golf—St. Andrews" inscribed on a crest on the front, Woods looked like a tourist who got carried away in the club shop. But in the Open Championship, quite literally realized by giant, newly crowned British amateur champion Gordon Sherry, Woods made the cut but struggled at the weekend, a final round of 78 giving him a total of 295 and a finish in a tie for sixty-eighth—one shot ahead of Jack Nicklaus.

In a remarkable conclusion to the competition, it was John Daly—the man who a thirteen-year-old Woods so nearly beat six years earlier when they played together at the Insurance Youth Golf Classic at the Texarkana Country Club—that took the Claret Jug, defeating Italy's Costantino Rocca in a playoff to land his second major championship win.

For Woods, it had proved to be a valuable reconnaissance mission at the Old Course. Not only he had been struck by the relative simplicity of the wide-open fairways and the huge double greens but also by the many subtle nuances that made it the intriguing challenge it had always been, especially when the North Sea wind blew in from St. Andrews Bay and played havoc with yardages and club selection. With notes made and lessons learned, Woods pledged to return when the Old Course would host the Open Championship in 2000, and next time, he told himself, it would be a very different story.

In the years to come, Woods would dominate at the home of golf unlike anyone before or since. A winner of two Open Championships over the Old Course, it was his performance in 2000 where he won with a record-breaking total of 19-under-par—eight shots clear of runners-up Thomas Bjørn and Ernie Els—that demonstrated not only his ability to change his game to suit the many varied demands of links golf but also how hard he had worked to eradicate the errant tee shots from his game. Indeed, across the four rounds of the tournament, Woods never went in a single one of the 112 bunkers peppering the Old Course and recorded just three bogeys across his four rounds, all of which were in the 60s.

In 2022, meanwhile, he declared St. Andrews to be his favorite track of all. "This golf course can present so many different ways to play it," he said. "You just have to open your mind to it. It's the way it should be."

All too often, however, it appeared that all Tiger Woods was required to do was turn up at competitions and wait for the intense pressure and scrutiny of the media and the larger crowds to ruin any chance his opponents may have of mounting anything resembling a stern challenge. But it wasn't always the case. In August, Woods returned to Benton Harbor and to Point O'Woods, the golf course that sounded as though it might already have been named in his honor and where, a year previously, he had taken the Western Amateur title for the first time.

Initially, it was another event that had seemed to be following the usual pattern, with Woods advancing ominously into the semifinals where he would meet Robert Floyd, a senior at the University of Florida, as well as the son of Raymond Floyd, the four-time major winner who, in 1993, had also become the oldest-ever player to feature in the Ryder Cup at age fifty-one years and twenty days. He appeared as a captain's pick for Tom Watson's victorious United States team in the matches at The Belfry, England.

Robert Floyd, who would turn professional later in the year, played with Woods in junior golf but had never been exposed to what he was about to experience. "I'd never played with him kind of head-to-head, coming down the stretch, or anything like that, but I was kind of happy to have gotten to that point and to be able to play him," he recalled.

But when they reached the first tee, he soon realized just what he was in for. "That was where I noticed the crowds. I was like, 'Holy shit!'" he said. "I had never experienced anything remotely close to that. They were six deep from the tee to the green."

Floyd turned to his caddie, a local boy from Point O'Woods. "Have all these people been here all day?" he asked.

The kid looked up and nodded. "Yep."

For Floyd, the principal objective of the game was: (a) to win; but, more likely, (b) to not get embarrassed, especially with his family's history weighing heavily on his shoulders. But after seven holes, his hopes were receding. At the next, a par-3, it looked as though Woods was destined to go four-up, but somehow, Floyd won the hole, chipping in while Woods missed his birdie putt. "Then I kind of just hung in there, and by the time I got to the thirteenth, I was like, 'Shit, I might beat him.'"

When they reached the final hole, Floyd, now one up, got a good break from a wayward tee shot and managed to find the green with his second shot, although faced with a putt of fifty feet, his chance of making a birdie were slim to nothing. Tiger, meanwhile, was fifteen feet closer to the hole and poised to take the game further. "I'm kind of thinking two putts and I win, or just two putts and make it to extra holes," he said.

Remarkably, and against all the odds, Tiger Woods didn't get a chance to make his birdie as Floyd stepped up and drained the greatest putt of his life to win 1 up. Watching greenside was Floyd's brother, Raymond Jr., who told him that when his putt dropped, the roar from the crowd was the loudest he had ever heard. "But I was so into the moment, I just didn't hear it," added Floyd.

The defeat to Floyd stung like no other. For both Earl and Tiger, these were the kind of routine matches that Woods should be winning. As far as preparation went for the defense of his US Amateur title at the Newport Country Club in Newport, Rhode Island, the venue for the inaugural US Amateur Championship, held one hundred years ago in 1895, his father said, "It could go two ways." Tiger could sulk and bemoan his misfortune at Point O'Woods, or he could take the feeling he had experienced in that reverse to Robert Floyd and channel them into something altogether more positive. Tiger chose the latter.

Thanks to the generosity of Tommy Hudson, a member at Point Judith Country Club in nearby Narragansett, Woods and his team had been given the full use of the kind of sprawling house that Tiger could see himself living in once the pro ranks started paying him his dues. It was the perfect base for a week where Woods was seeking to become just the ninth player in history to successfully defend the US Amateur Championship title, including the best amateur of all, Bobby Jones.

Again, Woods breezed through to the match play rounds, enjoying routine victories against five opponents, including Patrick Lee, who had beaten Robert Floyd in the final of the Western Amateur. His opponent in the final, meanwhile, would be a man old enough to be his father but one who was also able to sell him a premium quality European car if and when he hit the big time. Forty-three-year-old George Marucci, or "Buddy" as he was known, was a Mercedes-Benz dealer from Philadelphia who, when he wasn't selling motor vehicles, was one of the most renowned amateur players in the area, winning the Pennsylvania Amateur Championship on four occasions.

Before the final, Woods spoke with his mother, Tida, who told him to wear a red shirt, telling him it was a "power color" and that it was less of a fashion statement and more one of intent. "I wear red on Sundays because my mom thinks that's my power color—and you know you should always listen to your mom," he said later.

Tida may have had a point. A variety of academic studies have shown how the color red is pivotal in determining dominance. At the University of Cambridge in England, for example, anthropologist Dr. Joanna Setchell's studies of African monkeys suggest that it is those males boasting a distinct red coloration that have an advantage when it comes to mating, and that red, across all species, is the color indicating power and control. Even in the human world, a red face is often seen as a sign of anger and aggression, while a pale face tends to signify fear or nervousness.

Certainly, in the world of sports, there is a wealth of evidence reinforcing the idea that red maintains a strange hold over the opposition, but in the thirty-six-hole final, it didn't seem to affect Buddy Marucci, who eased into a 2-up lead, even though Woods pegged him back to draw level at the halfway stage. During the interval, Marucci had some lunch and freshened up while Woods found some quiet space outside the locker room and sat, silent, for an hour, gathering his thoughts.

Before they recommenced in the afternoon, Woods's caddie and sports psychologist Jay Brunza did what he always did in the pivotal moments: taking his student to one side and reminding him of all the work they had done together, the need to focus on his breathing, and how best to retain full and unwavering focus on the task at hand, whichever way the match was heading. From the outset, Brunza had always been impressed by Tiger's mental fortitude, believing it to be his greatest asset—better even than his actual golf game. "The process was to teach him to deal with critical situations by emotionally detaching himself from them, while, at the same time, being completely immersed mentally in the challenge of the moment," he said. "With the inhibition of the fear of the moment removed, Woods could respond to the best of his burgeoning physical ability."

It would be a similar story in the afternoon's eighteen holes with Marucci again grinding out a two-hole advantage, only for Woods to mount his customary comeback and head into the last with a 1-up lead.

Woods then produced one of the shots he had been working on with Butch Harmon, only this time, it was under the most intense pressure imaginable. With an 8-iron in his hand, his knockdown approach to the final green tracked right over the flag, pitched fifteen feet behind, and then sucked back toward the hole as the spin kicked in, leaving Woods just eighteen inches or so from victory. Marucci had put up a spirited fight but had no option but to concede Woods's short putt and the match itself. "The shot that he hit to close the match out was phenomenal, and it was really amazing to watch him do that," added Marucci. "But then he's done it throughout his whole career, hasn't he?"

There was no regret or remorse for Marucci. Despite coming up short in the biggest game of his life, he had played as well as he could and reveled in the challenge, especially as he had given Woods a scare he wouldn't easily forget. "You know, I really enjoyed it," Marucci said. "It was exciting for me, after all the years, to finally get into the final. I mean, I'd played in a lot of amateurs and been okay, but to get there was kind of cool for me."

While he hadn't landed the Havemeyer Trophy, Marucci's run to the final had helped fulfill a long-held dream of his. "The nice thing about the day for me was that it got me on the Walker Cup team, which is really what I was focused on my whole life," he added.

A successful defense mounted, and his fifth consecutive national amateur title safely secured, Tiger dedicated his win to his caddie and psychologist Jay Brunza. His father, Earl, meanwhile, had been otherwise detained in the clubhouse bar. When he emerged, he found Butch Harmon filling the Havemeyer Trophy with champagne, even though Harmon didn't drink himself. Earl did, though, and he swiped the trophy before taking a swig and telling anybody who cared to listen how "Bobby Jones can kiss my son's Black ass."

This, increasingly, was driving Tiger and especially his mother to despair. The more success Tiger enjoyed, the more entitled—and bombastic—Earl Woods appeared to become. Each triumph that Tiger managed seemed to vindicate everything that Earl had planned for Project Tiger. In other words, it was already hard enough being a mixed-race kid in the country clubs of America, and the last thing Tiger needed, especially in another glorious moment of triumph, was an embarrassing parent ruining the moment.

CHAPTER 16

THE PRINCE OF WALES

"God created golf for Tiger Woods."

— Lee Trevino, six-time major champion

What the Fanagans didn't know about death wasn't worth knowing. For nearly two hundred years, the family had been running their funeral home in Dublin, Ireland, with generation after generation taking the reins whenever they were called upon. While Jody Fanagan loved the family business, he loved golf just as much, maybe more, and as one of Ireland's leading amateurs, he took his place in Captain Clive Brown's Great Britain and Ireland team to face Downing Gray's United States in the 1995 Walker Cup at Royal Porthcawl Golf Club in Porthcawl, South Wales.

For Fanagan, like most other members of the Great Britain and Ireland team, there was only one name that caught their eye on the US side. "We knew all about Tiger Woods, but then everyone in golf did," he said. "He had just won his second US Amateur, having done three Junior Amateurs, and he was the guy getting all the press and media.

"He was their number one player by far. A real star in the making."

In a sport as individual as golf, where players live and die by their shot selection and the decisions made, it is always interesting to gauge how the elite-level golfers adapt to a team format when others, for once, are counting on you. Being an individual player and, perhaps more pertinently, always the best individual player within a team had never really been an issue for Tiger Woods, at least not up until the Walker Cup matches of 1995. With his unshakable self-belief and how well he played to back it up, the teenager had never relied on others. If he did his bit for his team—like he had so many times at Western High, Stanford, and at the Eisenhower Trophy in France in 1994—the chances were that any side he was a member of always stood a significantly greater chance of victory. His teammates, moreover, were largely glad of his presence, not least because Woods's reputation nearly always preceded him, and that alone always seemed like a head start on the opposition.

For those on the 1995 United States Walker Cup team, having Woods in their ranks was nothing but a godsend. Alan Bratton, whose Oklahoma State team had squeaked by Woods and Stanford to the NCAA title, would much rather have him on his side than facing him. "It was a blessing," he said. "How could it not be?"

But the Walker Cup matches of 1995 were different. Now, Woods arrived not only as the back-to-back US Amateur champion but also the Silver Cup winner at the Masters, and with it, a growing clamor surrounding his future in the game and all the unending questions as to just when he would be turning professional and taking his talents to the PGA Tour.

For his part, Woods batted the questions away and committed himself to his education, just as he had in the wake of his debut at the Masters in April. But it was clear, even in a wet and windswept South Wales, that resistance was futile. Even in an age before the internet and social media, Woods's mere presence at the Walker Cup in Porthcawl had seen ticket sales soar and media coverage grow exponentially.

Increasingly, Woods didn't appear entirely comfortable with the demands on his time, especially as now there wasn't any familiar faces of Team Tiger accompanying him. When the golf writer Martin Hardy had approached him for an interview at the Eisenhower Trophy in France in September 1994, for example, Woods had rebuffed him. Now, a year later, the answer was the same when Hardy tried to grab a couple of minutes with the star of the show.

"Tiger refused point blank—and amateurs don't do that. They just don't refuse to be interviewed. Most of them are just glad for the publicity," explained Gary Wolstenholme, the 1991 British Amateur Champion who was a member of that 1995 Great Britain and Ireland Walker Cup team. "I mean, he was nineteen. He'd won three US junior championships in a row. And two US Amateurs. You'd think that you'd be very open to being interviewed. And yet, he just wasn't interested."

Away from the media, Woods appeared most comfortable when talking to other golfers, where his character appeared to be entirely at odds with the one he displayed on the golf course. "He was only nineteen and a college kid. He was genuinely quiet, shy, and unassuming and just seemed happier out of the media gaze," said Jody Fanagan.

Despite spending his entire life in front of cameras and microphones, Woods's reluctance to engage with the media and, latterly, sponsors would continue long after he turned professional. Hughes Norton, the agent who represented him in the early days of his pro career, recalled a young man who viewed any of his media or commercial commitments as a chore. "His response was 'Fuck 'em,'" he said. "It really didn't matter whether the contract was for $100 or $100 million. If it brought a pain-in-the-ass time commitment, it was more trouble than it was worth."

It would only get worse. In 2005, a colleague at *Golf Punk* magazine, Danny Crouch, was given the opportunity to interview Woods in Florida. After flying the three thousand miles from the United Kingdom, Crouch arrived, tape recorder in hand, ready to speak with the world's number one. He was given six minutes and not a second more.

Woods, though, would have to accept that now, and for the rest of his career, he would always be the center of attention, on and off the golf course, and even in the amateur ranks and the Walker Cup.

Much like its professional counterpart, the Ryder Cup, the Walker Cup had been dying a slow and largely unnoticed death and had followed a similar pattern of predictable American dominance, punctuated by only a few surprise wins for Great Britain and Ireland dotted along the timeline. Indeed, in the thirty-four matches played since the inaugural event at the National Golf Links of America in Southampton, New York, in 1922, the Great Britain and Ireland team had won just three matches. But where the Ryder Cup had undergone a long-overdue renaissance, thanks largely to the Great Britain and Ireland team becoming a European team in 1979 and finally winning on a regular basis, the Walker Cup remained hugely one-sided.

At times, the gulf between the sides verged on embarrassing. Two years earlier, at Interlachen Country Club in Edina, Minnesota, for example, the United States—with a team including a glut of future PGA Tour stars like Justin Leonard, Tim Herron, and Brian Gay—had administered the kind of demoralizing demolition that should really have signaled the end of the event, winning 19–5 and prompting the press to start calling it the "Walkover Cup."

Expectations for anything resembling a competition in 1995 then weren't exactly high. As the reigning US Amateur champion, Woods took his place on a United States team that blended youth—in the shape of Woods, Trip Kuehne, Notah Begay, Chris Riley, and Alan Bratton as captain—with more experienced heads, such as John Harris, Jerry Courville Jr., and the man Woods had just defeated in the US Amateur Championship, Buddy Marucci.

For once, though, it seemed like Great Britain and Ireland might have a chance, not least as the Americans had lost Walker Cup stalwarts Jay Sigel and Allen Doyle to the professional ranks. The men included one who would win multiple majors in England, Scotland, and the US, the Irishman Pádraig Harrington; the English future Ryder Cup player David Howell; and European Tour pro in the making Stephen Gallacher. They also had the player billed as Britain's answer to Tiger Woods, the towering twenty-one-year-old Scotsman Gordon Sherry.

Standing six foot eight, Sherry had won the 1995 British Amateur title at Royal Liverpool and had made a hole in one in a practice round at that year's British Open at St. Andrews with his illustrious playing partners Jack Nicklaus and Tom Watson watching on. The following year, meanwhile, he would also become the tallest player to ever tee it up in the Masters at Augusta National too.

Sherry would also enjoy a friendly rivalry with Tiger Woods. At the Scottish Open, prior to the British Open, the Scot had won a one-pound-sterling bet from Woods when he finished fourth overall, ten shots and forty-three places ahead of his American counterpart. Woods, he maintains, never paid out.

There was also the small matter of the golf course itself, which was unlike anything most of the younger members of the US team had ever encountered. Located thirty-three miles west of the Welsh capital Cardiff, Royal Porthcawl is the quintessential British links course, and with frequent rain and savage gusts blowing in off the Bristol Channel, it was about as far removed from the short sleeves and sun-soaked fairways of California as Tiger Woods could have imagined.

On the suggestion of Michael Bonallack, the five-time British Amateur champion and secretary of the Royal & Ancient Golf Club of St. Andrews, the Great Britain and Ireland captain arranged a meal for the two teams on the Wednesday evening, ahead of the competition beginning on Saturday, at local restaurateur Eddie Rabaiotti's Caprice restaurant in Penarth. Caprice was the go-to place to eat in South Wales. In 1982, owner Eddie Rabaiotti had been asked to serve dinner to Pope John Paul II on his visit to the area, presenting the Polish pontiff with *Krakowska* sausage bought from Harrods and served on the family's own personal crockery set. The pope even signed his plate for them once he had finished his meal. The heir to the British throne, Prince Charles, had also turned up to see what all the fuss was about.

But there was a problem. As the teams sat on the bus waiting to take them on the thirty-mile journey, US skipper Downing Gray did a head count, only to find he was one man down. Twenty minutes passed before the figure of Chris Riley, with his shock of unkempt blond hair, appeared at the front of the bus, clambered up the steps, and took his seat as a spontaneous and sarcastic round of applause erupted. Meanwhile, Downing Gray turned to Gary Wolstenholme sitting behind him and, fully aware of the huge regard that Tiger Woods and his talent held among the team, whispered, "You know, if that had been Tiger, they wouldn't have said a word."

For the visit of the two teams, Eddie Rabaiotti had decked the restaurant out in the flags of the respective nations, covering up many of the photos of the celebrity visitors he had entertained over the years. Clive Brown, meanwhile, was responsible for the seating plan. "I had Tiger sitting with the Irish boys because Pádraig Harrington and Jody Fanagan are really good fun. So I thought it was a nice seating arrangement," he recalled. "But I remember sitting with Downing Gray, and we looked over, and it just looked like Tiger wasn't particularly excited to be there, to be honest."

Since touching down in the United Kingdom, Woods had stuck rigidly to the same diet of hamburgers and fries every day, just as he had in Paris at the Eisenhower Trophy, but come Thursday morning, hours after the teams' seafood meal, he woke up vomiting and doubled up with crippling stomach pains with another of his teammates, Jerry Courville Jr., also suffering the same debilitating symptoms.

Unable to play, Woods sat out his practice round on Thursday and only managed three holes on Friday when the discomfort got the better of him. His caddie that day was local sixteen-year-old Nathan Griffiths, who got the day off school to help out. "He was pretty rough, and I gave him a Trebor mint to help his stomach, and I remember Tiger thinking it was a giant aspirin," he said. "It seemed to help his stomach cramps, so that night, I got my mother to go to the local supermarket to buy a five-pack of the mints, and he ended up sucking on those for the rest of the week. You could have sworn I gave him twenty thousand pounds because he was really appreciative of the gesture," he told the press.

Saturday wasn't a day for golf, at least not for someone like Woods who could wear shorts all year round if he wanted to back at home. Cold, wet, and windy, it was the kind of day that, if you were meeting the guys for a four-ball, you might look at each other, shake your heads, and then retire to the comfort of the clubhouse instead. Whether it was his illness or the wild conditions, Woods was far from his imperious best on the first day's play. Though he and John Harris breezed past Gordon Sherry and Stephen Gallacher in the opening foursomes match, his match against Gary Wolstenholme in the afternoon singles showed that, for all his talent, Woods still had much to learn when it came to match-play strategy, especially when it was played on links golf courses.

In years to come, Woods would become a virtuoso of the links, winning the British Open Championship twice at the Old Course at St. Andrews, and a third time at Royal Liverpool where he used his driver just once in 72 holes and hit 86 percent of fairways on his way to a two-shot win over compatriot Chris DiMarco. But on a wet and windswept Saturday, Woods fell victim to one of the sharpest operators in the amateur game: the 1991 British Amateur champion, England's Gary Wolstenholme.

Wolstenholme's golf game was the polar opposite of that of Tiger Woods. Whereas Woods was the swashbuckling powerhouse, capable of reducing golf courses to a mere pitch and putt, Wolstenholme, the wily campaigner, was fifteen years Tiger's senior and fifteen light-years behind him on every tee shot.

"I was irritating to play against. I was a grinder. I put the ball in the fairway, found the green, and my short game was exceptional," he explained. "But Tiger had all that and so much more. Not only was he longer than every other player in either team, but he also had the short game, and that combination is incredibly rare. It's rare to see guys that bash it miles, that also have that kind of touch, but then there was also the mental fortitude that he obviously had. He was destined to be a superstar, no question."

Woods against Wolstenholme was the archetypal tortoise-versus-the-hare contest. On each hole, Wolstenholme would find himself sometimes one hundred yards behind Woods off the tee, but his canny course management, coupled with Woods's occasional waywardness off the tee, made for the tightest of matches. By the time the pair reached the eighteenth tee, still in their waterproof clothing, they were all square.

Woods inaccuracy off the tee, compounded by the conditions, had seen his ball nestle in the thick rough to the left of the fairway, high above the green. Worse still, he had already played two shots while Wolstenholme was already pin-high to the side of the putting surface in two.

With 160 yards to the green, Woods knew he needed something spectacular, maybe even something as sweet as the 8-iron that worked for Buddy Marucci at the Newport Country Club. Swapping his 6-iron for a 7-iron, and with hands down the grip, Woods lashed his ball forward, prompting the kind of "oohs" and "aahs" from the crowd usually associated with firework displays. As Tiger's ball sailed through the air, carried by the whistling Welsh wind, Lee James—who had lost on the last hole to Kris Cox in the second game out in the Sunday singles—was sitting by the final green, eager to see how the match would end. "I could see Tiger play his shot in the distance, and then I could see his ball fly miles over us before bouncing around in the out-of-bounds. It didn't even sniff us," he said.

Tiger's face, meanwhile, was a maddening mix of disappointment and total bewilderment—and it left his opponent in the driver's seat. Playing his fourth shot, Woods chipped onto the green but missed his par putt, and with Wolstenholme chipping up from the edge of the green to within a few feet, Woods strode forward and conceded the match.

After the game, Wolstenholme retired to the hotel room he was sharing with teammate Lee James, and the two laughed, not just because he had beaten Woods, but because the game itself had been so poor. "It was a good job it wasn't stroke play." James laughed.

But Wolstenholme's place in history was assured, even if he did lose heavily to Woods in the second round of singles on the Sunday when the result, a rare win for Great Britain and Ireland, had already been decided. "You could see that all he was trying to do was tick boxes, and that all he wanted to do was to beat what Jack Nicklaus had done, whether it was his records, the tournaments that he'd won, or the number of tournaments he'd won.

"But Jack won the Walker Cup. Tiger didn't."

Woods left Royal Porthcawl and Wales with a personal record of played four, won two and lost two, and, infuriatingly, with the knowledge that winning the Walker Cup was now one of Jack Nicklaus's achievements he would never emulate, given the grand and pressing plans for his professional future. Food poisoning aside, it had nevertheless been a useful experience for the youngster, but one that had already sewn doubts about his suitability and appetite for playing in team events like this and, in the future, the Ryder Cup. Yes, opposition players might find his very aura intimidating, especially after he turned professional, but his reputation inevitably meant there was now a much bigger target on his back, and the idea of taking down the Tiger was, as Gary Wolstenholme found, something to savor.

Likewise, Jody Fanagan meeting with Woods was the only time the pair ever met. In the years that passed, however, his playing partner on that damp day in South Wales, Pádraig Harrington, not only turned professional but went on to win three majors and star for the European Ryder Cup team, both as player and captain. Often, whenever Woods ran into Harrington at tournaments, he would invariably ask about Fanagan and their 1995 Walker Cup meeting, although he could never remember his name.

"Whatever happened to that undertaker fella?" he would ask. "Still burying people?"

CHAPTER 17
TURNING POINT

"Tiger Woods didn't just transcend golf; he transcended sport. He was a phenomenon."

— Brandel Chamblee, former PGA Tour pro and TV analyst

It felt like the end of the world. A megastorm, the worst in seventy years, had blown in from the Pacific, felling trees and power lines, battering the Bay Area with one-hundred-miles-per-hour winds, and soaking San Francisco with almost two months' worth of rain in a little over a day. From his new student home off-campus, Tiger Woods awoke to see the devastation wrought on the city. *Vegas might not have been so bad after all*, he thought.

After another summer traversing the country and wrapping up another US Amateur Championship, Woods returned to Stanford for his sophomore year, happier than he had ever been. During this first week, Woods caught up with Bill Walsh, coach of the university's football team, the Cardinal. Walsh first held the job in the late 1970s but had left to take over the San Francisco 49ers in the NFL where he masterminded three of their four Superbowl triumphs in the 1980s with his revolutionary "West Coast offense." His work done, Walsh called it a day in 1988 and returned to

Stanford in 1992 to see if he could work his magic with the Cardinal once again.

Bill Walsh knew genius when he saw it. More than that, he knew what to do with it. Now, as coach of the Stanford Cardinal (and with golf coach Wally Goodwin's blessing), he took Woods under his wing. Tiger was only too happy to listen. Their meetings weren't scheduled, formal mentorship sessions; rather just casual drop-ins to chat about anything and everything. Walsh, a keen observer of human nature as well as athletic potential, recognized Tiger's relentless drive, and their relationship proved pivotal in giving Woods a better perspective of just what it required to reach the very top of his craft. It is why Walsh even gave Woods his own key to the football team's weights room, something he didn't even do with his own team members. He would joke that Woods hit the weights more than any of his football team ever did.

Eager to bulk up and gain even more yards in his golf game, Woods took full advantage and set about transforming his physique from lithe and lanky to buff and built. "He was really thin, but he just had that supple, wiry strength," said teammate Dave Garcia. "We used to go into the weight room, and people would make fun of him, just about how skinny he was. But then he would get on the bench press, and it was very impressive, and everyone was like, 'Whoa! This guy is really strong!'"

While his sporting talent and now his physique set him apart from the computer geeks and math wizards, he was just as unsuccessful in love. Just like his days at Cerritos Elementary School, when his stammer inhibited his confidence, Woods was tongue-tied when he met girls. It didn't help that his "dynamite" dance moves didn't improve. Frustrated by his lack of success, Woods practiced golf even harder, figuring there would be plenty of opportunities to meet women later.

There was one girl, though. She was called Irene Folstrom, a brunette from Minnesota, and she had her heart set on becoming a lawyer. Initially, she thought Tiger was a bit of a dork and a little on the quiet side, but when they started talking, she decided she actually liked what she found. They had similar tastes in music, especially R&B, and she liked the self-control he seemed to have, unlike some of the other jocks she knew. "He was never a party animal, never reckless," she said. "He was always very guarded of himself and his friends. He kept his circle very tight.

"This may surprise some people, but Tiger was a great boyfriend."

Tiger even introduced Irene to his parents, and, occasionally, she would walk the golf course with Tida Woods as Tiger played for the Cardinal. Tida liked her, too, believing she held many of the values that she and her son held. Earl, meanwhile, would come along as well, teasing the pair about their blossoming romance and what might be in store for them down the line.

But it was a relationship all but doomed to fail, not least because of Tiger's decision to leave college prematurely and Folstrom's determination to finish her studies. "I decided to stay at Stanford and not follow him on the golf circuit. My education was more important than being a golf wife," she said.

After his leading amateur debut in the Masters in 1995, Woods returned to Augusta National in April 1996 to see just how much he had learned from that special week and to try and find those marginal gains required to take him even higher up the leaderboard. But it didn't quite pan out the way Woods had expected. Though he enjoyed a practice round with Jack Nicklaus, after which Nicklaus called him "absolutely the most fundamentally sound golfer that I've seen at almost any age," two rounds of 75 meant an early exit and a huge dent to his confidence, especially after the promise of his debut. It would not only be the first and the last time Woods would ever miss the cut at the Masters but a useful lesson in cutting him back down to size, lest he thought he had got the game of golf down pat.

Back in Palo Alto, there was surprise among all of his Stanford teammates that Woods had failed to replicate his showing at his Masters debut, especially as he had gone into the competition in a rich vein of form that had seen him win two NCAA events and claim a second and a third in his last five collegiate competitions.

But Tiger's blip in form didn't offer any crumbs of comfort for those students trying to catch Coach Goodwin's attention and make the Cardinal team. That said, just being around Tiger Woods and watching him play or practicing alongside him on the range was enough for many of them. Eri Crum, from Aspen, Colorado, was one. "I remember him intentionally hitting huge banana slices with his driver off the deck, starting the ball over the two-story suite dormitory that was to the left of our driving range and curving it back on to the range," he recalled. "The rest of us weren't willing to try that one."

The opportunities to make a mark for the Cardinal for players like Crum weren't just limited by the presence of Tiger Woods. Ahead of him in the pecking order over his years there were four All-Americans: Notah Begay, Casey Martin, Will Yanagisawa, and Steve Burdick. "I didn't stand a chance breaking into that lineup," Crum said. "But even compared to those guys, Tiger just had an extra gear. He could hit his 7-iron like sixty yards further than his stock shot when he really wanted to step on it." That Pac-10 tournament at Big Canyon, where Woods had honorary membership, was an astonishing case in point.

While Woods shot a four-round total of 270 to win by an unfathomable fourteen shots, destroying Corey Pavin's 1982 tournament record in the process, it was the first two rounds where teammates and opponents realized that they might not be playing the same game as Tiger. In his opening round, Woods racked up eleven birdies, an eagle, and two bogeys for a round of 61, as he went out in 30 and came home in 31 to beat the long-standing course record by five shots. Then, after a fifteen-minute break, he emerged for his second round and carried on in the same vein, once more going out in 31, taking just nine putts, and then birdieing three of the first five holes on the back nine on his way to a round of 65.

While NCAA officials reached for the record books to see if Woods's 61 was the lowest ever round in their history (and it was), his peerless performance had the rest of the field, coaches included, wondering what they had just witnessed. UCLA's Michael Miller, who played with him, was fulsome in his praise. "This guy for thirty-six holes was unbeatable by any person on this planet. No question about it, no doubt in my mind," he offered. "It is the best golf I've either seen on TV, seen in person, or even heard about."

Meanwhile, Randy Lein, coach at Arizona State, who comfortably won the team title by seventeen shots over runner-up University of Southern California, and twenty-six ahead of fourth-placed Stanford, was still scratching his head. He shrugged. "Everybody was shell-shocked."

Woods was imperious and never more so than at the NCAA Men's Championship, the one major amateur title yet not on Tiger's résumé. "It's one of the titles that a lot of great players have won, and I want to win it as well," he said. Held at the Honors Course in Ooltewah, Tennessee, located twenty miles east of Chattanooga, the club was founded by Jack Lupton, whose family had made their fortunes bottling Coca-Cola. The golf course was another of Pete Dye's more devious designs and was once ranked the second most difficult golf course in the United States. Measuring in excess of seven thousand yards and featuring fairways lined with the kind of thick, tall, and maddening grass guaranteed to swallow your golf ball whole, it held little or no danger to Tiger Woods, who set about with the kind of disregard he had on so many courses throughout the season.

Going into the championships, Woods had won all four of his previous NCAA competitions, taking his total to seven wins for the season, and he started in much the same fashion. By the end of the third round, Woods had recorded rounds of 69, 67, and 69—the second of which was another course record for the twenty-year-old. It gave him a mammoth nine-shot lead over his nearest challenger, the University of Arizona South African star Rory Sabbatini.

Though everyone, Woods included, expected him to breeze through the final round and go on to another convincing victory, what happened next was one of the few occasions in his sophomore year where Woods looked fallible, even human. With the memory of Greg Norman's spectacular collapse at the Masters—where he surrendered a six-shot lead to hand the Green Jacket to England's Nick Faldo, not to mention his own missed cut there—still fresh in the memory, Woods turned in the kind of round that nobody had anticipated. At the ninth hole, for example, he suffered a triple bogey after dunking his ball in the water, while the back nine saw a horror run of four straight bogeys. It left Woods with an 8-over-round of 80 that, on another day, would have seen him fall short of victory. Instead, his sizable lead proved sufficient to carry him to a three-shot victory over Sabbatini.

For once, Woods seemed genuinely perplexed by what had transpired but took comfort that he had become the first Stanford golfer since Frank "Sandy" Tatum in 1942 to win the NCAA individual title, and that it was also another of Jack Nicklaus's career milestones ticked off. "It doesn't feel like I shot 80. I mean, it's not like I gave up and shot an 80. I really dug deep, and I am pleased with the result," he said after the round.

But at the end of his sophomore year, however, Woods had made his first year's efforts for the Cardinal look distinctly average. Of the thirteen events he played for Stanford, he had won eight, taking his overall college total to eleven wins, matching the record for most victories in a Stanford career, but over just two years. His scoring average, meanwhile, had dropped by nearly a shot a round to 70.61, and he had doubled the number of rounds he had made in the 60s to 18. And while Stanford missed out again on the NCAA team title, finishing a distant fourth to champions Arizona State, inevitably, Woods landed even more personal accolades, including the Haskins Award, given to the most outstanding collegiate golfer in the United States.

After claiming the NCAA title, Woods traveled to Dublin, Ohio, and on to Jack Nicklaus's tournament, the Memorial, where he would also pick up the award for best collegiate golfer named in the host's honor. When Fuzzy Zoeller, the 1979 Masters champion and the PGA Tour's self-appointed wisecracker-in-chief, saw him, he yelled, "Nice three rounds, kid"—a reference to Tiger's uncharacteristically poor final round at the NCAA finals.

The disappointment of missing the cut at Augusta National had long since given way to a determination to silence a few of the doubters who stuck their heads above the parapet and suggest that maybe Tiger wasn't quite as ready as he and Earl Woods thought. There was vindication of sorts for Tiger at the US Open at Oakland Hills Country Club in Bloomfield Hills, Michigan, in mid-June when Woods made the cut, but his four-round total of 23-over-par, for a tie of eighty-second place, hardly had the fans and media buzzing. In fact, his first round, where he briefly held the lead but then played the last five holes in 9-over-par, turning a potential 67 into a 76, were about as bad as he had played since he started college. The *Los Angeles Times* reported that the wheels hadn't just come off for Tiger, but that he was "involved in a very serious one-car wreck" where "the tires went flat, the engine blew up, the frame collapsed, the bumper melted, and the radio got stuck playing 'Taps.'"

While Woods finished his first round with bogey, double bogey, quadruple bogey, bogey, and bogey, he was remarkably sanguine about what had just taken place. "I am fine," he said in the hospitality tent, as if he had actually just walked away from a potential life-threatening road traffic accident. "Life goes on. Tomorrow is another day."

Earl Woods was watching on, too, through the gaps in his fingers. "He's been through this before." He shrugged. "Maybe not in a tournament of this magnitude, but he's played like a bum before."

That week, Woods also appeared on *The Tonight Show with Jay Leno* where the host showed a photograph of baby Tiger in diapers and holding a golf club to the cameras. Leno said that it's not often you see a top golfer in diapers. Tiger replied, "I should have had one on at the Open."

It was a hard lesson learned for Woods, but one mitigated by the fact that the USGA always set up their US Open courses to be the most difficult of all the four major championships, and where making a par had always been the most precious of commodities. Yet the difference between the Woods that flailed so badly at Oakland Hills and the one who turned up at his next major, the British Open at Royal Lytham & St. Anne's on England's northwest coast, wasn't just noticeable; it was like watching an entirely different golfer.

For his week in Lancashire, Woods had a new caddie in tow. Richard Noon had been a member at Royal Lytham & St. Anne's since he was a young boy and had now come home to the United Kingdom for the summer from his studies at Texas Wesleyan University in Fort Worth, Texas. "One of my close friends, Colin Maclaine, was Mark McCormack's right-hand man at IMG, and he facilitated the introduction," he explained. "They were looking for a good player familiar with the course to caddie for Tiger."

With Woods missing the cut at the Scottish Open the week before the Open Championship, Tiger arrived early with his father and met up with Noon on the practice ground on Sunday before playing a practice round in two-ball with Costantino Rocca the following day. It didn't take long for the two men, the same age, to gel. "At one point, Earl Woods told me he had never seen anyone get along so well with his son," recalled Noon.

With Noon on his bag, and His Royal Highness Prince Andrew waving him off on the tee, Woods soon found the relatively wide-open spaces of the Lancashire links to his liking, not to mention the way it required all manner of creative shots to the ones he might ordinarily be required to play on the flat tracks back home. "After about three holes, I realized I could club Tiger pretty accurately—I was also a long hitter in my youth and could relate to his distances, especially with irons," added Noon. "As the round progressed, he saw he could trust my local knowledge and course insight. From then on, every shot that week became a collaboration between the two of us."

That week, Woods posted a total of 281 (3-under-par) for a share of twenty-second place and the Silver Medal as the British Open's leading amateur, something Jack Nicklaus never achieved. Not only did it tie the record for the lowest British Open score by an amateur (he could have beaten it had a twelve-foot putt fell at the last) but his second round 66 broke the record for the lowest ever single round by an amateur. "I remember I got hot in that second round,"

Woods said later. "I think I made seven birdies on an eleven-hole stretch or twelve-hole stretch there. I thought that was a pretty great accomplishment."

For Richard Noon, meanwhile, it was a week to remember. "I received a small compensation from IMG," he said, "but the memories I have from it are truly priceless."

Inevitably, all the talk after the final round at Royal Lytham & St. Anne's was about when Tiger would turn professional, not least as the likes of Seve Ballesteros, Nick Faldo, and Jack Nicklaus—all multiple winners of the Open Championship—were already professional by the time they were Woods's age. Tiger didn't take the bait, though. "So far, my plans right now are to return to school," he said. "I'll know when [to turn pro]. I can't tell you when. I can't tell you because I've never been there. When I get there, I'll tell you."

In the years to come, Woods reflected on his week on the Lancashire coast and explained how it had actually been a pivotal event in his golf career, a moment that convinced him that he was ready for the challenges of the professional game and not a return to his studies at Stanford University. "The Open Championship that year basically, I thought, pushed me toward turning pro versus going back to college," he said. "I was still kind of iffy about whether I should turn pro or not, but that gave me so much confidence that I could do it at a high level, I could shoot those scores, and I could play against the top players in the world on a very difficult track."

As Tiger received his silver medal for being the competition's leading amateur, he looked on in envy as his compatriot, Tom Lehman, lifted the most famous trophy in golf for the one and only major win of his career. "Heck, I was looking for the Claret Jug, that's what I came here for," he said.

Lehman, meanwhile, was in no doubt about what the future held for Woods and the game itself. "I'm the player of the year, but Tiger is the player of the next two decades," he suggested. "I'm holding off the inevitable, like I'm trying to bail water out of a sinking boat."

CHAPTER 18
HELLO, WORLD

"The world has not seen anything like what he's going to do for the sport. I wasn't alive to see Monet paint, but I am alive to see Tiger play, and that's pretty great."

—Phil Knight, Chief Executive, Nike

At the end of a sophomore year in which he became the first Stanford golfer in half a century to win the NCAA Individual Championship, Tiger Woods assured his college coach Wally Goodwin that it would be business as normal when he returned to college in the fall. But they both knew that was bullshit.

Though Stanford had provided Woods with a much-needed haven away from the escalating attention he received whenever he set foot on a fairway, the professional game offered far too much temptation—and remuneration—to keep the young man's head in his books for the next two years. Besides, Arnold Palmer and Jack Nicklaus never finished college either, and they didn't do too bad, figured Tiger.

His father was even more keen to see Woods turn pro. Yes, it meant financial security for his son, and, in turn, for him and his estranged wife, Tida, but Tiger's frequent disagreements with what Earl saw as an overzealous NCAA had all but made his mind up for him, despite Tiger's public statements to the contrary. For Earl Woods, the NCAA's compliance officers had always seemed to have Tiger in their sights, for no other reason than he was in the public eye much more than most other college athletes. From the moment he was reprimanded for accepting a dinner from Arnold Palmer in San Francisco in his freshman year, there had been a succession of incidents where Tiger appeared to be on the receiving end of the kind of attention that nobody else suffered. If Tiger used a different ball or some new irons, the NCAA wanted to know where they came from. If Tiger put on a clinic for youngsters, they wanted to know who, if anyone, was getting paid. They even denied him an honorary membership at the Olympic Club in San Francisco even though no money was involved.

Earl Woods also had reason to be upset with the NCAA. In 1996, he had started work on a book called *Training a Tiger: The Official Book on How to Be the Best* and been hamstrung by the NCAA as to just how much input his son could have in it. Eventually, the NCAA struck a compromise, allowing Tiger to write the foreword and appear in a few instructional photographs within it, but any promotion of the title that involved him was banned.

Again, it seemed as though Tiger was being singled out. "The NCAA is picking on me," he told his father. "They are watching me. They are looking for something wrong. And it is inevitable that, one of these times, they are going to get something on me they can embellish to bring me down.

"I don't have to put up with this."

When Tiger then told Earl Woods that he was now ready to leave college and turn professional, his father couldn't have been more delighted. "If you look at this situation objectively," he said, "this is the perfect opportunity for Tiger to say, 'Kiss my yin-yang,' and leave school," then added, "Goodbye NCAA! And good riddance!"

Besides, he said, there was an unprecedented third consecutive US Amateur title to win, this time at Pumpkin Ridge in Portland, Oregon, which, following his decision, would now be his last ever tournament as an amateur. Within a week, his pro contracts would be signed and sealed, he would have more money than he could imagine and the kind of celebrity few athletes ever achieve. He didn't need to complete an economics degree to realize it made no sense to stay at Stanford.

When he finally got around to telling Wally Goodwin he was leaving, the conversation was short, largely because the coach already guessed why Woods was calling. But Woods's Stanford teammates weren't afforded the same courtesy. One minute Woods was a Stanford student; the next he would be a multimillionaire billed as the savior of professional golf.

But as many people had found—Tiger's family included—this kind of behavior wasn't unusual. When Woods was about to begin at Stanford, he had promised his half-sister, Royce, that when he hit the big time, as he surely would, he would buy her a house but only on the condition that she did all his laundry when he was at college.

But while Woods's farewell, or lack of it, was increasingly typical of the manner in which he seemed to jettison those who were no longer of any use to him, there were no hard feelings. Besides, most of the Cardinal golf team, like Dave Garcia, suspected he was never coming back to Stanford anyway. "I think we all knew, because you had to apply for housing at the end of your year for the following year to secure your on-campus housing, and he didn't do that," he recalled. "So I think we all thought he's probably not coming back. He never said he was leaving, but we all knew."

Woods's progress in the US Amateur competition at Pumpkin Ridge was solid if unspectacular and included victories over future PGA Tour winners D. A. Points and Charles Howell III and his Stanford teammate Joel Kribel in the semifinal. Awaiting Woods in the final over the Witch Hollow course was Steve Scott, a nineteen-year-old about to enter his sophomore year at the University of Florida. Certainly, he knew the scale of the task ahead of him. "It was the ninety-sixth edition of the US Amateur, and nobody had ever won three straight. You could say I was the only guy in the way of history that day," he said. "It was this David versus Goliath sort of match. It was all pretty remarkable. That moment, that day, that event—it was kind of surreal."

Nine months before their final, Scott had played with Woods in a collegiate event where, having heard all about his opponent's prodigious talent, he got hypnotized by the hoopla surrounding Tiger. "The first time I played with him, I got caught up watching him, as most people do, and so part of my game plan was to not watch him hit a shot and not get caught up in his swing," he recalled. "It was one of those survival mechanisms, really, because you can get caught up in what he's doing."

When Scott stepped on to the first tee, with his girlfriend Kristi Hommel on his bag, he was taken aback by the sheer volume of the galleries watching. Ten, twelve deep, it was estimated that as many as fifteen thousand people had turned up to watch the final. "For an amateur match, it was pretty something," said Scott. "One thing I'll never forget was that it was seven fifteen in the morning, and the whole first hole, a 420-yard par-4, was completely lined with people, right and left, all the way around it. That was pretty shocking, considering it was out in the farm country near Portland. It was pretty crazy that there was that many people there."

Also watching was Tiger's old Stanford teammate Casey Martin. Having turned professional in 1995, Martin, like everyone else, still had no idea as to when Woods was going to turn pro. Yes, it was inevitable, he said, but still there had been no confirmation. "I mean, there were thousands of people out watching him," he recalled. "But then I remember Phil Knight came out, and there was chatter in the crowd, like, 'Wow, the Nike CEO is here to watch Tiger.' And I remember thinking like, *Okay, Phil Knight doesn't come to these kind of events very often. Something is definitely going on.*"

When Phil Knight started the company that would become Nike in 1964, he hadn't envisaged that the operation would become one of the coolest sports brands around, but having hit the big time in running and athletics, and, later, in basketball and tennis, the idea that they could make inroads into a game as sedate as golf seemed fanciful at best. But when Knight first saw Tiger Woods, he knew that here was one golfer who might just be able to pull it off.

Knight had been tracking Woods since his junior year at Western High, and nothing he had seen since had dissuaded him that Woods was the one and only player who could launch Nike into the golf market. "I hope we sign him," he said. "If not, I hope he goes to medical school."

As he watched the action, ABC's *World News Tonight* reporter Carol Lin stopped him to see if he could reveal when Tiger might turn professional. Knight didn't say much. Then Lin asked him what Woods had to lose by staying in school, especially one as good as Stanford. Knight smiled. "Millions of dollars."

But if Tiger thought the crowds would faze Steve Scott, he was wrong. If anything, it had the polar opposite effect. Scott started strongly and powered into a commanding lead while Woods was uncharacteristically erratic. "He came out very, very flat. It was a very poor performance, honestly. He hit one in the water on the fifth hole, he was hooking shots, and he missed several putts. He did not do anything well," added Scott.

After eighteen holes and six birdies in his first round, Scott held a healthy 5-up lead, and with Woods a shadow of his usual dominant self, Scott used the ninety-minute break before the second round to buy some souvenirs from the club shop.

Back at the Navy Club, Joe Grohman's phone in the club shop exploded with people calling to tell him how Tiger was heading for defeat. "They kept saying, 'He's going down!' but there was absolutely no doubt in my mind that he was going to win this because Steve Scott had no clue who he was in the octagon with."

Then Tida called him. She wasn't at all worried. "She was the only one that I could talk to that completely understood how I felt because we both knew he was going to win. There's no way this kid's going to lose," he added.

"If it had been stroke play, I would have shot 68 or something, and he shot maybe 75 or 76," added Scott. "But having watched some of his previous US Amateur and USGA Finals, I knew that he was going to come back, because that's just what he does."

Woods took to the practice range to seek advice from his caddie and sports psychologist Jay Brunza and his swing coach Butch Harmon. With a change of clothes and after giving himself a dressing down, he emerged for the afternoon round with a newfound determination. "It was like a completely new golfer. As though he had flipped a switch, and now the lights were on," said Scott.

Woods powered his way back into contention, preferring a 2-iron off the tee rather than his wayward driver. Within five holes, he had reduced Scott's lead to just two holes, and by the time they reached the turn, it was down to just one. "I don't think I've ever seen such a dramatic change in form in such a short time," added Scott.

Remarkably, Scott rallied, and when they arrived at the par-4 sixteenth hole (the thirty-fourth hole), he had stretched his lead to two, with just three holes to play. By the time the pair reached the green, Scott had a ten-foot putt for his par while Woods had a glorious chance for his birdie after his wedged approach spun back to just six feet from the hole. Crucially, however, Woods's ball was directly in Scott's line to the hole, and having marked his ball, Scott asked that he move it again so he could get a clear sight of the hole.

His route clear, Scott made his par putt, leaving Woods with his shorter effort to win the hole and reduce the deficit to just one hole with two to play. When Woods returned to his marker, though, he placed his ball behind it, forgetting to move it back into its original position, an error that could have cost him the hole and the match itself. Instead, Scott intervened. "Hey, Tiger," he said instinctively. "Did you move that back?"

Tiger didn't say anything. No thank-you or even a nod of appreciation for Scott's sportsmanship. He just placed his marker back where it should have been, drained his birdie putt, and headed off to the seventeenth and penultimate tee.

As so many other opponents had found, Tiger Woods in game mode was never one to talk on the way around a golf course, but to not even acknowledge Scott's gesture smacked of arrogance, not least because Scott could have been crowned US Amateur champion if he had kept his mouth shut.

From that moment, it was almost inevitable what would transpire.

At the seventeenth, a birdie from Woods made the game all square going down the last, and when both players matched each other on the thirty-sixth hole, the final went into a sudden-death playoff that ended on just the second extra hole. As Scott's short par putt failed to drop, Woods stepped up, tapped in, and claimed an unprecedented third consecutive US Amateur Championship, something not even Bobby Jones—the man routinely hailed as the greatest-ever amateur golfer in history—could boast. "I saw how great he could be in that afternoon eighteen that he played against me," added Scott. "I guess on paper he shot 65, but it could have been 61 or 62 pretty easily."

As Tiger was engulfed on the green by his emotional parents and assorted well-wishers, he eventually found time to offer a cursory handshake to Steve Scott, who had been waiting patiently to congratulate his opponent. When NBC's Roger Maltbie interviewed the pair soon after, he said that Tiger now had "a place in golf history," which was undeniably true. But so, too, did Steve Scott, the nineteen-year-old who would go on to be a three-time All-American at the University of Florida. After all, without his magnanimity and innate sense of fair play, Tiger's peerless amateur record would have an almighty hole in it.

Today, Scott bears no ill will toward Tiger Woods. "It was pretty crazy, but I guess what I did was just my way of honoring the game, and looking back on it, that was my victory that day," he said. "I didn't win the match at the end, but I think I won a lot of fans."

The natural, inevitable question, of course, is what would have happened if the roles had been reversed, if it was Tiger Woods watching on as Steve Scott stood on the verge of a catastrophic, game-ending mistake?

What would he have done?

Almost anybody who had ever played against Woods—a player whose ruthlessness on the golf course had been hardwired into him by his parents—in those key matches over the amateur years would almost certainly know the answer.

. . .

In six years, from ages fifteen to twenty, Tiger Woods had won six consecutive USGA National Championships, in juniors and seniors, triumphing in thirty-six straight matches on six different courses across the United States, from Portland to Ponte Vedra Beach. But sitting in Pumpkin Ridge's locker room with the gleaming Havemeyer Trophy once again by his side—and his vanquished opponent slumped just a couple of yards away—Woods had little time to celebrate. Hughes Norton, the powerhouse agent from IMG, had assumed that Woods would emerge triumphant and arranged an important meeting for his client directly after the presentation. And so, accompanied by his parents, Earl and Tida, and his coach Butch Harmon, Woods headed with Norton to a private room in the clubhouse.

Waiting for them was Phil Knight, the founder and CEO of Woods's new sponsor, Nike, and Jim Riswold, creative director of Nike's ad agency, Wieden+Kennedy. Riswold, who was not yet forty, had been hired by the agency as their first copywriter in 1984, fresh out of the University of Washington. In the twelve years since, he had become the creative force behind a host of audacious and game-changing commercials for the sportswear giant, including 1992's "Air Rabbit," featuring Michael Jordan and Bugs Bunny. Now, he was tasked with writing an ad to announce Tiger's much-anticipated arrival in professional golf.

His brief was to make Tiger—and by extension golf—*cool.*

Jim Riswold wasn't interested in any polite endorsements; he wanted a seismic cultural shift in the game of golf. He understood that Tiger Woods wasn't just another golfer; he was a phenomenon poised to shatter norms, and now Riswold's challenge was to somehow capture the essence of a mixed-race prodigy entering a white sport and show how Tiger's power lay not simply in his golf game, astonishing though it was, but in his very presence in the professional ranks.

As the guests took their seats, Knight motioned to Riswold, who was standing by a TV and VCR. He thanked everyone for coming, dimmed the lights, inserted a video cassette, and pressed play.

> *A choir sings as a succession of images and video footage from Woods's childhood and amateur career flash across the screen. Then a script appears:*
>
> *I shot in the 70s when I was eight.*
> *I shot in the 60s when I was twelve.*
> *I played in the Nissan Open when I was sixteen.*
> *Hello, World.*
>
> *I won the US Amateur when I was eighteen.*
> *I played in the Masters when I was nineteen.*
> *I am the only man to win three consecutive US Amateur titles.*
> *Hello, World.*
>
> *There are still courses in the US I am not allowed to play—because of the color of my skin.*
> *Hello, World.*
>
> *I've heard I'm not ready for you.*
> *Are you ready for me?*

Sixty seconds later, the commercial ended. Tiger, shy and uncertain, his face impassive, scanned the room, trying to gauge reaction.

Hughes Norton, standing at the back, wasn't sure. "To say it was unlike any golf commercial I'd ever seen was an understatement," he recalled. "But I kept my thoughts to myself."

Meanwhile Earl Woods, sitting next to his wife, Tida, offered only the slightest of smiles. At Tiger's request, they ran the tape again.

Still, silence.

Finally, Woods's swing coach Butch Harmon broke cover.

"*That*," he declared, "is the best fuckin' ad *I've* ever seen . . ."

CHAPTER 19

THE TIGER CHANNEL

"He's inspired a whole generation of golfers, myself included, and we wouldn't be here without him."

— Rory McIlroy, career Grand Slam winner

Not so fresh from winning the US Amateur at Pumpkin Ridge in Oregon, Tiger and Earl Woods moved on to Milwaukee to prepare for his professional debut. First held in 1968, the Greater Milwaukee Open had never been one of the most celebrated events on the PGA Tour, but in its twenty-eighth installment, it suddenly became the very epicenter of the golf world. Held at Brown Deer Park Golf Club, ten miles north of the city, it was never intended to be the place where Tiger finally turned pro, but now, with an unprecedented third consecutive victory in the US Amateur under his belt, resistance was futile.

Tiger was exhausted. On the flight from the US Amateur Championship in Portland to Milwaukee, laid on by Phil Knight and Nike, he crashed out as soon as he took his window seat and only woke up when the pilot announced they were beginning their descent into General Mitchell International Airport, nearly four hours later.

Thanks to Nike's whopping endorsement waiting in the wings, this was the first time Woods hadn't had to slum it on commercial airlines. Slumped in his chair, his long legs outstretched, he looked out of the window of his private jet and thought, *I'm never flying coach again.*

When he arrived at his hotel room, Woods found bag after bag of Nike clothes, all made especially for him. Later, when he turned up at Brown Deer Park to practice, he opened his locker to find more Titleist golf gloves than he would ever need and three dozen new Titleist Tour Balata balls. "He was like a ten-year-old dropped into the middle of Toys 'R' Us," recalled his swing coach Butch Harmon.

A day after they arrived, Hughes Norton dropped by Tiger's hotel suite, armed with the Nike apparel and Titleist equipment contracts for Tiger to sign. Norton tossed them on the table.

"Do you know you're now earning four times what Greg Norman makes on his equipment deal, Tiger?" He laughed. "And double what he's getting for his shoes and apparel deal? And he's the world number one!"

Woods seemed uninterested. He shrugged. "Not bad."

Norton was taken aback. "I thought a more appropriate response might have been, 'Holy shit, Hughes, that's incredible!'" he said. "But Tiger just signed them and went off to get a Coke and a burger, like he always did."

Some of the deals Norton had secured for Woods were unheard of in the pro game, not least for a twenty-year-old kid who had just dropped out of college after a couple of years, had never won a pro tournament, and who missed the cut in nine of the sixteen professional events he had already played as an amateur. The clothing deal with Nike, for example, guaranteed Woods $40 million over five years, regardless of how he actually performed, but also featured dramatic, escalating bonuses for tournament wins and world-ranking improvements. The contract struck with Titleist was similarly impressive, with the equipment manufacturer agreeing to pay Woods $20 million over five years, also with lucrative add-ons based on his results.

Soon, there would be even more money sloshing around Project Tiger's coffers: credit card company Amex paid him $25 million to be a brand spokesman for five years. Rolex put him on an annual retainer and even made a Tiger Woods–signature Tudor watch with a guaranteed $645,000 in royalties annually. Asahi beer signed a $4.6 million deal with him. *Golf Digest* paid him $320,000 for just four hours of his time each year. You could also find Tiger's face on Wheaties cereal boxes.

When he was asked about the money his son was now earning, Earl Woods was typically dismissive, describing it as "chump change," as though whatever amount anyone was prepared to pay Tiger wouldn't ever be sufficient recognition for his extraordinary talent.

For the young Woods, though, the riches earned off the golf course, or "paper money" as he called it, meant little compared to the cash made on it. "It honestly never mattered to him," said Norton. "But then why would it? He had $60 million in the bank at twenty, guaranteed. Why worry?"

But while his record-breaking contracts with Nike and Titleist had been signed, Woods had yet to receive any money. On his first night, he had paid for dinner at a Kopp's burger joint using a gift certificate he had been given on his arrival.

Woods also met up with Butch Harmon again, and the pair drove to Brown Deer Park Golf Course in the suburb of Glendale, the site of his professional debut. As they approached the clubhouse, Woods nervously raised a delicate subject. "Butch," he muttered. "I don't have the hundred-dollar entry fee."

Harmon laughed. Then laughed again.

Here was Tiger Woods, the young man with the megabucks deals, a player already revered as the savior of modern golf, and he didn't even have the cash to enter his first professional tournament. "I haven't seen a penny yet," he continued. "I haven't seen any check in the mail yet. I'm still broke."

As the pair walked into the clubhouse and to the tournament registration office, Harmon patted him on the shoulder, told him not to worry, and pulled a hundred-dollar bill from his wallet. Moments later, Woods gave his name to the officials, handed over his entry fee, and waited till they found his name on the entry list before checking it off. It had been two decades since he first picked up the little putter in his dad's garage, but Eldrick "Tiger" Woods was finally a professional golfer.

He also had a new caddie. Mike "Fluff" Cowan was a seasoned bagman who had been Peter Jacobsen's caddie for the best part of twenty years, helping him win six times on the PGA Tour, including the Bob Hope Chrysler Classic in 1990 and the AT&T Pebble Beach National Pro-Am in 1995. With his distinctive white moustache, perpetually unbuttoned top button, and easy-going manner, Cowan would prove the perfect fit for Woods in the nascent stages of his professional career. But more than that, he was very good at his job.

To his credit, Jacobsen appreciated that working with a once-in-a-generation talent like Woods was too good a bag to turn down, and although Cowan was determined to fulfil his commitments to his boss, Jacobsen insisted he move fast, giving his blessing to the new partnership.

IMG had intended to announce Tiger turning pro at Niketown in Chicago on Tuesday, August 27, but instead decided to do it at Brown Deer Park Golf Course instead, commandeering the large marquee of a local catering company, Saz's, to introduce Tiger to the world's media. The press conference included journalists from organizations like *People* and *Newsweek* magazines, titles that, ordinarily, would rarely or never cover golf. And at 2:30 p.m. on Wednesday, August 28, 1996, Tiger Woods took to the makeshift podium, dressed in a striped polo shirt and with a mile-wide smile dazzling the room, and his father, Earl, sitting next to him in an armchair, uttered his first words as a professional golfer. "I guess, hello, world, huh?" he said, echoing Nike's slogan from Jim Riswold's ad that was about to drop.

With the news now public, Earl Woods was also free to offer his opinions. Not surprisingly, they were hyperbolic in the extreme. "Tiger will do more than any other man in history to change the course of humanity," he said. "He's the bridge between the East and the West. There is no limit, because he has the guidance. I don't know yet exactly what form this will take, but he is the Chosen One. He'll have the power to impact nations. Not people. Nations. The world is just getting a taste of his power."

On Tuesday morning, just after 7:00 a.m., Dave Stockton Jr., son of the two-time PGA Championship winner and 1991 Ryder Cup–winning captain Dave Stockton, wandered into the players' locker room at Brown Deer Park to find Tiger Woods nearby. "Hey, Tiger, welcome to the tour. Good to have you out here," he said.

Tiger smiled. "Want to play a practice round?"

"Sure," said Stockton Jr., who then roped in Billy Andrade, who had already won twice on the PGA Tour, to make up a three-ball. As one of the longest hitters on tour, Stockton soon found himself being outdriven by Woods by twenty or thirty yards. "And he was hitting shots that I can't hit," he added. "Whatever he needed to hit, he could do it. I didn't see a single weakness. He could work it left, work it right. He had an extra gear to hit it as far as he wanted to hit it. He had tremendous control. It was very impressive."

The round over, the trio shook hands on the final green, and Stockton wished Woods well for the week. "Then I turned to my caddie and said, 'Come on, we got to go to the range. I don't know what we're going to work on, but we've got to work more,'" he said. As Stockton Jr. headed straight to the range, he was approached by a couple of reporters eager to talk about the main event. "I knew they didn't want to talk about me or my game." He laughed. "They asked me what I thought about Tiger's game instead, and I remember distinctly saying, 'Don't worry, guys. Tiger's gonna do just fine out there,' and left it at that."

It was a similar story for Allen Doyle, who, at forty-six, had finally turned professional, becoming the oldest rookie in tour history. When he finished his practice round on Tuesday, he returned to the locker room to find a note stuck to his locker, asking him to attend the press center. "I thought, *What the hell would they want me in the media tent for?*" he said. Ever obliging, though, Doyle did as requested and took his seat at the podium at the front where his name was announced over the public address system. "Suddenly, there's this rush of people coming in. I'd say a couple of hundred," he continued.

Baffled by his newfound popularity, Doyle asked what was going on, only to be told by a press officer that he was the only one in the field that week that had actually played with Tiger, when they were on the same United States team at the World Amateur Team Championship in France two years earlier. "I said, 'Son of a gun, I just might be,'" he added. "So then it was just question after question about Tiger and how I thought he would do. And I just said, 'He'll do just fine.'"

According to Dave Stockton Jr., the number of media representatives at Brown Deer Park that week was "fifty times what was normally there," but then everybody wanted to see him. Everyone was there, from *Golf Digest* and *Sports Illustrated* to less-familiar names on the PGA Tour accreditation list like *Newsweek* and *People* magazine. Even the television show *Live with Regis and Kathie Lee* was broadcast from Brown Deer Park as an expectant nation tuned in.

When the Virginian professional Robert Wrenn was at the practice range right next to Woods, meanwhile, his caddie became preoccupied with watching the youngster, prompting Wrenn to reprimand him for not doing his job properly. "It was like a girlfriend that catches the boyfriend looking at another girl." He laughed.

That afternoon, Jeff Hart, who was back on the PGA Tour after dropping off in 1990, was having lunch after his practice round. In the pre-internet age, players would typically find out who they were playing with by referring to the tee times that tournament officials would post around the venue in locations like the clubhouse, the locker room, or, as was the case at Brown Deer Park, on the door of the dining area. Hart was just finishing his food and about to get up to see who his playing partners were when an excitable Carl Paulson, who he had just played a practice round with, broke the news. He smiled. "You're not going to believe who you're paired with."

"Obviously, I knew who he was talking about, and that's how I found out," said Hart. "But there was a lot of media surrounding Tiger turning pro, and of course I knew all about him and knew that it was going to be quite a circus."

As the golf writer for the *Milwaukee Journal Sentinel*, Gary D'Amato had been to more Greater Milwaukee Opens than he cared to remember. "It was always a nice community event, but it attracted a weak field because of when it was and the smaller purse on offer. The galleries were enthusiastic but on the small side, so it really generated minimal buzz," he said.

But that year, D'Amato suddenly found it had become the most popular golf venue in the world. For the first time, the national and international media had turned up and so, too, had the crowds. "I would estimate that the galleries were three or four times bigger than normal, with a large percentage of those spectators following Tiger," he said. Crucially, added D'Amato, it wasn't simply a bigger crowd, it was a different crowd. "For the first time ever, I saw numerous people of color in the crowds," he added.

Come Thursday, the crowds and the media attention had swelled still further. As Tiger made his way to the first tee for his maiden round as a professional, he stopped beneath some trees near the Brown Deer Park clubhouse just as his caddie Fluff Cowan emerged with a brand-new black-and-white Titleist staff bag, still wrapped in its plastic covering. In full view of D'Amato, now a senior writer for the website Wisconsin.Golf, the pair ripped off the plastic before transferring Tiger's clubs from his trusty Stanford carry bag to the new one that Titleist were paying him $20 million over three years to use. "As I observed this exchange, I just thought to myself that I was witnessing the symbolic moment that Tiger was actually turning pro," he added.

At 1:36 p.m., wearing his new black Nike cap and shirt fresh from the packet, Tiger Woods stood on the first tee at Brown Deer Park, smiling, as he was introduced to the thousands of fans eager to get a glimpse of golf's newest phenomenon.

"From Orlando, Florida, and playing his first tournament as a professional: Tiger Woods," boomed the official.

Tiger smirked. The last time he had even been in Florida was two years earlier when he won his first US Amateur Championship at Sawgrass, and while he was intending to move to the Sunshine

State soon—the state tax breaks made perfect sense—he hadn't even started to look for a house yet.

No matter. He took his driver from his caddie Fluff Cowan and addressed his ball. He waggled the club a couple of times and then laced a 336-yard drive down the right side of the fairway. A few holes later, his playing partner John Elliott was dumbfounded as Woods reached the par-5 sixth hole with a driver and a 5-iron, leaving his ball just twelve feet from the cup.

"Pretty good, isn't he?" Elliott joked with the gallery. Everyone nodded in agreement.

Woods's other playing partner that day, Jeff Hart, agreed. "It was very apparent that he was a special talent. Nobody hit the ball that far back then, except for John Daly and maybe a couple of others," he recalled. "But he had the complete game and obviously, looking back, a very strong mind as well."

That said, Hart did find the experience of playing with Woods slightly disconcerting. "It was far from my usual gallery, and the holes were lined with people three or four deep from the tee to the green. My normal galleries consisted mostly of family and friends," he added. "But there also seemed to be a lot of photographers who weren't used to covering golf. One even parked himself a few inches from my ball just over the green on the first hole, forcing me to politely ask him to move."

Back at Stanford, meanwhile, the golf team was watching events unfold in Milwaukee, scarcely believing what they were seeing. Having already seen Tiger play in many professional events, missing the cut in the vast majority, they began betting between themselves on just how his pro career would pan out. "Some of us were saying he's going to be the greatest ever, but others were saying he can't even make a cut on the PGA Tour," recalled Dave Garcia. "Greg Norman was the best player in the world at the time, and most of the guys thought he might get to that level. You know, two or three majors. But I went out on a limb. I said he'll get between twelve and fifteen. And everyone laughed at me."

Though he shot a round of 67 in his first round, Brown Deer Park wasn't really Tiger's kind of golf course. Comparatively short at 6,739 yards and with tree-lined fairways and doglegs that took the driver out of Woods's hand on many holes, he resorted to one of this stock shots—the so-called stinger—on several holes, drilling low, piercing 2-irons down the fairways instead.

After his first round in professional golf, Woods sat down for an interview with Curtis Strange, the double US Open winner, now working as a golf analyst for ESPN on ABC. Amid unprecedented interest in Woods, Strange had been chosen to conduct the interview, largely because they were both represented by IMG. As the pair sat down to chat, producer Jack Graham sat on the floor between them, listening in.

"There was more access to Tiger back then because he was new, but he was still pretty guarded and did very few things," said Graham. "But I guess the good thing for us was that he and Curtis knew each other, and he liked Curtis, so we were able to get that long sit-down with him."

What transpired was an interview that not only demonstrated Woods's drive and motivation but also a more general skepticism among the older guard of the PGA Tour about just how successful Woods might be.

"What would be a successful week here in Milwaukee?" asked Strange.

"Two things," replied Tiger, wearing his new black Nike cap. "I think if I play for solid rounds—and we're off to a good start today—if I can do that for three more days, I'll be very happy, and a victory would be awfully nice too."

Strange paused, looked down, and laughed.

"A victory? To me that comes off as a little cocky or brash, especially talking to the other guys on tour who have been out here years and years and years. Certainly, [you have] an incredible amateur record, but what do you say to those guys?"

Tiger looked puzzled and tried to reply, but Strange continued. "You know what I'm saying. You come out here, your first pro tournament, and you say, 'I can win!'"

"I understand that. I've always figured that why go to a tournament if you're not going there to try and win? There's really no point. That's the attitude I've had my entire life, and that's the attitude I will always have. That will explain to my dad that second sucks and third's even worse. It's just a feeling . . ."

"But on tour, that's not too bad sometimes though."

"That's not too bad, but I want to win. That's just my nature."

Strange smiled again and looked at his question sheet. "You'll learn," he said.

In the years to come, when Woods had proved his caliber beyond all doubt, Strange would finally admit that he might have got it wrong during the interview, but for producer Jack Graham, it was television gold. "At the time when Curtis said, 'You'll learn,' I think everyone agreed that he was exactly right. Guys finishing second and third out there, that's a lot of money," he recalled. "But you could sense Tiger bristle slightly. I don't think he necessarily came across as cocky when you just stood and talked to him, but in an interview like that, I think he just truly believed in what he was saying."

Certainly, Robert Wrenn, who played a practice round with Woods that week, sensed some resentment among older professionals, not just because Woods was only twenty, but because he was already earning more than the world's number one, Greg

Norman, and he hadn't even got his tour card yet. "Candidly, a lot of people were thinking the same thing," he said. "Here was this kid that just signed a $40 million deal with Nike. We all hope to get a deal with a comma in it, but he had two in his. I mean, multiple commas is what we all aspire to, right?"

The tournament's executive director Tom Strong certainly sensed a little discontent too. "There are a lot of good players who don't get the recognition they deserve," he said. "What we have to keep in mind is he's one of 156 players here. We want to do what we can to be sure Tiger's stay in Milwaukee is successful, but we'd do that for anybody who is attracting this much attention."

Not everyone felt the same. Younger players, like Dave Stockton Jr., were only too glad to have Woods in the pro ranks, not least because he could see the impact he was going to have on the game's popularity and, as a result, the bearing it would have on the earning potential of all tour pros, young and old. "I was twenty-seven years old at the time, in my third year on tour, and all the guys I knew were looking forward to playing against him, even if we maybe didn't realize just how much we were going to get our head beat in." He laughed. "I guess it was like taking a world title bout against Mike Tyson in his prime. I'll take it because it's really well paid, but I am gonna get my head pummeled."

Jack Graham started working in television sports at ABC in 1979 "when Jack Nicklaus was still a very big deal," he said. But having produced Tiger's first US Amateur win, when he defeated Trip Kuehne in that epic comeback at Sawgrass in 1994, he knew instantly that here was a golfer destined to take the game to a new level, especially as the likes of Greg Norman and Nick Faldo—elite players though they undoubtedly were—weren't exactly the kind of characters to draw more viewers to television coverage of golf. "I haven't seen a buzz like that about many sports stars over the years, let alone a golfer," he said. "At the time, Michael Jordan was the biggest guy in sport, but to think that Tiger would go on to become the world's most famous athlete playing what is really a niche sports is really amazing."

Indeed, other than the Masters, the US Open, and the Bob Hope Chrysler Classic that year, the highest television ratings for any golf tournament came during Tiger's final-round comeback against Steve Scott in the US Amateur Championship at Pumpkin Ridge.

Increasingly, however, Graham was already fielding complaints from viewers, irritated by the amount of coverage that Tiger Woods was receiving compared to the rest of the field. "I would never go to Tiger Woods over a shot of one of the guys who's really in contention, but I was a fan, and I wanted to see every shot of Tiger Woods," he said. "I never believed any of the people saying it's overkill, because it just wasn't reflected by the general public and the fans and the ratings. I never believed that small minority that screamed and yelled about showing too much of him."

What was clear to Jack Graham was that Woods's appeal was almost universal and went far beyond anything he had ever seen before and would in the months to come. The Golf Channel would morph into what people were calling the "Tiger Channel" while the increase in television audiences, all driven by the Tiger phenomenon, had PGA Tour bean counters rubbing their hands in glee at the prospect of the major networks purchasing broadcasting rights at much higher prices. Tournaments like the Walt Disney World / Oldsmobile Classic in Lake Buena Vista, Florida, meanwhile, would even have to print more tickets just to satisfy unprecedented demand.

From the moment he uttered, "Hello, world," Tiger Woods wasn't just a golfer; he was a cultural-phenomenon-in-waiting. His arrival wasn't just a different face on the leaderboard; it was a new kind of gravitational pull, sucking in viewers who had never before considered watching the game.

Everything about Woods was box office; they called it "the Tiger Effect." Not only did he play golf in a way nobody else did, with raw power and aggression on one hand and jaw-dropping creativity on the other, but his rounds guaranteed thrilling drama. But it was more than just his game. Tiger brought an undeniable charisma, a compelling narrative. He was young, articulate, and of mixed heritage—a figure who defied easy categorization and resonated with audiences far beyond golf's traditional boundaries. He would transform golf from a niche pursuit into must-see TV, turning Sunday afternoons into communal gatherings around the screen. People who had never touched a club suddenly found themselves invested in his every birdie and bogey.

But as Dave Stockton Jr. explained, the Tiger Effect on the pro ranks was also a wake-up call for all tour players, even the very best. "Prior to Tiger coming up, the biggest players were Norman and Faldo, and those two guys dominated the number-one ranking for a long time," he said. "When Tiger came on the scene, both of those guys stopped playing not that long after. It's not a coincidence, is it?"

While a second round of 69 saw Woods comfortably make the cut in Milwaukee and take his place in the weekend field, his total of 136 saw him trailing the leaders by eight shots. "Welcome to the real world of golf," joked fellow tour player Kelly Gibson.

It didn't get much better. A third round of 73 and a final round of 68 left him at 7-under-par. Woods did manage to grab more headlines late in his final round on Sunday though. At the fourteenth hole—a 202-yard par-3—he pulled out a 6-iron from his Titleist bag and sent a soaring shot onto the green, watching as his ball took a couple of hops and disappeared straight into the cup.

Some golfers go lifetimes without making a hole in one. This was Tiger Woods's ninth—and he was only twenty.

Allen Doyle was two groups ahead of Woods when he made his ace. "The place went wild. You just knew it had to be Tiger," he recalled. "I equate the roar to like what you would hear in Southeastern Conference football. I've been to Auburn games, I've been to Alabama games, I've been to Georgia games, I've been to Clemson games, and the crowd noise in those places is unbelievable. But Tiger outdid those decibel levels."

As he plucked the ball from the hole, Woods tossed it into the crowd where it deflected off the arm of watching fan David Beck and straight into the hands of Beck's brother-in-law, construction worker Bob Gustin. Twenty-six years later, Gustin auctioned the ball, selling it for $186,000 and splitting the money with Beck.

Despite his impressive first two rounds, Woods faded over the weekend, finishing in a tie for sixtieth place, twelve shots adrift of the winner, Loren Roberts, who defeated Jerry Kelly in a playoff. And while Tiger waited for his millions from Nike and Titleist to hit his bank account, he at least had his first winnings as a professional—a check for $2,544—to tide him over. "That's my money," he said later. "I earned this."

And so what if it wasn't the victory he and the thousands at Brown Deer Park had craved? At least he could pay Butch Harmon back.

When Tiger finally escaped the clamor for his attention and got back to Teakwood Street, it was clear that his life had now changed beyond all recognition. Hearing that he was back home, Joe Grohman decided to drop by to see how he was getting on since becoming a global superstar and the richest kid in Orange County. "I go over to the house, and there's like twenty or thirty people in there, and they're all wearing suits. I didn't know any of them," he recalled. "And Tiger was there, and he literally had a phone in each ear. They were corded phones too!

"It was just crazy."

Sensing Tiger was just a little busy, Joe Grohman made his excuses, telling Tida Woods he would come back the following day, and they could catch up then. The next day, Grohman returned to Teakwood Street to find only Earl and Tida at home.

"Where's Tiger? Where's Champ?" he asked.

"He's moved," replied Tida.

Grohman was perplexed. "I was thinking maybe he's gone to Redondo Beach or Manhattan Beach, just to be a little bit closer to LA, but then Tida told me," added Grohman.

"Florida," said Tida. "He's gone to Florida."

"But I was here last night? Nobody said you had better say your goodbyes to Tiger?"

To his dismay, Grohman, like so many others in Tiger's life, was now, without a word of thanks or a forwarding address, surplus to requirements in the world of Project Tiger. "I couldn't believe it. My spirit was broken. Just walked right out of my life, and that was that," he added.

Joe Grohman wasn't the first, and he wouldn't be the last to be jettisoned as Project Tiger moved on to a new phase. Caddies, friends, girlfriends, even the man who made millions for him, IMG agent Hughes Norton, soon found themselves out in the cold. In Tiger's first year as a professional, Norton had received 1,545 requests for Woods's time, nearly all of which were rejected. "Managing Tiger had put us in the business of pissing people off," he said.

Now, though, it was Norton that was irritating Woods. In early 1998, the agent had agreed to be interviewed and photographed for a *Golf World* cover story about Woods's huge commercial success, and Tiger, incensed at what he viewed as a betrayal of confidence, decided to take action. It was, said Norton, "the worst strategic decision of my career."

Summoning him to Isleworth Golf & Country Club in Orlando, Woods met Norton outside the clubhouse where the "expressionless" and "zombielike" golfer confirmed he was firing him. "It was a shock, especially when you feel like you've done a great job," he said. "But that's how Tiger operates. One minute you're on the inside, the next you're out.

"He just cuts you right out."

For Earl, Tida, and Tiger Woods, though, it was all part and parcel of Project Tiger.

EPILOGUE

"I want to be professionally excellent."

—Tiger Woods, aged nine

Saturday, April 12, 1997

Lee Elder had arrived back at his home in Pompano Beach, Florida, after playing in a charity tournament in Palm Beach County.

A man of his word, the sixty-two-year-old had cut short his trip to the Masters at Augusta to fulfill a promise he had made to a friend. Now, his duties over, he was back home and desperate to know what had happened in the third round at Augusta.

His second wife, Sharon, had the latest.

"Tiger's leading by nine!" she yelled.

"Better pack a bag then," replied Elder. "I guess we're going back to Augusta."

The following morning, the Elders rose early to catch a flight from Fort Lauderdale to Atlanta, before renting a car and heading off on the I-20 for the two-hour drive east to Augusta. Thirty minutes into the journey, however, Elder noticed the flashing lights of a Georgia Highway Patrol car in his rearview mirror, and an officer at the wheel demanding he pull over. When the traffic cop asked him why he was doing eighty-five miles per hour in a seventy-miles-per-hour area, Elder began making his excuses.

"I've got to get to the Masters," he pleaded. "I have to see Tiger Woods."

The cop didn't buy it.

"I don't know who Tiger Woods is," replied the officer. "And I don't like golf."

May 3, 2006

Earl Woods died from a heart attack at 6704 Teakwood Street, collapsing just three steps from Tiger's old bedroom. Three days later, after Earl's cremation, Tiger Woods; his mother, Tida; wife, Elin; and his three half-siblings, Earl Jr., Kevin, and Royce, met at a private airstrip in Anaheim where they boarded Tiger's Gulfstream IV jet and flew the two-hour journey to Manhattan, Kansas, so they could bury his ashes in the place where he grew up.

Earl Woods was a husband, a father, a soldier, a mentor, and a philanderer. A proud but flawed man, it wasn't just his verbosity that drove his wife, Tida, away but also his sexual proclivities, and while they remained married up until his death, Earl continued to live in Teakwood Street while Tida, who died nineteen years later in February 2025, aged eighty, lived in her own house in Tustin, bought for her by her son when he turned professional. As one interviewee told me, "[Tiger] hated the fact that his father cheated on his mother, and yet, guess what? He turned around and did exactly the same thing."

That they were both devoted to their only child together is inarguable. In many ways, Tiger received more love and attention than most kids, his parents looking out for him every step of the way, but the obsession—Earl's obsession—with making him the greatest golfer of all time clearly had unintended consequences.

Earl Woods was the ultimate Svengali. He didn't just teach Tiger golf; he crafted a phenomenon, instilling a relentless mental toughness, a sense of destiny, and a unique, almost military-precision approach to life and sport. When Tiger turned professional, the world knew Earl. His voice was the omnipresent backdrop to Tiger's early triumphs—guiding, defending, and often provoking. To Earl, every facet of Tiger's development was meticulously planned, and that included bringing in the best technical mind, Butch Harmon, to refine his prodigy's swing.

The flip side, of course, is what would have happened if Earl hadn't have driven him on? Would we still have had that seismic Masters win in 1997? That chip-in at the sixteenth at Augusta in 2005? The Tiger Slam? Might this be a book about David Duval, or Phil Mickelson, instead?

For Tiger Woods, who broke down in tears on the final green when, in the wake of his father's passing, he won the British Open at Royal Liverpool that summer, it had been a relationship that had made him the man he was, both good and bad.

But was it also one that ultimately broke him?

Repeatedly, Earl Woods always said he never bullied Tiger to play the game, and that all he ever wanted to do was raise a good person, not a good golfer. "The idea of me as a controlling father is 180 degrees from the truth," he once said. "It was never a question of me forcing Tiger to play golf. Everything came from him. We transcended the father–son thing . . . We became best friends, equals."

Only they weren't. Tiger's future was predetermined, almost from the moment he was born. Shoved in front of television cameras as soon as he could walk and talk, paraded around like a circus act, he had little or no choice in the route his life might take. That Earl—and, to a lesser extent, Tida—got the result they wanted with Tiger is undeniable, but the happy-go-lucky kid who went along with it all, the TV shows and the magazine profiles, vanished long before he turned professional. Several interviewees in this book have mentioned how the only people they ever saw Tiger hanging out with when he was younger were Earl's friends at the Navy Club, all retirees. They were never kids his age.

Tiger never bought into his father's predictions or proclamations about the impact he might have on golf and the wider world; it's why he never really ventured any opinions on those issues his father was only too happy to address publicly.

Was Tiger scared of his parents? Possibly. Probably. While Earl admitted he would scold Tiger whenever he stepped out of line, he said he left the physical discipline to Tida. "I'm still deathly afraid of her," Tiger said in 2017. "I love her so much, but she was tough."

For everything that has been said about Earl Woods and his profound influence on Tiger, perhaps the true bedrock of Tiger's formidable character, the steel in his spine, actually came from his mother. While Earl played the part of the outspoken mentor, Tida was the quiet, unyielding force, the embodiment of a stoic discipline that few could really comprehend, let alone emulate. It was Tida who instilled the relentless work ethic, the ruthless competitive edge, and an almost monastic focus, at least on the golf course, if not off it.

Tida's Buddhist faith wasn't just a spiritual guide; for her, it was a practical framework for mental fortitude. Like her husband and Jay Brunza, she also taught Tiger to block out distractions, to channel his emotions, and to use an inner calm to his advantage. When others saw a prodigy, Tida saw a son who needed grounding, who needed to understand that true greatness wasn't just about talent but about unshakable self-belief and an almost brutal dedication to perfection. She wasn't one for platitudes; her lessons were forged in quiet intensity and maternal expectation.

When Tiger's world imploded in 2009, it was Tida who stood by him with unwavering support. Her public reaction, famously striking him with a firm, disciplinary look, spoke volumes. It was the stern love of a mother who had poured her life into her son, only for him to stray wildly from the principles she had so lovingly taught him. She became his fierce, often silent, protector and his emotional anchor, navigating a storm that would have shattered lesser bonds.

The relationship between Tiger and Tida was a bond built on respect, a shared understanding of sacrifice, and a deep-seated love that transcended public scrutiny. While Earl shaped the public persona, Tida honed the private person, ensuring that even when his game faltered, the man himself possessed the inner resilience he needed to continue.

When Tida Woods died on February 4, 2025, Woods said, "My mom was a force of nature all her own. Her spirit was simply undeniable.

"She was quick with the needle and a laugh. She was my biggest fan, [my] greatest supporter. Without her, none of my personal achievements would have been possible."

Yes, it was a different time, but the idea that Woods, ostensibly a single child without any siblings in his house to call upon or confide in, could hold any sway in his household as he grew up was for the birds. Put simply, he had to do as he was told, irrespective of what Earl might want others to believe.

While Tiger Woods's story is unprecedented in golf, it is a story seen in so many other sports and in entertainment, typically ending in burnout, failure, or worse. Perhaps the closest comparison is that of the Williams sisters, Venus and Serena, in professional tennis who, driven on by their father, Richard, achieved huge success, amassing thirty individual Grand Slam titles between them. Like Earl Woods, Richard Williams controlled their careers from an early age, emphasizing mental toughness, discipline, and a strong work ethic as the principal routes to success in a sport that wasn't used to having people of color not just participating but winning in abundance. He even wrote a detailed eighty-five-page plan for their careers before they were born. And like Earl, Richard Williams did all he could to prepare his daughters for what was to come, heckling them during practice and even using old tennis balls that bounced lower and forced them to work harder.

The difference between the Williams sisters and Tiger Woods, however, was that they managed to stay on an even keel, perhaps because they had each other. Tiger Woods had nobody, other than Earl and Tida, and while his rise to become the greatest golfer of all time was remarkable, especially given the weight of expectation he faced from an early age, the fact that his life imploded in such spectacular fashion in 2009, when he publicly admitted to a string of extramarital affairs and blamed his "irresponsible behavior" on a sense of entitlement where the "normal rules didn't apply" to him was hardly surprising. After all, his father was the same.

Long before he turned professional and became the world's most recognizable sports star, Tiger's amateur record had set him apart from any other golfer in history, and his undefeated run of three consecutive US Junior Amateur titles, followed by three US Amateur Championships will, in all likelihood, never be repeated. Today, any player who ever came remotely close to emulating it would be professional long before it became reality.

What is depressing is that with a record like that, Tiger Woods had a chance—a genuine opportunity—to make a difference in a game steeped in elitism and riddled with discrimination.

And he blew it.

The truth is that golf got to Tiger Woods, as it always got to people. And that is the single biggest failure of Project Tiger. The facts speak for themselves. Since he won his first major at the Masters in 1997, there hasn't been another Black major winner, and there have been just two Asian winners: Y.E. Yang at the 2009 PGA Championship (where he overhauled Tiger in the final round to win) and the Japanese star Hideki Matsuyama, who won the Masters in 2021. Today, you can still count the number of African Americans competing on the PGA Tour on one hand (sometimes on one finger at certain tour stops). At the PGA Tour's flagship event, the Players Championship at TPC Sawgrass in 2025, there wasn't a single Black player in the field of 144 players. Golf, it seems, is as impenetrable as it has ever been.

Despite Earl Woods's occasionally outlandish proclamations about what his son may achieve not so much in golf but in the wider world, Tiger never really bought into it, except, of course, when he started out as a professional golfer and had been only too happy to sign off on a Nike commercial that openly bemoaned the egregious racial discrimination he had suffered on America's golf courses. But once the $40 million contract was banked, he always seemed to steer clear of such issues, lest it scare away the many other sponsors that turned up, checkbooks in hand. In May 2000, for example, the National Association for the Advancement of Colored People (NAACP) asked Black athletes to boycott events in South Carolina while the state continued to fly the Confederate flag over its capitol building. Certainly, it gained some high-profile support. Tennis superstar Serena Williams, for example, withdrew from the Family Circle Cup tournament held in Hilton Head Island, South Carolina, stating, "My decision to not play in South Carolina was based on a much deeper issue, and one that I feel strongly about." The NBA's

New York Knicks also stopped holding preseason training camps in Charleston, too, in response to the NAACP's request. What did Tiger Woods say? "I'm a golfer. That's their deal, not mine."

Despite all of Earl Woods's early predictions for his son and the heavenly levels of greatness he would almost inevitably achieve on and off the golf course, Woods's decision, conscious or otherwise, to navigate a wide, circuitous route around anything remotely controversial is perhaps the biggest missed opportunity of his life and career. That's why he can never be mentioned in the same breath as, say, Jackie Robinson, Muhammad Ali, or Arthur Ashe. They took a stand. Tiger never did.

In reality, Tiger Woods didn't need his father to make racism part of his story (though it certainly was, not least at the Navy Club), nor did he need Nike to make stuff up. He didn't need an aura or an attitude. His freakish natural talent spoke for itself and gave him all he would ever need. But Earl Woods never shut up. Commendable in many ways, but to then saddle his son with the burden of being the golfer that might finally render irrelevant the color barrier that Pete Brown, Charlie Sifford, and Lee Elder fought so hard to break through was, in retrospect, something he wasn't equipped to deal with.

The depressing fact is that Tiger Woods didn't really change the dial as much as he could have. Like every other successful golfer, with their shirts bought and branded, he soon realized that the best way—the only way—to keep sponsors happy was to play the game, both on and off the golf course.

When Tiger Woods won the 1997 Masters at Augusta, it had seemed as though golf might finally turn a corner and move away from a status quo rooted in exclusion. Here, after all, was a twenty-one-year-old with a mixed-race background not just winning at one of the very places that fought so long to prevent men like him playing there, but doing so in a fashion that rendered everything that had happened there previously almost irrelevant. Even after the victory, Tiger was still keen to tackle the issue that was on everyone's lips. "I hoped my win would encourage them to play, or to chase their dreams, whatever they were," he said. "But it would have been naive of me to think my win would mean the end of 'the look' when a person from any minority walked into some golf clubs, especially the game's private clubs."

Even as Woods cantered to victory on Sunday, there was a stark reminder of all the prejudice that his father said would inevitably come his way when Fuzzy Zoeller, a Masters champion himself, spoke to a reporter from CNN. When asked about Tiger's dominant performance, Zoeller replied, "That little boy is driving well, and he's putting well. He's doing everything it takes to win. So you know what you guys do when he gets in here. Pat him on the back, say congratulations, enjoy it, and tell him not to serve fried chicken next year. Got it? Or collard greens, or whatever the hell they serve."

In the context of a sport that, for far too long, had struggled with issues of inclusivity and racial barriers, Zoeller's remarks, regardless of intent, reeked of an old, uncomfortable stereotype. It was a stark, jarring reminder that, for all of Tiger's barrier-breaking talent, the undercurrents of prejudice still ran deep within the sport's traditional enclaves.

The fallout was swift and severe. Sponsors, sensing the public outrage and a shift in golf's demographic, began to distance themselves from Zoeller. K-Swiss dropped him. His reputation, built on affability, was tarnished. Zoeller quickly issued apologies, claiming his comments were misinterpreted, that he was merely joking, and that he held no racial animosity toward Woods, but the incident proved to be an uncomfortable asterisk on what was otherwise a glorious week in Georgia.

Most of the interviewees in this book, especially his fellow players, have commented on how Woods was playing a "different game" around 2000 and later, when he won his fourteenth major title at the 2008 US Open at Torrey Pines, beating the veteran Rocco Mediate in a playoff, it appeared for all the world that there was nothing that could stop Woods in his lifelong pursuit to eclipse the record eighteen majors that Jack Nicklaus achieved.

But then, in the early hours of Friday, November 27, 2009, his personal indiscretions finally caught up with him, when he fled his house after an argument with his wife, Elin, and crashed his Cadillac Escalade into a fire hydrant, which, in doing so, fired the starting pistol on the biggest sex scandal in living memory as cocktail waitresses and porn stars, models and moms, all came forward to tell of their affairs with Woods.

That was the day Tiger Woods stopped smiling. The day it seemed he all but gave up.

It was also the moment the true extent of Tiger's celebrity became apparent, not because of the news bulletins he dominated or the column inches devoted to him but because of the extraordinary thirteen-minute mea culpa press conference he conducted later at the PGA Tour's headquarters in Ponte Vedra, Florida, on February 19, 2010, that was broadcast live on all the major networks. With a stern-faced Tida Woods sitting in the front row, staring intently at him, Woods apologized for his actions, saying, "I felt that I had worked hard my entire life and deserved to enjoy all the temptations around me. I felt I was entitled. Thanks to money and fame, I didn't have to go far to find them."

In his first public appearance since the scandal broke a little more than two months earlier, Woods explained how he had spent forty-five days at the Pine Grove sex addiction center in Hattiesburg, Mississippi, in a bid to understand why he behaved the way he did and to try and salvage his marriage and career. He also announced an indefinite break from the professional game before heading back to Pine Grove for further treatment.

Whether it was a prudent move is a moot point, given that his marriage didn't survive, but it's worth remembering that this wasn't a president or a prime minister admitting their mistakes to the electorate; it was a professional golfer, a thirty-five-year-old married man, a father, addressing his many failings not just to a room full of people in Ponte Vedra but the entire world watching. Imagine if had been any other golfer in Woods's shoes? A Phil Mickelson maybe, or a Sergio García? Do you think they would have appeared for the world in such an eye-opening confessional? Of course they wouldn't.

But Woods's demise was as spectacular as it was rapid. In jeopardizing his career and wrecking his marriage, that teenage Tiger whose smile lit up golf courses across America in the 1980s and 1990s made way for a more somber specimen, all too often sidelined by injuries, incidents, and accidents. Here was a player who had built his career, his entire life, on what he could do with a golf club in his hands and a ball at his feet, now a shadow of his former self.

In many respects, the only real surprise was that Woods was able to keep this unseemly side to his character secret for so long. But he was his father's son, and his demise, shocking as it was, seemed to be the almost inevitable conclusion of a life spent turning a blind eye to the same kind of behavior that Earl Woods exhibited around women.

That he could continue to live a double life and yet still be the game's most dominant player might not have been in any way admirable, but it was remarkable. It was as though all of the many years of dedication to his craft had gradually ceded power to the darker side of his character, irrespective of the painful and far-reaching consequences.

Think back to 2000 when Woods was just twenty-four. In June, he had decimated the field in the US Open at Pebble Beach, winning by a record fifteen shots and finishing 12-under-par, the only player under-par for the tournament. The next month, at the British Open Championship on the Old Course at St. Andrews, he won by eight strokes, setting a new record for the lowest 72-hole score in relation to par (-19) and becoming the youngest player in history to win all four of golf's major championships, breaking Jack Nicklaus's record by two years. It got better. A month later, he took the PGA Championship as well, defeating Bob May in a playoff at Kentucky's fabled Valhalla Golf Club.

To give an idea of just how exceptional he was in that stretch in 2000, you only have to examine his scoring in the four majors, where he boasted a total of 53-under-par, and his nearest rival, South Africa's Ernie Els, was just 18-under. The following year, in April 2001, Woods would win his second Masters at Augusta to simultaneously hold all four major titles. Of course, there were some curmudgeons who maintained that it wasn't a "grand slam" as such, given that all four titles were not won in the same calendar year, but the Tiger Slam, as people began to call it, was a phenomenal and unique achievement whichever way you looked at it.

Somewhere along the way, around the time he turned professional, a switch flipped in Tiger's head. Single-minded to the point of rudeness on the golf course, he was ruthless and calculating off it too. It's perhaps why it is difficult to feel any sympathy for what happened to him.

What made Tiger's later indiscretions all the more unsavory was that his two children, Sam and Charlie, were just two years old and nine months old, respectively, when the scandal broke.

Sixteen years on, and Elin now has three children with her new partner, the former NFL tight end Jordan Cameron. Woods, his hair all but gone, has had a number of new partners, including the Olympic gold medalist skier Lindsey Vonn as well as Erica Herman, the woman who used to manage his restaurant, the Woods Jupiter. Following their breakup, Herman filed lawsuits against Woods, seeking to nullify a nondisclosure agreement she had signed and also claiming she was improperly evicted from his mansion. She later withdrew the claims. More recently, Woods has been dating Vanessa Trump, the ex-wife of President Donald Trump's son, Donald Jr.

What is encouraging is that the turmoil that engulfed Woods's private life doesn't appear to have affected his relationship with his children. When he was inducted into the World Golf Hall of Fame in 2022, his daughter, Sam, introduced him with a speech filled with love and admiration. Son Charlie, meanwhile, is often seen playing golf with his father in the PGA Tour's annual Father/Son Challenge, the PNC Championship, where the similarities and idiosyncrasies of the pair's golf swings and on-course mannerisms, right down to the way they lean on their putters, isn't just noticeable but actually quite remarkable.

It's there where the comparisons end though. Extremely talented though Charlie Woods is, he isn't yet a scratch handicap—something his father achieved at the age of thirteen—and, to date, has just one American Junior Golf Association victory to his name when he won the Team TaylorMade Invitational in May 2025, although he did defeat the nation's number-one ranked player in the process.

While he is almost certainly assured of a college golf scholarship, it is not fair to compare him to his father at a similar age. When he was sixteen, Tiger Woods had won two US Junior Amateur titles and pretty much everything else there was to win on the junior circuit, so the idea he might fill the golf shoes of his father, simply by his genes, isn't realistic.

But while Charlie has played from a young age, it is only post-pandemic where he has really concentrated on the game, suggesting that Tiger's way of raising his children differs remarkably from that of his own father. Of course, that may also be down to the fact that while Tiger and Elin are no longer married, they still have the kind of coparenting relationship where the children's interests always take precedence.

That said, like Earl Woods, Tiger does coach him and has caddied for him in a number of tournaments but, conversely, has always spoken publicly about how he never wanted to pressure Charlie into playing golf for fear he might end up hating the game. Similarly, he is also extremely protective about his son. You won't see Charlie on the chat show circuit, nor will you ever hear Tiger making the same kind of ridiculous predictions and proclamations that Earl Woods used to make about him.

Since the sex scandal, there seems to be a weariness about Tiger Woods, not to mention a realization that his halcyon days are gone and won't ever be coming back, desperate though golf fans are to see him back in contention. Yes, he won the Masters again in 2019 for the fifth time (still one behind Jack Nicklaus's record of six wins in the event), but a near fatal car crash in Los Angeles in February 2021, where Woods nearly lost his right leg after going almost double the speed limit, has all but ended his career. Will he compete on the Champions Tour now that he's fifty years old? He might, given you can use a golf cart there, but still, you can't really picture it, can you?

Yes, whatever the future holds for Tiger Woods remains to be seen, but one thing is for sure, and that is that certain key aspects of the game of golf never changed in his wake and, in all likelihood, never will. Or rather, some did, but perhaps not in the way that Earl Woods's Project Tiger had hoped. It is, after all, still as white and middle-class as it has ever been, and even more so on the pro ranks of the PGA Tour where 80 percent of players are white and just three are of African American heritage.

If Tiger, indeed, changed anything, it was the idea of what was possible in the game of golf. His was a talent unmatched in the modern game, and his swashbuckling style not only ensured he became one of the most recognizable and richest athletes on the planet, but ensured that every other professional on the major tours benefitted from increased exposure, better sponsorship deals, and, of course, much bigger purses. As Dave Stockton Jr. told me, "We went from purses with first places of maybe $180,000 to high six-figure and sometimes seven-figure winners' checks in no time at all, and that was all driven by him."

It's why Tiger is still widely liked and respected in the game, despite everything that has happened to him off the golf course, much of it self-inflicted. Players know that without him, they wouldn't have the lives or the opportunities they do today. It's why even the ninety-first ranked player on the PGA Tour Money List—Will Zalatoris at the time of writing—has earned over $1 million in the current season. In many ways, it's even why LIV Golf exists and why they offered Woods a reported $800 million to jump ship from the PGA Tour and join the breakaway competition, even though he barely plays any more, as his injuries and ailments take an ever-deleterious toll.

As golf fans, we should all be grateful for what Tiger Woods did for golf, even if the wider game, and the attitudes within, never really changed that much. Some of the memories he has provided will live forever: the miraculous chip-in at the sixteenth at Augusta in the final round of the Masters in 2005, winning the 2008 US

Open with a fractured leg, or completing the Tiger Slam—yes, his has been a career for the ages.

But there's also the unknown, the many what-ifs and maybes. Where would Tiger Woods be now without the scandal that destroyed his marriage and his golf game? What if he didn't crash his car that day? Would Tiger Woods, the kid who targeted every milestone and record that Jack Nicklaus ever set, now be miles ahead of his idol? The answer, in all likelihood, is yes. He might now have had twenty or more major titles, and while he shares the record for the most PGA Tour titles with Sam Snead at eighty-two, he would now be well clear, probably with over one hundred victories.

Does that diminish what Woods did achieve? Of course not. But how it imploded so spectacularly wasn't just shocking but, in many ways, predictable, given the childhood he missed out on, his father's behavior, and the entitlement he felt as the world's greatest golfer. But the 2019 Masters aside, when he won his fifteenth major title against all the odds, the spectacle of Woods struggling around golf courses on the increasingly rare occasions his various ailments allow him to play is one of the saddest sights in sport, bringing to mind those last few years of the late Seve Ballesteros's career when the Spanish golfing legend and five-time major winner didn't seem to know where the ball was going to go, or even Muhammad Ali in those agonizing final fights against Larry Holmes in 1980 and Trevor Berbick in 1981. Nobody enjoys it, not Seve, not Ali, and certainly not Woods.

This, after all, is a golfer for whom winning is, or was, everything.

TIGER'S ACCOMPLISHMENTS

MILESTONES 1975–1997

1976 Hits his first golf shots in the family's garage, aged ten months

1978 Makes television debut (aged two), putting against James Stewart and Bob Hope on *The Mike Douglas Show*

1981 Shoots 48 over nine holes at the Navy Golf Club in Los Alamitos

1982 Makes his first hole in one at Heartwell Golf Park, aged six

1984 Aged eight, wins his first Junior World Championships against boys two years older than him, going on to five more Junior World Championships

1987 Breaks 70 for the first time on a regulation golf course, aged twelve

1988 Makes his fifth hole in one

1989 Achieves a scratch handicap at age thirteen

1991 Aged fifteen, Woods becomes the youngest US Junior Amateur champion in history and was named AJGA, *Golf Digest*, and Southern California Player of the Year

1992 Plays his first PGA Tour event at the Los Angeles Open

1993 Accepts a full-ride scholarship to Stanford University

1994 Becomes the youngest ever US Amateur Champion, aged eighteen

1995 Plays in the Walker Cup and ties for forty-first place in his debut at the Masters

1996 Wins a third consecutive US Amateur title and is the leading amateur at the British Open Championship. Turns professional and wins his first professional event at the 1996 Las Vegas Invitational. Also named PGA Tour Rookie of the Year

1997 Aged twenty-one, wins Masters by twelve strokes on his way to the top of the world rankings, breaking twenty-one records in the process. Named PGA Player of the Year

STANFORD UNIVERSITY, NATIONAL COLLEGIATE ATHELETIC ASSOCIATION RECORD

1994–95

TOURNAMENTS:	13
ROUNDS:	35
AVERAGE SCORE:	71.37
AGAINST PAR:	-0.51
NATIONAL RATING:	2nd
LOWEST ROUND:	66
ROUNDS IN 60s:	9
PAR OR BETTER:	25
WINS:	3

1995–96

TOURNAMENTS:	13
ROUNDS:	41
AVERAGE SCORE:	70.61
AGAINST PAR:	-0.95
NATIONAL RATING:	1st
LOWEST ROUND:	61
ROUNDS IN 60s:	18
PAR OR BETTER:	27
WINS:	8

NATIONAL COLLEGIATE ATHLETIC ASSOCIATION TOURNAMENT VICTORIES

1994

September 16–19

William H. Tucker Invitational, Championship Golf Course at the University of New Mexico, Albuquerque, New Mexico

October 24-25

Jerry Pate Invitational, Shoal Creek, Alabama

1995

November 3–4

Stanford Invitational, Stanford Golf Course, Palo Alto, California

1996

February 21–23

John Burns Invitational, Klipper Golf Course, Kaneohe, Hawaii

March 25-26

Southwestern Intercollegiate, North Ranch Country Club, Westlake Village, California

April 20

The Brawl, Stanford Golf Course, Palo Alto, California

April 26-27

Cougar Classic, Riverside Country Club, Provo, Utah

April 29–May 1
Pac-10 Championship, Big Canyon Country Club, Newport Beach, California

May 16–18
NCAA West Regional, Stanford Golf Course, Palo Alto, California

May 29–June 1
NCAA Championship (individual title), The Honors Course, Chattanooga, Tennessee

NATIONAL COLLEGIATE ATHLETIC ASSOCIATION HONORS

1995
First Team All-American
First Team All-Conference
Pac-10 Player of the Year

1996
First Team All-American
First Team All-Conference
Pac-10 Player of the Year
Pac-10 Conference Champion
NCAA Division 1 Individual Champion
Jack Nicklaus National Player of the Year
Haskins Award Winner
Ben Hogan Award Winner

OTHER NOTABLE VICTORIES

US Junior Amateur Championship 1991, 1992, 1993
US Amateur Championship 1994, 1995, 1996
Optimist International Junior World Championship 1984, 1985, 1988, 1989, 1990, 1991

SOURCES

BIBLIOGRAPHY

Aaron, Hank, with Lonnie Wheeler. *I Had a Hammer: The Hank Aaron Story*, Harper Collins, 1991.

Anselmo, John. *A-Game Golf: The Complete Starter Kit for Golfers from Tiger Woods' Amateur Instructor*, Doubleday, 2001.

Barkley, Charles, with Michael Wilbon. *Who's Afraid of a Large Black Man?*, Penguin Press, 2005.

Benedict, Jeff, and Armen Keteyian. *Tiger Woods*, Simon & Schuster, 2018.

Callahan, Tom. *His Father's Son: Earl and Tiger Woods,* Mainstream, 2011.

Cook, Kevin. *The Tiger Slam: The Inside Story of the Greatest Golf Ever Played (Tiger Woods in 2000–2001)*, Avid Reader Press, 2024.

Crosby, Don, with James Dale. *Tiger Woods Made Me Look Like a Genius: 5 Simple Ways to Take 10 Strokes Off Your Game*, Andrews McMeel Publishing, 2000.

Duran, Rudy, with Rick Lipsey. *In Every Kid There Lurks a Tiger*, Grand Central, 2002.

Grohman, Joe. *How To Golf: Beginners Guide*, self-published, 1995.

Harig, Bob. *Drive: The Lasting Legacy of Tiger Woods*, St. Martin's Press, 2024.

Hayes, Neil, and Brian Murphy. *The Last Putt: Two Teams, One Dream, and a Freshman Named Tiger*, Mariner Books, 2010.

Newsham, Gavin. *Sportonomics: A Sideways Look at Sports Statistics*, Carlton Books, 2013.

Newsham, Gavin. *John Daly: Letting The Big Dog Eat: The Biography*, Virgin Publishing, 2003.

Newsham, Gavin. *Two Tribes: The Rebirth of the Ryder Cup*, Atlantic, 2010.

Norton, Hughes, and George Pepper. *Rainmaker: Superagent Hughes Norton and the Money-Grab Explosion of Golf from Tiger to LIV and Beyond*, Atria Books, 2024.

Patterson, James. *Tiger, Tiger: His Life, As It's Never Been Told Before*, Little, Brown & Company, 2024.

Sampson, Curt. *Roaring Back: The Fall and Rise of Tiger Woods*, Diversion Books, 2019

Strege, John. *Tiger: A Biography of Tiger Woods*, Broadway, 1997.

Woods, Barbara Gary. *At All Costs: My Life with the Man Behind the Tiger*, BookSurge Publishing, 2008.

Woods, Earl, with Fred Mitchell. *Playing Through: Straight Talk on Hard Work, Big Dreams, and Adventures with Tiger*, Harper Collins, 1998.

Woods, Earl, with Pete McDaniel. *Training a Tiger: A Father's Guide to Raising a Winner in Both Golf and Life*, William Morrow, 1997.

ORIGINAL INTERVIEWS

Alan Bratton, Walker Cup teammate and OSU opponent

Allen Doyle, Presidents Cup teammate and played in Tiger's professional debut

Bob Friend, played with Woods at LA Open in 1992

Brad Zwetschke, army chaplain who lost to Woods in the US Junior final

Buddy Marucci, car dealer who lost to Woods in US Amateur final

Casey Martin, Stanford friend and teammate, ex-pro, and now coach at University of Oregon

Chip Spratlin, beat Woods to the 1995 NCAA title

Clive Brown, GB and Ireland captain Walker Cup 1995

Dave Garcia, Stanford teammate

Dave Stockton Jr., pro golfer and played with Woods in his first pro event

Eri Crum, Stanford teammate

Gary D'Amato, reporter for *Milwaukee Journal Sentinel* and for *Wisconsin.Golf*

Gary Wolstenholme, British Walker Cup player who beat Woods in 1995

Hughes Norton, Tiger's first agent

Jack Graham, TV producer of Woods's first pro appearance

Jeff Anderson, friend and teammate from Western High School

Jeff Hart, played with Tiger in his first ever round as a pro

Jim Dale, cowrote coach Don Crosby's book with him

Jody Fanagan, Irish Walker Cup player who beat Woods

Joe Grohman, former pro at the Navy Golf Club and Tiger's friend and confidante

José María Olazábal, Masters winner and played with Woods at the event

Kevin Mihailoff, junior golf opponent at the US Junior

Lawrence Donegan, golf writer and former European Tour caddie

Lee James, British amateur champion who played with Woods several times

Paul Page, last person to beat Tiger in a national amateur event

Robert Floyd, son of Raymond Floyd and a pro golfer who played with Woods frequently

Robert Wrenn, played at Brown Deer Park during Tiger's professional debut

Rudy Duran, Tiger's first ever coach from the age of four

Steve Bowen, rules official who oversaw many of Woods's games

Steve Scott, beaten opponent in US Amateur final

Todd Demsey, Presidents Cup teammate and college opponent

Tom Sargent, junior golf expert in California who worked with Tiger as a child

Trip Kuehne, close friend and beaten opponent in US Amateur final

ACKNOWLEDGMENTS

In writing this book, I interviewed scores of people who had come across Tiger in his childhood and amateur career, and it really wouldn't have been possible without their assistance. From school friends to college teammates, coaches to fellow professionals, they were all extremely generous with their insights, and I would like to thank each and every one who volunteered their time. It's very much appreciated. Special mentions go to Joe Grohman, Steve Scott, Trip Kuehne, Eri Crum, Dave Garcia, Alan Bratton, and Casey Martin for their much-valued input.

Thanks also to Mary Flanagan and Stuart Moffat at the Royal & Ancient, Pat Kravitz at Augusta National, and Ron Driscoll at the USGA, all of whom were really helpful whenever I needed a contact or a fact checked.

Thanks, too, to Evan Phail, Keith Wallman, and everyone at Diversion Books for giving me the opportunity to do this, and to my agent, Toby Mundy, at Aevitas Creative Management for helping to get it over the line.

To my kids, Betsy, Frank, and Cissy. I want to say thanks for always making me laugh and smile. You're all a source of light relief when I need it and, invariably, a massive distraction when I don't.

Finally, to Ann, my wife and plate spinner par excellence, I want to say thank you, although that doesn't seem anywhere near sufficient for the love and support you always give me. This book was written in the wake of her losing her beloved mum, the force of nature that was Betty Farragher, and the strength and resilience she has shown has been nothing short of inspirational. I've said it before, and I'll say it again: I don't know how you manage to do what you do, but I'm so grateful you can and that you do. I love you.